DENALI'S HOWL

DENALI'S HOWL

THE DEADLIEST CLIMBING DISASTER ON AMERICA'S WILDEST PEAK

ANDY HALL

DUTTON
— est. 1852 —

DUTTON
— est. 1852 —

Published by the Penguin Group
Penguin Group (USA) LLC
375 Hudson Street
New York, New York 10014

USA | Canada | UK | Ireland | Australia | New Zealand | India | South Africa | China
penguin.com
A Penguin Random House Company

LIBRARY OF CONGRESS CATALOGING-IN-PUBLICATION DATA
has been applied for.

ISBN 978-0-525-95406-4

Printed in the United States of America
1 3 5 7 9 10 8 6 4 2

Set in Times New Roman MT
Designed by Amy Hill
Maps copyright © 2014 by Jeffrey L. Ward

To Melissa, who believed in me when I didn't,
and to my father, who knew that putting more people at risk
would not save those who were already gone.

CONTENTS

Contents

THE WILCOX EXPEDITION*

JOE WILCOX, *twenty-four years old*

HOMETOWN: Provo, Utah

OCCUPATION: Graduate student studying mathematics

EXPERIENCE: More than fifty ascents above 10,000 feet; Mount Rainier National Park Rescue Team rope leader; snow, glacier, and crevasse training; participant in several rescue operations

SUMMITS: Tooth of Time, Clear Creek Mountain, Baldy Mountain, Touch-Me-Not Mountain, Wheeler Peak, Mount Rainier, Mount St. Helens, Mount Adams, Mount Hood, Mount Olympus, Mount Timpanogos, Mount Nebo

STEVE TAYLOR, *twenty-three years old*

HOMETOWN: Mount Prospect, Illinois

OCCUPATION: Graduated May 1967 with a bachelor's degree in physics

EXPERIENCE: Snow cave building, mountain-rescue techniques class, member of Brigham Young University Rescue Team, outdoor survival class, first aid training, ice climbing experience, instructor for BYU Alpine Club winter mountaineering school

SUMMITS: Mount Timpanogos, Mount Nebo, Mount Rainier

* Information compiled from Joe Wilcox's *White Winds* (Los Alamitos, CA: Hwong Publishing Company, 1981); Howard Snyder's *The Hall of the Mountain King* (New York: Scribner, 1973); DENA13611 1967 Wilcox Expedition Folder, and an undated letter to Joe Wilcox from Mark McLaughlin.

MARK MCLAUGHLIN, *twenty-four years old*

HOMETOWN: Eugene, Oregon

OCCUPATION: Part-time student

EXPERIENCE: Cross-country and alpine skiing; Eugene Unit Leader, Mountain Rescue and Safety Council of Oregon Alpine Club; Climbing Committee chairman, Eugene, Oregon, Obsidians club

SUMMITS: Mount Olympus, Middle Olympus, Mount Rainier, Mount Washington, Three Fingered Jack, Mount Jefferson, Mount St. Helens, Mount Adams, Mount Hood

JERRY CLARK, *thirty-one years old*

HOMETOWN: Eugene, Oregon

OCCUPATION: Electrical engineer

EXPERIENCE: Thirteen years' climbing experience; two six-month stints in Antarctica—duties included climbing and ice-safety instructor for the United States Antarctic Program; mountain leader, Purdue Outing Club; University of Oregon Alpine Club; University of Wisconsin Hoofer Mountaineering Club; Eugene Oregon Obsidians Club Rescue Team

SUMMITS: Grand Teton, Mount Owen, Hagerman Peak, Medicine Mountain, Symmetry Spire, Pinnacle Peak, Middle Teton, Mount Moran, Mount Oldenburg, Gannett Peak, Mount Oliver, Pingora Peak, Mount Rainier, Mount Jefferson, North Sister, Mount Adams, Mount Hood

ANSHEL SCHIFF, *thirty years old*

HOMETOWN: West Lafayette, Indiana

OCCUPATION: Assistant college professor of engineering sciences

EXPERIENCE: Backpacking and scrambling western US mountains; Sierra Club Rock and Snow Climbing School; rock climbing at Devil's Lake, Wisconsin, and Mississippi Palisades

SUMMITS: Grand Teton, Tahquitz Rock, Fingertip Traverse, Pingora Peak

HANK JANES, *twenty-five years old*

HOMETOWN: Portland, Oregon

OCCUPATION: Teacher

EXPERIENCE: Climbed several of Colorado's 14,000-foot peaks; winter camping and ski mountaineering; experience in technical ice climbing; Mountain Rescue and Safety Council of Oregon

SUMMITS: Shadow Peak, Longs Peak, Mount Hood, Capitol Peak, Mount Sneffels, Mount Adams, Three Fingered Jack, Crestone Needle, Mount Rainier, Mount St. Helens, Grand and Middle Tetons

DENNIS LUCHTERHAND, *twenty-three years old*

HOMETOWN: Madison, Wisconsin

OCCUPATION: Graduate student studying geology

EXPERIENCE: Mountain leader, University of Wisconsin Hoofer Mountaineering Club; snowshoeing, backpacking, and winter camping near Lake Superior

SUMMITS: East Lester Peak, Middle Lester Peak, West Lester Peak, Jackson Peak, Ice Point, Mount St. John, Disappointment Peak, Teewinot Mountain, Cloudveil Dome, Buck Mountain, Rockchuck Peak, Gannett Peak, Mount St. Helens, Mount Sacagawea, Winifred Peak, Fremont Peak, Wilder Freiger, Grossvenediger, Rainer Horn, Schwarze Wand, Hoher Zaun, Kristallwand, Mount Rainier

WALT TAYLOR, *twenty-four years old*

HOMETOWN: West Lafayette, Indiana

OCCUPATION: Student; completed his second year of medical school and simultaneously working on a master's degree in philosophy

EXPERIENCE: Three years as a technical climbing instructor at Ashcrofters mountaineering school; extensive alpine skiing experience

SUMMITS: Hagerman Peak, Disappointment Peak, Mount Owen, Grand Teton, Capitol Peak, Middle Teton, Pinnacle Peak, Lincoln Gulch Split Rock, Snowmass Peak

JOHN RUSSELL, *twenty-three years old*

HOMETOWN: Auburn, Washington

OCCUPATION: Logger

EXPERIENCE: Two-week solo hike in the High Sierra; carried one-hundred-pound loads above 10,000 feet; assisted in mountain-rescue operations

SUMMITS: Mount St. Helens, Mount Adams, Mount Rainier, Mount Baker, Mount Shuksan, Mount Hood, Mount Whitney, Pillars of Hercules, Mount Yoran, The Tooth

HOWARD SNYDER, *twenty-two years old*

HOMETOWN: Boulder, Colorado

OCCUPATION: College graduate; studied geography and geology

EXPERIENCE: Led twenty-four climbs on Longs Peak; climbed thirteen other 14,000-foot peaks in Colorado; numerous winter climbs above 14,000 feet; winter camping, snowshoeing, ice climbing, and glacier travel experience; climbing leader for Colorado Mountain Club Canadian Outing

SUMMITS: Matterhorn, Monte Rosa, Mont Blanc, Aiguilles de Triolet, Mönch, Jungfrau, Eiger, Mount Brazeau, Charlton Peak, Mount Unwin, Orizaba, Popocatépetl, Iztaccihuatl

PAUL SCHLICHTER, *twenty-two years old*

HOMETOWN: Lakewood, Colorado

OCCUPATION: US Air Force cadet

EXPERIENCE: Extensive climbing on Colorado's 14,000-plus peaks, US Air Force one- and four-week survival training; US Army Mountain Troops Climbing School training student, US Army Mountain Troops Climbing School instructor

SUMMITS: Longs Peak, Middle Teton, Orizaba, Popocatépetl, Iztaccihuatl

JERRY LEWIS, *thirty years old*

HOMETOWN: Boulder, Colorado

OCCUPATION: Army veteran; college student studying electrical engineering

EXPERIENCE: Rock climbing, snowshoe travel, and ice climbing experience; cold-weather camping in Greenland; climbed several of Colorado's 14,000-plus peaks

SUMMITS: Navajo Peak, Longs Peak, Snowmass Peak, Boulder Flatirons

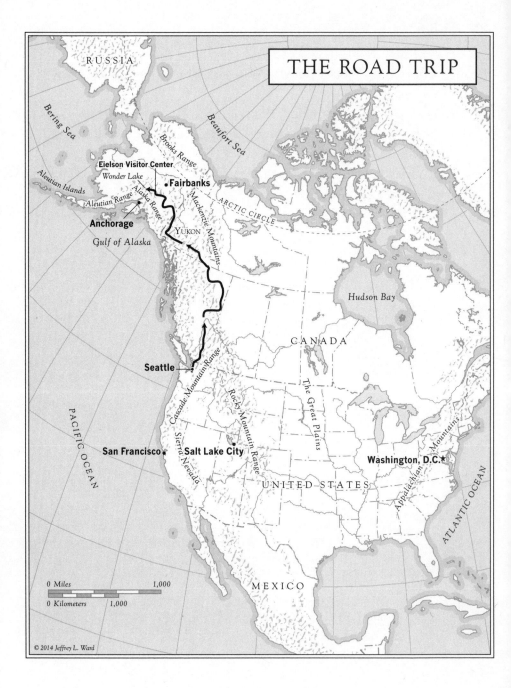

THE ROAD TRIP

RUSSIA

Bering Sea

Aleutian Islands

Beaufort Sea

Brooks Range

Eielson Visitor Center
Wonder Lake
Fairbanks

Aleutian Range

Alaska Range

Anchorage

Gulf of Alaska

YUKON

Mackenzie Mountains

ARCTIC CIRCLE

Hudson Bay

CANADA

Cascade Mountain Range

Rocky Mountain Range

The Great Plains

Seattle

San Francisco

Sierra Nevada

Salt Lake City

UNITED STATES

Washington, D.C.★

Appalachian Mountains

PACIFIC OCEAN

ATLANTIC OCEAN

MEXICO

0 Miles   1,000
0 Kilometers   1,000

© 2014 Jeffrey L. Ward

DENALI'S HOWL

A STRANGER IN THE WILDERNESS

Joe Wilcox may not have been the first man to reach the summit of Denali, but on Saturday afternoon, July 15, 1967, he felt like it. A rare clear day reigned on the mountain outsiders call Mount McKinley. Wilcox and his three companions had savored it for the last few hours as they trudged upward on crusty, wind-carved snow. Atop the continent, Joe's deep-set eyes swept over the Alaska Range—some of the tallest and most rugged peaks in North America—reduced to so many white waves of rock and ice lapping at the mountain's base. But along with the grandeur there was an edge of tension. After twenty-seven days on the mountain, Wilcox knew that the window of good weather could close just as quickly as it had opened. The four men on the summit, along with the rest of their twelve-man team waiting for their turn just a couple of thousand feet below, had no time to waste.

Wilcox had been on the mountain for nearly a month, and as he approached the summit the final steps seemed insignificant when compared to the tremendous effort the team had made to get there. The sweeping panorama instilled in him a sense of gratitude. He had worked hard, but that hard work did not guarantee success; he felt lucky.

Two weather systems had been developing as Wilcox and his companions worked their way toward the summit: one to the northeast and one to the southwest. Rainclouds mustered over the Beaufort Sea, a stretch of ice-bound ocean that spans 1,200 unbroken miles between Alaska's North Slope and the North Pole. In those days the sea was largely devoid of human traffic, save the occasional Eskimo* hunter. The low-pressure system spun to life and grew in intensity as it marched southwest carrying potent moisture-laden winds toward the Alaska Range. At the same time an equally strong high-pressure system developed over the Aleutian Islands, a wind-swept, treeless archipelago, known by mariners as the Cradle of Storms, southwest of Denali. The development and location of both weather systems at that time of year was unusual.

These massive weather systems, separated by a thousand miles of forest, mountain, tundra, and taiga, were on a collision course, headed straight toward Joe Wilcox.

On the summit at an elevation of 20,320 feet, Wilcox watched wind-whipped cirrus clouds high above him. These clouds marked the margins of the two massive weather systems as they began to brush against each other. In a matter of hours one of the most violent storms ever recorded on the mountain would engulf the peak and leave seven of Joe Wilcox's twelve-man expedition dead.

Joe stood six foot one inch tall. He was twenty-four years old.

---

* "Eskimo" is commonly used in Alaska to refer to all Inuit and Yupik people of the world. It is considered derogatory in many other places because it was given by non-Inuit people and was said to mean "eater of raw meat." Linguists now believe that "Eskimo" is derived from an Ojibwa word meaning "to net snowshoes."

I was five. I don't know why my dad took me along on the drive in his light-green Park Service sedan deep into the park that midsummer night. It might have been because I'd been cooped up in the house by days of rain, or maybe he just wanted the company of his son. Whatever the reason, there I was, wearing my red-topped rubber boots next to Dad on the wide bench seat as we weaved along the endless muddy road deep inside Mount McKinley National Park. Two more light-green park vehicles, with rangers at the wheels, followed behind. With the sun low on the horizon it was light out, but low-hanging clouds obscured Denali and the alpine vistas that flanked the road. The small black spruce and willow trees, stunted by the high altitude and latitude, marched up the hillsides and disappeared into the mist as we passed by. The creek beds roiled with muddy, brown water from bank to bank, the result of the steady rain that had not yet stopped.

Most of the time, I loved riding shotgun with Dad. He was a gregarious man who sang while he drove, mostly military songs he learned in the Army Air Corps during World War II. When he wasn't singing, *"Over hill, over dale, as we hit the dusty trail . . ."* he was whistling, telling stories, pointing out landmarks and wildlife, or expounding on historical facts that were usually without much meaning to my young mind. I'd lean against him on the seat and steer the car while he kept us on the road with his thumbs secretly pressed against the bottom of the steering wheel.

That night, he was a different man. His National Park Service–issue tan Stetson sat between us on the seat; it rarely left the hat rack at park headquarters. I was used to being quiet, since he usually did all the talking, but this time Dad was almost as mute as I was. The air hung heavy with the absence of his chatter and gave the car a closed-in, somber feel. He whistled a little at first, but the songs trailed off, like his heart wasn't in it. Soon the rhythm of the windshield wipers and the slosh and ping of the muddy gravel road under our wheels was our only accompaniment.

We drove far into the park, the distance elongated by the strange silence, and finally stopped at a pullout near a rain-swollen river. Dad got out, slipped a green raincoat over his uniform, and huddled with the other men. The air was sharply cool and carried the tang of freshly cut earth. I noticed places where the riverbank had fallen into rushing water. Bored, I walked toward the river, tossed in sticks, and watched the current sweep them away. The last time we'd stopped here on a family outing, the river looked completely different—a series of gravel bars laced with narrow braids of flowing water. Now it was a single channel of brown water, wider than the park road.

Dad returned to my side, but the others waited in their vehicles with engines idling and headlights shining in the rainy gloom. We ambled slowly along the swollen river. I skipped stones while Dad trailed behind, one eye on me while he scanned up and down the riverbank. He didn't join in the rock skipping or find flat rocks for me; I was on my own. The turbulent water made skipping difficult, so I turned my attention to bigger rocks, heaving in big clunkers to hear the satisfying thunk and the muffled, bowling-alley crashes as they careened along the rocky riverbed in the swift current.

We were nearly out of sight of the vehicles when Dad looked up and suddenly stiffened.

"Andy, get back to the car," he said. "Now."

I froze and looked at him in confusion.

He didn't look back at me but gazed downstream. "Go," he said, calmly but firmly.

I turned, took a step, and promptly tripped and fell onto the rocks. I saw blood trickle onto my palms. He moved quickly and grabbed my hand, took two strides, and then swung me ahead of him, repeating the process as we scrambled over the rocks and driftwood along the riverbank. He set me down on a sandy stretch and I ran, but I was too small to keep up, so he reached down and grabbed my hand again. I held his hand with both of mine, lifted my feet off of the ground, and ventured a look behind as he swung me ahead toward the idling cars. Far downstream, maybe a couple hundred yards, a dark, hulking shape had emerged from the brush along the river and loped toward us.

Grizzly bear, I thought. He never said the words, but I was pretty sure Dad was thinking the same thing.

Fear seized me. I'd seen plenty of grizzly bears, but always from the safety of our car, never on foot with nothing between us but rain and wind. Children who lived in the park were warned to retreat indoors at the first sign of the big animal. Doors to the homes in the small enclave that surrounded park headquarters were not locked, and we all understood that it was OK to enter any home at any time, if necessary, to avoid wildlife. Running wasn't advised when encountering a bear, but we'd also been told that when refuge is close, it's always wise to seek it. Dad was following that advice. Paralyzed with fear and dangling from Dad's grip like a rag doll, I looked backward rather than forward, watching the intruder's slow progress as Dad hustled us to where the others waited.

Back in the car, we watched as the dark shape shambled along the bank where we had stood minutes earlier. Just as suddenly as he had grabbed my hand and retreated, Dad relaxed, his shoulders slumping and the firm, set line of his lips upturning in relief. He opened the door and walked toward the approaching figure as it came into focus. I stayed in the backseat, still scared, even though I could see that it was no grizzly but a man wearing a huge backpack and caped by a billowing brown rain poncho.

Mountaineers were rare in those days. About twenty came to the park each year to climb, and they were enigmas to me, even more unusual than the moose and bear and sheep that frequented this two-million-acre wilderness preserve. Somehow I knew he was a climber, though he was the first one I'd seen. He was tall and his wet clothes hung loosely on his lean frame. I peered over the dashboard to get a closer look at this rare creature, taking in his unbuttoned flannel shirt, mud-covered high-water pants, thick-knuckled fingers, and battered boots. At first I thought he was as ancient as Dad, but when he turned his head and saw me watching him, he smiled. His teeth were dazzling against his brown beard and sunburned face, and I realized he was not much older than the teenage boys who lived next door.

I don't know what they said to each other—I stayed in the car, watching from my perch behind the dashboard as they talked. The young man unshouldered his pack and did most of the talking, gesturing with his hands and occasionally pointing into the foggy distance. Dad and the rangers listened intently, their faces serious, rain dripping from the brims of their Stetsons. After what seemed like hours, the circle of men broke, the climber got into one of the other vehicles, and we began the long drive home, slithering and bouncing along the muddy park road.

I peppered Dad with questions about the strange man who had emerged from a wilderness that I thought was home only to moose, caribou, sheep, and bear: Who is he? Where did he come from? Why had we come all this way to meet him?

After a long silence my father said there had been a climbing accident on Denali and some boys had died. His voice was heavy and sounded tired, as if the words were difficult to pronounce. His tone told me the moment was grave, and part of me knew I should share his sadness. But I was just a kid and I was both scared and excited by the thrilling sprint along the river.

"What happened, Daddy, did they fall off a cliff?" I asked.

"There was a bad storm, kiddo. We don't know what happened to them yet, but we're trying to find out."

"Why don't you just fly up and get them?" I continued.

"We did, but the boys we found were already dead."

"Are you going to bring them down?"

"No, we'll probably leave them buried in the snow."

"What if the snow melts?"

"They're in snow that never melts."

CHAPTER 1

THOSE WHO CAME
BEFORE

The Athabaskan people have lived in the shadow of the great mountain for ten thousand years and know it by many names. To the people of the Lower Tanana, it is Deenaadheet or Deennadhee. The Dena'ina call it Dghelay Ka'a; the Koyukon, Deenaali. Each tribe's name, though unique, translates to roughly the same meaning: the Big One, the High One, the Great One.

Neither legends nor oral tradition indicate that Alaska's Native people desired or attempted to climb it. Though it was revered, no taboo appears to have kept Alaska's indigenous people from standing on the summit. A healthy aversion to the treacheries of glacier travel and perhaps common sense were enough.

The subsistence life was hard. The icy slopes and inhospitable mountaintop held no allure to those whose lives were focused on the already-difficult challenge of surviving off the subarctic wilderness; in fact, they avoided the desolate terrain. When Alfred Brooks made the first approach to the mountain in 1902 during a US Geological Survey he knew he was the first white man to see it up close, and speculated that no Alaska Native had been so near to it either.

> I was far beyond, where the moccasined foot of the roving Indian had never trod. The Alaska Native seldom goes beyond the limit of smooth walking and has a superstitious horror of even approaching glacial ice.

▲▲

Among the world's high mountains, summits in excess of 20,000 feet are surprisingly common. In the South American Andes, more than forty exceed 20,000 feet in height; in the Himalayas, hundreds rise higher. But height alone does not define a mountain. While Denali is the tallest mountain in North America at 20,320 feet, it also is arguably the biggest mountain on the planet.

The Denali massif is bounded on the west by Kahiltna Pass and to the east by the Traleika Col. The Peters Glacier, at the base of the Wickersham Wall, is its northern boundary. The Ruth Gap marks its southern edge. Within those margins is Denali, a 144-square-mile mass of rock, snow, and ice that rises abruptly from a 2,000-foot plateau, soaring 18,000 feet from base to summit, the greatest vertical relief of any mountain on Earth, with the exception of the Hawaiian seamount Mauna Kea, the bulk of which lies beneath the Pacific Ocean. In comparison, Mount Everest, though 29,029 feet above sea level, rests on the 17,000-foot-high Tibetan Plateau and rises just 12,000 feet from base to summit. A similar plateau boosts the Andes; without those geologic booster seats, those peaks all would lie in Denali's shadow.

Denali is the apex of the Alaska Range, a cordillera that arcs 600 miles across Alaska, dividing the coastal lowlands around Cook Inlet from the Yukon lowlands of interior Alaska. The great range is about 60 miles wide near Denali and home to twenty peaks taller than 10,000 feet.

Most of the cordillera is composed of sedimentary shale, limestone, and sandstone that is between 100 and 400 million years old, but a handful of peaks—among them Denali, Foraker, Hunter, and the Moose's Tooth—arise from a younger 35-million-year-old granite intrusion. Tectonic activity continues to push the entire range upward at a rate of about one millimeter a year even as the erosive action of wind, water, and ice wear it down. The durable gray-and-pink granite ensures that millions of years from now Denali and its granite brothers will endure long after their sedimentary neighbors have been reduced to glacial dust and carried away by wind and water.

Europeans began exploring Alaska a little more than two hundred years ago and, upon seeing the mountain dominating the interior skyline, were immediately impressed by its evident size. Russian trappers were the earliest to push into the hinterlands and, like the Alaska Natives, were prosaic about the mountain, referring to it as Bolshaya Gora, or Big Mountain. British Navy captain George Vancouver made the earliest written reference to Denali in 1794 after navigating the silty shoals of Knik Arm at the head of Cook Inlet. Standing on the deck of the HMS *Discovery,* he looked north and noted the horizon "bounded by distant stupendous snow mountains."

When prospector Frank Densmore visited Lake Minchumina in 1889, the big mountain rising to the south so enthralled him that he couldn't stop talking about it—so much so that for years it was known among prospectors as Densmore's Peak.

Denali was already well known in Alaska when it entered into the national consciousness on January 24, 1897. An article in *The*

New York Sun written by William Dickey ignored millennia of indigenous tradition and decades of local custom by replacing the name Denali with Mount McKinley, after an Ohio politician who had just been nominated for the presidency of the United States. William McKinley had no connection to Alaska, but was a proponent of the gold standard, a fact not lost on Dickey, a gold prospector. Alaskans and others familiar with the territory challenged Dickey's label, saying a traditional name was more appropriate. The issue had not yet been settled four years later when an assassin killed President McKinley, and his name became permanently affixed to the mountain. In the same article, Dickey estimated the mountain's elevation at 20,000 feet. His controversial christening and astonishingly accurate elevation estimate put the mountain on the map, and for the next twenty years virtually all travel to the region was for exploration and mountaineering.

Judge James Wickersham and four companions made the first serious attempt to climb Denali during the summer of 1903. The party journeyed into the remote region aboard the riverboat *Tanana Chief,* starting on the Chena River and navigating down the Tanana and up the Kantishna River before disembarking for the final overland approach. On May 19, Wickersham and his party left the little steamboat behind and camped with "Nachereah, the moose hunter" and "Olyman the wise." Their hunting party was composed of fifty Athabaskan Indians and a hundred malamute dogs.

With the help of an interpreter, Wickersham described the quest to their nomadic hosts.

> At my request he tells them of our journey to the big mountain and our wish to reach its summit. Ju-dan told us in broken English, "Mountain Sheep fall off that mountain— guess white man no stick 'um." Incredulity appeared on

every unwashed face at the statement of our purpose. "What for you go top—gold?" No, we go merely to see the top, to be the first men to reach the summit. This information imparted by the interpreter caused Olyman to remark in brief Indian phrases, which McLeod translated after the rude laughter had subsided as; "He says you are a fool."

Undaunted by the ridicule of the pragmatic Natives, the party hiked south and entered the folds of the mountain via the Peters and Jeffery Glaciers. They soon came to the mountain's massive north face, a nearly vertical escarpment that rises all the way to the 19,470-foot north summit. But they could find no way to the top and ended their quest at an elevation of about 8,000 feet on what has since proved to be one of the mountain's most technically challenging routes. Wickersham's party wore wool, canvas, and leather, adequate to protect them from the cold weather encountered on the mountain. Their climbing tools, however, were rudimentary by today's standards. They climbed with alpenstocks—six-foot-long, steel-tipped, wooden staffs first used during the Middle Ages by shepherds in the Swiss Alps. In the latter half of the eighteenth century mountaineers added an ax head with a pointed pick on one side and a flattened adz blade on the other. The pick was used to gain purchase on the steep slopes and the adz blade was used to chip out ice steps. Crampons of the day were more like spiked horseshoes, providing good traction underfoot, but little help on steep or vertical ice. In light of the many obstacles found on the impossibly steep wall, including overhanging rock and ice, chimneys, and fissures, the long-handled ax would have been unwieldy at best. In the hands of Wickersham and his companions, hardened Alaska sourdoughs but novice mountaineers, they weren't enough to assist them in getting where they wanted to go—the summit.

Wickersham's June 20 journal entry captures the moment of surrender.

> I was then convinced that no possibility existed of our overcoming the apparent obstacles to our higher climb— we were climbing on a spur as sharp as a house roof, rapidly rising to where it was nearly perpendicular—solid glare ice, and above it rose thousands of feet of glacial ice undermined and even falling by reason of the hot weather and constant sliding out of the softer snow.

Though he never made the summit, the north face of the mountain, where he ended his quest, was named for him, today known as the Wickersham Wall, a 3-mile-wide precipice that sweeps skyward for 14,000 feet from the Peters Glacier to the summit of the north peak, making the facade of rock, ice, and snow one of the largest on Earth.

Snow falls down to 6,000 feet on Denali in every month of the year, giving it one of Earth's greatest permanently snow-covered vertical reliefs. And that extraordinary snowfall spawns some of the highest and longest glaciers in the Alaska Range. The Harper Glacier originates in the perpetual snow between Denali's twin summits and feeds the Muldrow, a 41-mile-long ice river that scours a U-shaped valley on the mountain's northeast side. To the south, the 44-mile-long Kahiltna is the longest glacier in the range. The Ruth Glacier spans 38 miles as it flows through the spectacular Don Sheldon Amphitheater. There the ice is a mile thick and the granite walls rise a mile above that.

Two months after Wickersham's attempt, Dr. Frederick Cook's expedition followed a similar route, pushing deeper into the massif to the Peters Basin and ascending the steep and treacherous

Northwest Buttress to an elevation of 11,000 feet. Cook, like Wickersham, was just a mile from the summit as the crow flies, but then, crows can fly. He had underestimated the size of the wall and soon realized the route was too difficult and time-consuming for him and his companions. Still, it was a notable achievement for the four men, three climbing with the aid of alpenstocks and the fourth relying on a tent pole. Undaunted, Cook returned to Denali in 1906 with three other climbers, including Belmore Browne and Herschel Parker. After an initial summit bid failed, Cook set out again while Browne and Parker remained in camp, and returned claiming to have reached the top. Irrefutable evidence soon revealed that this claim was fraudulent, though the Frederick A. Cook Society claims to this day that Cook was the first to summit.

During the winter of 1910, four Kantishna miners, incensed at Cook's deception and fueled by a barroom bet, set out for the summit. The Sourdough Expedition spent three months approaching the mountain by dogsled and ascending via the Muldrow Glacier. Three men climbed an astounding 8,000 feet on their summit day, carrying two thermoses of hot chocolate and half a dozen doughnuts in a burlap sack. Two of them, William Taylor and Pete Anderson, reached the top and spent two and a half hours on the north summit taking in the view and planting a fourteen-foot spruce pole in a location they thought could be seen in Fairbanks, 150 miles distant. They had topped the 19,470-foot north peak not realizing, or not caring, that it was 850 feet lower than the south peak. Alaskans were enthused that a group of hardened Alaska miners found success where East Coast cheechakos had failed. Still, the highest summit in North America had yet to be conquered.

On February 1, 1912, with spring still far off, Browne and Parker set out from the port town of Seward for the great mountain, at first hitching rides on dogsleds to the settlement of Knik near present-day

Anchorage. With neither road nor rail links yet established, it was the only mode of overland travel that would get them to the interior in winter. At Knik they met up with Arthur Aten and Merl LaVoy, veterans of an unsuccessful 1910 expedition mounted by Browne. The two men arrived two months earlier to begin caching food and supplies along the trail. They kept to the Iditarod Trail mail route at first but not long after leaving Knik set out across the trackless wilderness ascending the Susitna River. Highways and a railroad now span much of the 500-mile route they and their dogs would follow.

The four-month odyssey took the adventurers north from tidewater, across the Cook Inlet lowlands, and through the Alaska Range, a tremendous feat in and of itself. Once on the north side of the range, they established base camp in the willows at the head of Cache Creek. While Aten tended the lower camp, Browne, Parker, and LaVoy began their ascent, following the route the Sourdough miners had established in 1910, accessing the upper mountain via the Muldrow Glacier and climbing what would later be named Karstens Ridge. On June 29, after three weeks of arduous climbing, Browne, LaVoy, and Parker left their camp at 16,600 feet on the Harper Glacier, intent on reaching the summit. A blizzard blew up as they methodically cut steps into the icy slope above them. Cresting a rise, the full force of the gale struck Browne and he realized that even though the summit was enticingly close, to continue would be suicide.

> As I brushed the frost from my glasses and squinted upward through the stinging snow I saw a sight that will haunt me to my dying day. The slope above me was no longer steep! That was all I could see. What it meant I will never know for certain—all I can say is that we were close to the top!

Browne's party most likely reached Farthing Horn at 20,125 feet, a few hundred yards away, and just 200 feet lower than the summit. There, they tried to wait out the weather but quickly realized their extremities were freezing and began a harrowing return to camp. They spent June 30 resting and set out the following day, only to be thwarted again by dense, wind-driven snow.

Exhausted and heartbroken, the party descended to base camp two weeks later than planned, where they reunited with a relieved Aten and turned for home. On July 6 a massive earthquake jolted interior Alaska, bringing down avalanches and rock falls on Denali and the surrounding peaks.

Had they remained to make another summit attempt rather than turning back when they did, Browne and his companions almost certainly would have died there.

The race for the top ended in 1913 when Archdeacon Hudson Stuck, Harry Karstens, Robert Tatum, and Walter Harper set out from Fairbanks by dogsled, headed for the Kantishna mining district and on to McGonagall Pass, the gateway to the Muldrow Glacier. Though Stuck organized the expedition, Karstens, a veteran of the Klondike Gold Rush, led the climb. The expedition lasted three months and again followed in the footsteps of the Sourdoughs even though the earthquake had shattered Karstens Ridge, leaving it a jumble of massive ice blocks.

Where deception, confusion, and poor weather had stymied earlier attempts, the Karstens/Stuck Expedition succeeded with hard work and no small amount of good luck. Harper, an Athabaskan Indian, was the first to set foot on the summit.

On June 7, 1913, Karstens, who later would become the first superintendent of Mount McKinley National Park, noted the event with pride, compassion, and poor grammar:

Cold & Clear. "Hurrah" The south summit of Mt. McKinley has been conquered. Everyone out of condition on last
night & no one slept we tried from 7 to 10 but not go so we
all sat arround primus stove with quilts on our backs waiting for 4 Oclock. My stumach was bad and I had one of
the most severe Headaches if it where not final climb I
should have stayed in camp but being the final climb &
such a promising day I managed to pull through I put
Walter in lead an kept him there all day with never a
change. I took 2nd place on rope so I could direct Walter
and he worked all day without a murmur.

During the ascent, Walter Harper had spotted the spruce pole
planted on the north peak by the Sourdoughs. Once he pointed it
out, Tatum and Karstens confirmed it with field glasses, saying "it
was plain and prominent and unmistakable." A monument to the
power of hot chocolate, doughnuts, and perhaps barroom bets.

Even during the long days of the boreal summer, when the sun
barely sets and midnight is more like dusk, the summit is known as
one of the coldest places on the planet with the average temperature
remaining below zero. During the dark days of January the average
temperature is closer to minus 30 degrees Fahrenheit.

The mountain's subarctic latitude and great elevation combine
to produce its especially harsh conditions. Earth's atmosphere ta-
pers at the North and South Poles and as a result, the troposphere—
the life-supporting lowest layer—is shallower at extreme northern
and southern latitudes. At the equator it is 10 miles thick, at the
North Pole, about 5. A mere 1,800 miles from the North Pole, Denali
rises 4 miles high and is closer to the top of the troposphere than
many higher peaks at lower latitudes, like Mount Everest.

Proximity to the top of the troposphere means two things. First, there is less oxygen near the summit of Denali than there would be at a mountain of identical elevation at the equator, and 42 percent less than at sea level. At the summit it takes two gasps to bring in the amount of oxygen that one breath delivers on the beach in Hawaii. Second, the thinner troposphere means the jet stream, wind that constantly moves through the upper troposphere near the boundary with the stratosphere, is closer than anywhere on the planet. Atmospheric conditions can drive the jet stream lower, commonly bringing winds of 100 miles per hour or more to bear on Denali's heights.

And when those high-speed air currents encounter the peak's morphology (the shape of the mountaintop), their velocity can increase dramatically. At Denali Pass, between the north and south summits, a stream of air moving perpendicular to the peaks creates a relative vacuum and pulls wind through the pass at speeds much greater than that of the prevailing wind. When the wind blows through Denali Pass, it is compressed and accelerated like water through the nozzle of a fire hose.

On Denali, where 100-mile-per-hour winds are common, meteorologists agree that downslope winds three times that velocity are possible, peeling away snow, ice, loose rock, and any climber unfortunate enough to be in their path. The phenomenon takes place when fast-moving air piles up against a peak or ridge, boils over the top, and plummets down the lee side. Denali, with its particular geography, is the perfect crucible for such extreme wind events. Mountaineers have never reported such velocities, but then again, surviving such conditions would be unlikely.

The fastest wind speed ever recorded on land by a measuring device was a gust of 231 miles per hour on Mount Washington in Maine on April 12, 1934. A comparison can be made between both the 1967 storm and the storm that produced that record-setting gust.

Both involved strengthening high- and low-pressure systems that created an abnormally powerful pressure gradient between them that was also precisely over a large mountain—Denali in one case and Mount Washington in the other.

While the rest of the Alaska Range bathes in sunlight, Denali often is shrouded in mist or capped by saucer-shaped lenticular clouds. Because of its height, bulk, and permanently icy mantle, it often creates its own weather. The Alaska Range acts like a mountainous bulwark, separating the moist coastal air coming from Cook Inlet to the south from the drier conditions to the north. The great wall arcs across the lower third of the state of Alaska, from Canada to the Alaska Peninsula, with Denali at its apex acting like a sentry to the comings and goings of snow and wind and rain. When the cool highs and moist lows breach the wall and clash over the range, storms can arise with little warning. Moisture, condensing when pushed into the air surrounding the frigid peak, can transform visibility from crystal-clear to something like being on the inside of a Ping-Pong ball in a matter of minutes. Avalanches are frequent, as year-round snowfalls are released by changing temperatures; crevasses are strewn everywhere, hidden beneath thin layers of snow and ice.

The idea that such a place can be conquered may seem foolish.

▲▲

As the decades passed following the first ascent of Denali, climbing waxed and waned as the Depression, two world wars, and finally peace and postwar prosperity brought mountain climbing into the mainstream. In 1954, my father joined the National Park Service as the first historian at the Sitka National Historic Park. The parameters of the job were unclear, so he defined them himself. The federal government was actively suppressing the religion, language, and customs of the Tlingit people who had lived in the region for thousands of years. When he arrived in Sitka, my father realized that young Tlingit people were not learning about their own culture and an entire generation of tradition bearers were dying—and with them the region's indigenous culture and language. Carrying a suitcase-size reel-to-reel tape recorder, he visited villages throughout Southeast Alaska, interviewing elders and recording their songs, stories, and traditions.

My father worked out an agreement that put many Tlingit artifacts on permanent loan from Tlingit clans and families to the Sitka National Historical Park with the understanding that they would remain available to the owners when needed for ceremonial or other purposes. The agreement remains in place today and those totem poles, blankets, robes, hats, house fronts, and other cultural items are still held in trust at the Sitka National Historical Park's visitor center. To honor his work, Tlingit elder Alex Andrew adopted my father, made him a member of the Kiks.adi clan, and they named him Shakshanee Ish. He later learned that a man named Shakshanee Ish had lived in Sitka and died in the early part of the century. Reincarnation is part of the Tlingit belief system and many of the elders in Sitka had known the first Shakshanee Ish. They told my father, "You're just like him."

Perhaps due to his demonstrated success in working with Tlingit people, the National Park Service drafted my father for a management training program in Washington, DC. With the birth of my sister, Gerianne, in 1960 and me two years later, he began to think about his career. Gone were the days of roaming the islands of the Alexander Archipelago in the Park Service boat to interview ancient men and women who spoke of an earlier time in Tlingit, the only language they'd ever known. In late 1964 our family traveled to Washington, DC, where my father went to work at the Department of the Interior, ultimately working in the office of National Park Service director George Hartzog.

My parents had met and started our family in Sitka, a small island town. Though my father grew up in Chicago, and my mother in Connecticut, Alaska had changed them. The heat, the traffic, the social pecking order, and the proximity to so many other people in Washington, DC, was oppressive after life among the giant spruce trees and dignified Tlingit elders. Early in their tenure back East they agreed that if they could get back to Alaska, they'd never leave. When the Mount McKinley superintendent's job was offered, my father called my mother to tell her the news and by the time he got home, she had already listed our house with a Realtor.

When my family and I arrived at Mount McKinley National Park in April of 1967, barely fifty years had passed since Walter Harper first stood on the summit. In that half century, 420 mountaineers had attempted to scale the mountain, 213 had succeeded, and 4 had died trying. Allen Carpe and Theodore Koven fell into Muldrow Glacier crevasses in 1932. Park ranger Elton Thayer tumbled to his death while descending Karstens Ridge in 1954, and just prior to our arrival, in February of 1967, Jacques Batkin had died in a crevasse on the Kahiltna Glacier.

Denali was still a remote and exotic climbing destination, known to be a challenging and unpredictable mountain, but not particularly deadly.

That was about to change.

CHAPTER 2

WHAT MAKES AN EXPEDITION?

J oe Wilcox first experienced Alaska sweating over a chainsaw on slopes crowded with Sitka spruce in the summer of 1966. He was in the islands of the state's southeast, cutting transects through the temperate rain forest for the United States Forest Service. During those long days amid majestic scenery, his thoughts turned to the highest peak in North America. Though hundreds of miles away, and much too far away to see, Denali called. During the trip home to Utah he hatched a plan a return to Alaska in the summer of 1967. The obstacles piled up before him, but he was intent on climbing the big mountain. Before all the practical matters of equipment, food, timing, and transportation were addressed, he would need to assemble a team.

Back home in Utah, his newlywed wife, Cheryl, was agreeable. They had recently arrived at Brigham Young University, where they were both pursuing studies. Wilcox was already acquainted with many climbers there and began trying to enlist expedition members. He imagined a six-man team, but the experienced climbers he hoped to draft declined, one after another. Each man had a good excuse, but Wilcox wondered if his personality had something to do with the dearth of willing expedition members. "I was rather non-gregarious . . . sometimes lacking in tactful social amenities."

When Jerry Clark and Mark McLaughlin signed on in November, the Wilcox McKinley Expedition suddenly grew wings. McLaughlin was recommended to Wilcox by a mutual friend and brought excellent climbing credentials, including several ascents of Mount Rainier. He recommended Jerry Clark, who offered even more experience. Clark was a gregarious thirty-one-year-old who had an extensive climbing résumé, including eight trips to the Tetons, two in the Wind River Range, and two trips to Antarctica. Though he was on the southern continent for scientific work, he taught mountaineering and got to the top of one unnamed peak before spending the remainder of his time driving around in a snowcat measuring ice thickness. Clark had been climbing for fourteen years and, a few years prior, had been approved to lead a Denali climb. He was small at five foot seven and 145 pounds, and while not known for tremendous strength he was a smart and careful climber.

So Clark had deeper mountaineering experience than Wilcox, and where Wilcox appeared blunt and distant, Clark was open and friendly. Between classes, Wilcox dove into planning and organizing the climb—something he could do on his own, which suited his nature better than the social aspects of recruitment. He decided that the team would climb via the Muldrow Glacier on the north side of the mountain. This was an arduous route to the summit, but less expensive for a large, cost-conscious party, and none of these young men had much money to spare.

Wilcox mailed out fourteen copies of an expedition newsletter on November 16, 1966—the first of several—to potential expedition members in five states. The blue ink of the Ditto copies spelled out the cost as $300 per person (equivalent to about $2,000 nowadays), which would cover "food and group gear" as well as transportation from Seattle to Alaska and back. While the cost was a stretch for most of the young men interested in joining Wilcox's expedition, it was still a bargain. Forty years later, climbers pay $6,000 to $8,000 per person to join a guided expedition.

While the official start date was not set, the letter spelled out a "get acquainted workout" to be held on Mount Rainier immediately prior to leaving for Alaska. Rainier would be where the group would get a feel for one another's abilities and personalities before they roped up at McGonagall Pass and headed up Denali's Muldrow Glacier. "Every person will be expected to be in attendance," Wilcox wrote, "unless arrangements are made with the leader"—a phrase he appears to have grown fond of, at least in his missives.

Though Wilcox was the expedition leader "primarily because I conceived of it and organized it," most of the men signing on to the expedition were strangers to him, joining by Clark's invitation. "I was a bit uncomfortable leading an expedition composed largely of Jerry Clark's friends," he wrote. "But Jerry's complete cooperation and support was reassuring."

A mail-order expedition like Wilcox's was not unusual at the time. The climbing community was small and assembling a large expedition sometimes meant bringing strangers together. Wilcox trusted Clark's judgment, but he knew significant variation in skill levels might prove to be a problem. Meanwhile, there were other, more mundane, problems to consider.

▲▲▲

In early December, Joe Wilcox continued his planning and research. He applied to Mount McKinley National Park for permission to climb and at the same time wrote to Bradford Washburn, who was the director of the Boston Museum of Science.

Bradford Washburn's opinion mattered. He was virtually synonymous with Denali for the latter half of the twentieth century, first visiting the mountain in 1936 at the request of Gilbert M. Grosvenor, the longtime editor of *National Geographic*. On assignment for the world-renowned publication, Washburn hired a pilot who removed the door to accommodate the large camera and then circled the mountain just below the summit. Wearing a cold-weather flying suit, mittens, and an oxygen mask, Washburn spent two days perched on a gas can, photographing the great mountain. He made two more photo expeditions to the mountain in 1937 and 1938. Washburn had scaled mountains all over the world, but it was 1942 before he set foot on Denali for the first time as part of the US Army Test Expedition. He returned in 1947 to lead Operation White Tower, an expedition fueled by an odd mix of hard science and Hollywood. RKO Pictures had acquired the movie rights to a wartime novel called *The White Tower,* about a mythical peak in the Alps. When a movie executive called to ask if he would lead an expedition to Mount Everest to capture film footage, Washburn convinced him to film on Denali. He also proposed conducting a series of scientific studies in concert with the filming, and soon several Harvard scientists, handpicked by Washburn, had signed on. The major scientific goal was cosmic ray research that could be effectively conducted only at high altitudes, where the atmosphere was thin. The Air Force supported prior research from high-altitude aircraft but experiments were limited by the duration of the flights. A camp at 18,000 feet on Denali would provide a unique vantage point and allow experiments to run longer. Given the scientific element of the operation, the Air Force agreed to provide air support to Operation White Tower. Though a nine-day storm hampered progress and damaged equipment early on, the research was conducted over a ten-day period from a camp at Denali Pass. Between the storm and the start of the research, several expedition members, including Washburn and his wife, Barbara, climbed the south peak. Washburn had melded science and showbiz, and he had managed to get himself and his wife to the summit, making her the first woman to climb Denali.

Washburn was known to be both imperious and generous, equally comfortable discussing the mountain with John F. Kennedy, who had served on the museum's board, or a penniless climber looking for a new route to the summit.

Joe Wilcox wrote to Washburn on December 2, 1966, during the winter before the proposed expedition, describing his plan and seeking the endorsement of Washburn's museum. Such support would bring financial advantages, but Wilcox wanted to make a scientific contribution to the mountain's knowledge base as well.

> I have organized and will be leading a ten man expedition on Mt. McKinley this summer (Muldrow Route). The expedition has been divided into two groups: a high climbing group composed of six climbers with the primary purpose of reaching the summit and a four man scientific group with the primary objective of carrying out scientific experiments on the Muldrow Glacier between McGonagall Pass and the base of Karstens Ridge (they will not go above this elevation).

Wilcox described the team and their educational background in detail but did not fully describe the study, saying only that Dr. Marion Millett of the BYU Geography Department was supervising the planning of the scientific group.

His plea for help was vague, specifying that he did not want money, just an endorsement that would convince the National Park Service to relax its flight rules, which allowed aircraft on and around the mountain only to support scientific research or search and rescue activity. The no-fly rule meant mountaineers carried all the food and gear they'd need to get to and from the summit on their backs. Ferrying supplies onto the mountain by small plane could save time, and Wilcox knew that.

Washburn promptly and politely replied, noting that the Muldrow Glacier was more passable than it had been in recent years. He offered to sell Wilcox maps and photos that might help with planning and then addressed the scientific study, saying that geologists with PhDs would be necessary. This was not what Wilcox had hoped for. With no such expertise available, endorsement by the Boston Museum of Science was out of the question.

Wilcox's glacier study involved using a theodolite to align a row of bamboo wands at intervals across the surface of the glaciers to be studied. Three weeks after the initial alignment, another theodolite reading of the wand positions would be extrapolated to reveal surface-ice movement. The study may well have been merely a ruse to get around the no-fly rule, as others in the group believed. But it is indisputable that such data is useful—in retrospect all the more so, thanks to global climate change.

Brad Washburn had discouraged the scientific component of the expedition. But Wilcox wondered if perhaps he could be of some help with publicity for sponsorship purposes. After all, he had been very successful in publicizing his own climbs. Months later, and just weeks before the expedition would get on the road to Denali, Wilcox reached out again to Washburn. On May 12, after disclosing his plans to news organizations, he wrote seeking advice on the veracity of the "firsts" he was considering for his climb:

Dear Dr. Washburn:

I will be leading a nine-man expedition on Mount McKinley this June. It appears that we will receive considerable publicity from area newspapers and TV stations to the extent that they may send me to Alaska to cover the expedition. They seem excited by the fact that we may put a camp on the summit, climb both summits simultaneously, or put a camp on each summit. According to the Park Service, some climbers spent the night on the summit in 1960. To the best of your knowledge.

Has anyone else spent the night on the summit?

Has any group climbed both peaks simultaneously?

Has anyone camped on the north summit?

Has anyone camped on both summits simultaneously?

Your help will be greatly appreciated. I do not want my group to claim a "first" unless it is indeed, a "first." Please reply soon, because the news media are anxious to start releases.

Sincerely,
Joseph F. Wilcox.

Washburn didn't delay in responding, though Wilcox probably wished he had. It was written on Museum of Science letterhead and dated May 17.

Dear Mr. Wilcox:

We have received your extraordinary letter regarding the plans for your record-breaking efforts this year on Mt. McKinley. I have answered hundreds of queries about McKinley over a long period of time, but never before have I been faced with the problem of answering one quite like this. In fact, I am amazed that the National Park Service would grant a permit for such a weird undertaking.

A Japanese party spent a very comfortable night on top of the South Peak and another party climbed both peaks of McKinley in the same day. In fact, the 1942 Army Expedition and our 1947 expedition lived comfortably for literally weeks above 15,000 feet and could easily have spent a week or more on top of either or both of the peaks if we had had the slightest inclination to do so—or any conceivable practical reason for it. After all, climbers have spent week after week on Everest, K-2, Nanga Parbat and scores of other Himalayan giants far in excess of McKinley's altitude, packing heavy loads and climbing difficult rock and ice simply for the sheer love of it—not just sleeping their way into headlines!

For your information, according to our records, McKinley has not yet been climbed blindfolded or backwards, nor has any party of nine persons yet fallen simultaneously into the same crevasse. We hope that you may wish to arise to one of these compelling challenges.

Very truly yours,
Bradford Washburn
Director

Washburn's vitriol didn't end at the sarcastic evisceration of Wilcox's proposed "firsts." Washburn went on to share his response with other climbers and with the Park Service.

My father wrote to Washburn on June 6, chiding him for attacking Wilcox and saying there were no grounds for denying the Wilcox

Expedition's application to climb. My father described his predicament in a 1999 interview: "Here I've got this guy who was important yet difficult and influential screaming about not letting them on the mountain and I've got no basis that I knew of to not let them on the mountain."

Washburn wrote back to my father on June 12, acknowledging that he had misinterpreted Wilcox's letter, but defended his motivation. Washburn goes on to defend firsts achieved during "regular climbing" and scientific expeditions but says, "It is very much another thing to go off record seeking as an end in itself." He concludes the letter with a prescient warning:

> In chatting with Mr. Wilcox about all this (as I assume he will bring it up in his discussions with you) It might be worthwhile for you to point out these suggestions to him, as my remarks about his plans were not of a wholly negative nature—as record-breaking for the sake of records alone has resulted in an astonishing succession of serious accidents scattered pretty much all over the world— whereas the same sort of operations resulting in the same kind of records but carried out carefully and seriously with practical scientific objectives, seem to have resulted in almost no casualties at all!
>
> Sincerely yours,
> Brad

Joe Wilcox typed more than twenty state-of-the-expedition reports before the full group gathered at Mount Rainier, just south of Seattle. The reports included everything from discussions of proposed

31

menus to gear lists and advice on preparing both the body and the mind for the climb. To prepare the body, he recommended running, swimming, weight lifting, and carrying a heavy pack for long distances. For mental preparation, he required each expedition member to read *The ABCs of Avalanche Safety, The Mountain World,* and *Freedom of the Hills* and to memorize a pamphlet written by none other than Bradford Washburn titled "Frostbite."

In January 1967, Wilcox sent out a report identifying Jerry Clark as deputy leader of the climbing team and Anshel Schiff, PhD, as deputy leader of the scientific/support team. Expedition members were Hank Janes, Dennis Luchterhand, Mark McLaughlin, and Steve Taylor. The names of Walt Taylor and John Russell had been added in blue ink alongside the typed names. Five others were listed, but each would drop out over the next few months for various reasons. The core of the team had formed.

As the summer of 1967 approached, Chief Ranger Art Hayes remained concerned about the lack of experience among some members of the Wilcox Expedition. He had earlier suggested that the group merge with another smaller, yet stronger, group from Colorado comprised of Howard Snyder, Paul Schlichter, Jerry Lewis, and Lewis's younger brother, Steve. The two groups agreed to explore the idea.

In a letter to Wilcox dated May 10, 1967, Chief Ranger Hayes approved the Wilcox Expedition's climbing application, with some caveats requiring the carrying of a radio for communications, less experienced climbers always being in the company of more experienced climbers, and those less experienced climbers receiving days of intensive training on Mount Rainier focusing on "crevasse rescue, belays, self-arrest, etc."

Hayes also made clear that while he felt many in the party had inadequate experience, Wilcox's careful planning, organization, training program, scheduled Rainier climb, and an arrangement with the Alaska Rescue Group to be standing by had convinced him to grant approval. Finally, he wanted to know to what degree the Wilcox and Colorado expeditions would work together.

Though the Wilcox and Colorado contingent had by May agreed to pool resources when mutually beneficial, both parties remained reluctant to unite their expeditions. Colorado expedition leader Howard Snyder's letter to Jerry Clark, written the day after Chief Ranger Hayes wrote to Wilcox, captures this reticence: "It is my intention that we coordinate our efforts, not completely combine them."

Then in June, just seven hours before heading north, a car accident threatened to ground the Colorado Mount McKinley Expedition before it even left Colorado. Steve Lewis, Jerry's younger brother, had broken his nose and hand and could not climb. Howard Snyder had received approval to climb from Chief Ranger Art Hayes, but with the loss of one of their climbers, the expedition no longer met Park Service requirements. The three remaining climbers discussed their options. Rather than climb elsewhere, they decided to approach Wilcox about formally joining his party. In Snyder's words, "We had to either combine with the Wilcox Expedition, or we had to abandon the hopes, plans, and expenditures of the past two years."

Joe Wilcox, along with Hank Janes, Dennis Luchterhand, Mark McLaughlin, Steve Taylor, and John Russell were already at Joe's wife Cheryl's parents' home in Puyallup, Washington, near the foot of Mount Rainier. Howard Snyder called Wilcox and explained their predicament. Wilcox said a merger was possible, but only with the approval of his entire expedition, and invited the three men to come to Rainier for the June 11 training climb. The three remaining climbers of what had been the Colorado Expedition loaded member Jerry Lewis's new Dodge Power Wagon and left Boulder for Mount Rainier on June 9.

CHAPTER 3

A DOZEN KIDS

That June, pop star Scott McKenzie sang, *"If you're going to San Francisco, be sure to wear some flowers in your hair,"* and had a huge Billboard hit, but no one in the Wilcox Expedition was listening.

The house in Puyallup was soon bustling with activity. The sewing machine ran nonstop and vehicles shuttled the young men to and from area sporting-goods stores gathering last-minute supplies. On the night before departing for Rainier, Jerry Clark and Hank Janes called to say they would be delayed. Clark, who had already become the Wilcox team's electronics guru, was modifying the Citizens Band radios they'd be carrying. Hank Janes was altering their rented tents. Walt Taylor had yet to be heard from.

Wilcox and his five companions reached Mount Rainier National Park on June 10, but the Colorado climbers were also nowhere to be seen. After a long wait, they headed to the Nisqually River Bridge to practice ascending ropes using Prusik hitches* and then on to a steep slope to practice self-arrests. After lunch they went on to the Nisqually Glacier to make camp for the night and run through crevasse-rescue techniques. Out on the glacier, a man dressed in oversized wool suit pants and suspenders, his nose and lips slathered in white sun cream, overtook them.

Humorous yet functional garb, thought Wilcox. Walt Taylor had arrived.

After a rainy night on the glacier they spent the foggy morning practicing crevasse rescue and then returned to the parking lot at the mountain's base. There, Denny Luchterhand pulled Wilcox aside and said he was pulling out of the expedition.

"Why?" asked Wilcox.

"I just don't feel good about it; I have a feeling there will be problems on the climb."

They talked a little, but Luchterhand couldn't shake a feeling that "something will go wrong."

"Think it over," concluded Wilcox, presuming Luchterhand's decision was the effect of a couple of days at high altitudes.

While they were talking, Walt Taylor and John Russell had decided to free-climb a rock wall inside the visitor center. Park rangers had halted the fun and Wilcox had to retrieve his wayward team members. So Joe Wilcox was probably a little agitated when he heard the Colorado group had arrived and were camped nearby. They drove to the campsite, where their first meeting was cordial but short. Wilcox didn't

---

* A Prusik is a friction knot used to attach a loop of cord around a climbing rope. The Prusik grips the rope under pressure but can slip when the pressure is relieved. Two Prusiks are used in tandem on one rope, allowing a climber to ascend by shifting weight from one Prusik to the other. While one Prusik holds the climber's weight, the other is moved higher on the rope; then weight is transferred to that one, allowing the other to be loosened and moved up the rope.

get out of his car while speaking to Howard Snyder, who felt that he was being surveyed "like a Hong Kong tailor sizing up a customer."

As Paul Schlichter, one of the Colorado climbers recalls with a chuckle, the exchange was "frosty." "You've got two guys who were going to be leading expeditions, and now one is going to be somewhat the subordinate. Howard is somewhat strong-willed, and he wasn't looking forward to being in a subservient position."

However frostily, Wilcox invited the three newcomers to the house in Puyallup to discuss the merger. By the time they got there, Jerry Clark and Hank Janes had arrived, so all twelve men gathered for the first time in the backyard to talk it through. Of the Wilcox team members, Steve Taylor was most concerned with the intermingling of personnel and equipment and strident in his opposition. Some of Steve's reasons were well thought out, Joe Wilcox said, others were not. Howard Snyder characterized them as inane and said they revealed Steve Taylor's "apparent lack of basic mountaineering knowledge."

Sometime late that night the discussion ended and the merger was approved unanimously. A formal eleven-point written agreement was composed that identified Wilcox as the leader and outlined members' responsibilities and of course the sharing of anticipated costs. Over the decades since Joe Wilcox and Howard Snyder signed their Expedition Agreement, the merger has been portrayed as having been forced on them by the National Park Service. However, former Wonder Lake District Ranger Wayne Merry, the last NPS employee to see the climbers before their ascent, is unequivocal: "Wilcox was under no obligation to accept anybody he didn't want on his team."

In any case, after agreement was reached, the three Colorado climbers—Jerry Lewis, Paul Schlichter, and Howard Snyder—left immediately. While for all practical purposes they would gradually integrate themselves into the group, they always remained the guys from Colorado who joined at the last minute.

▲▲

The Colorado contingent left Puyallup's famous daffodil fields behind and headed for a campground overlooking the gray waters of Puget Sound. It was 3:00 A.M. when they rolled as silently as possible through the campground, the tires of the pickup crackling atop the gravel. Exhausted, but happy that matters were settled with the Wilcox Expedition, they threw out their bedrolls and settled in for a short sleep. The Big Dipper, the brightest stars in the constellation Ursa Major and the symbol on Alaska's iconic state flag, loomed brightly above them. It would be one of the last times they'd see these twinkling lights as they drove north into latitudes where the sun doesn't set in the summer and the starry sky becomes a distant memory until autumn.

The next day, Jerry Lewis, Paul Schlichter, and Howard Snyder awoke early, stuffed their sleeping bags into the nearest open space in the bed of Jerry's Dodge truck, piled into the cab, and headed toward Seattle. They had a few last-minute shopping errands but were eager to turn the truck north. The Canadian border was 114 miles north on Highway 5. The road runs parallel to the coastline, a dozen or so miles inland, passing through Everett, Mount Vernon, and Bellingham before turning inland toward Sumas, Washington, and the Canadian border. The men chatted about past climbs they'd done together and shared thoughts on the coming adventure. At Canadian customs, agents viewed the numerous pairs of snowshoes suspiciously since it was summer, took a look at the clean-cut young men—so unlike the Jim Morrison wannabes and assorted hippies they were increasingly seeing heading north to Alaska—and finally waved them through. Lewis, Schlichter, and Snyder thanked the agents and crossed into British Columbia. Now it was only the 800-mile Cariboo Highway between them and Dawson Creek, the start of the Alaska Highway.

The Wilcox men had planned to hit Canadian customs the same day, but they were still in Puyallup. Some made gear modifications while others made a final run into Seattle to look for bamboo poles to be used as crevasse probes and markers for their unofficial glacier study. They finally found them at a carpet shop. The last thing on the list was down pants for Walt Taylor, a specialty item not easily found but an absolute necessity on Denali. Taylor didn't trust mail-order catalogues, insisting on finding a sporting-goods store where he could try on the pants before purchasing them.

Back at the house, the men reconvened. Food and equipment were split between Hank Janes's Dodge van and Joe Wilcox's sixteen-year-old Chevy Carryall.

"The Hankmobile and the Green Bomb," announced Jerry Clark, christening the vehicles.

What didn't fit in the vehicles, the men placed in a small trailer. Hank Janes, inspired by the coming trip, etched the words "MT. MCKINLEY" onto the back of the trailer and stepped back to admire his work. It would be the caboose to the Green Bomb. But by the time all the packing, christening, hitching, and repacking was done, it was too late to hit the road.

The next morning, Tuesday, June 13, they pooled a few extra bucks to buy roses and gave the bouquet to Joe Wilcox's in-laws, who had put up with them for longer than anyone expected. And then they headed north. It was a road trip in the summer of '67, but this was no band of Merry Pranksters on a psychedelic tour. These former Boy Scouts climbed to get high.

Schiff, Russell, and both Taylors rode with Wilcox in the road-weary Green Bomb. Clark had allayed Luchterhand's concerns about the climb and the two decided to join McLaughlin and Hank Janes, who captained his namesake van. Wilcox's plan called for round-the-clock driving in order to arrive on schedule, and they were already a day behind. In this way, the marathon road trip began with drivers trading off every few hours in order to keep the pace.

No loud music blared—the radio reception through middle-of-nowhere Canada was spotty if it existed at all and they had no other music source. They stayed within the speed limit.

The Hankmobile and the Green Bomb covered 800 miles of paved road the first day to reach Dawson Creek. From there, the Alaska Highway was a two-lane dirt road, rutted in places, muddy in others, and mostly bumpy and dusty.

"You going to eat that?" Russell asked for what seemed like the eight hundredth time. He had been under the impression that his financial contribution to the expedition covered food during the drive.

"You'll have to buy your own food at grocery stores or gas stations," Wilcox admonished. "Or go hungry." Like the rest of these young men, Russell had little money—and he had spent his last dime just to join the expedition.

Though they had left twenty-four hours behind the Colorado team, the Hankmobile and the Green Bomb leapfrogged ahead of the trio in the Dodge Power Wagon sometime during the night. The Colorado Three weren't in as big a hurry as the others, since their gear would be packed in from Wonder Lake to McGonagall Pass three days after that of the Wilcox group. Wilcox had handled all the application procedures as well as virtually all the planning, which included the logistics of getting nine men and all their supplies and equipment from the trailhead at Wonder Lake, where the dirt road stopped, to McGonagall Pass, where they would step onto the Muldrow Glacier. Berle Mercer, a rancher in Lignite, a stop on the Alaska Railroad just a few miles north of the park boundary, had agreed to pack the expedition's gear the 18 miles from Wonder Lake to McGonagall Pass at 30 cents a pound. Snyder signed up for the same deal, but Mercer had only so many packhorses, so the Colorado contingent would have to wait a few days while the horses made their first round-trip.

Meanwhile, the Power Wagon again caught up with the Wilcox vehicles on the Alaska Highway. The Green Bomb was pulled off the road with a flat tire. With the Dodge pickup and Hankmobile all parked on the shoulder, everyone was out of their vehicles complaining and commiserating about the potholes and ruts, which frequently slowed them to a crawl. When the Colorado climbers later stopped for the night at Wolf Creek, the Green Bomb and the Hankmobile took the lead again, maintaining the round-the-clock pace in order to make their date with Berle Mercer and his horses.

The days lengthened and the cost of fuel rose along with the latitude as they drove north. The big trees of the coastal forests had long since given way to stunted black spruce and tundra pocked with kettle lakes. The weather was good but dry; dry meant dust, which now seemed to have permeated everything.

With Janes at the wheel, and Luchterhand, McLaughlin, and the slightly older Clark as passengers, the atmosphere in the Hankmobile was relaxed and full of talk of the big mountain that lay before them. They all knew one another well and had counted on one another during many climbs past.

Mark McLaughlin was known for his ready smile and his ability to see humor in just about any situation. At twenty-four, the same age as Joe Wilcox, he had made a couple of attempts at higher education, first studying architecture and art and later geology at the University of Oregon. It was in mountaineering, however, that he found his passion, topping seventeen peaks in Washington and

Oregon, exploring the Olympic Mountains and several glaciers and icefalls, though he'd never been higher than the 14,410-foot summit of Rainier. When it came to gear, he knew what he wanted. When over-the-counter outdoor equipment didn't meet his standards, he made his own. One of the tents the team would carry up Denali was a McLaughlin creation.

Prior to the Denali expedition, McLaughlin was coming to grips with the consequences of his lack of education, specifically working fifty-hour weeks filling orders for the Oregon Screw Machine Products company.

"This last fall I finally realized that I didn't want to spend my life working at some half-assed job, and started back to night school to get my grades up and my study habits into some sort of shape," he wrote. McLaughlin planned to reapply to the University of Oregon to continue his studies in geology when he returned home.

His close friend Jerry Clark, also riding in the Hankmobile, was seven years older and, unlike McLaughlin, had excelled in academic studies. He already had completed a master's degree in geophysics, done PhD work in psychology, and been working as an electrical engineer. Both were strong climbers, yet their styles contrasted greatly. McLaughlin was a more aggressive climber than thirty-one-year-old Clark, who drew on fourteen years of experience and perhaps because of that took a more conservative approach to climbing.

Luchterhand—his friends called him Denny—tried his best to lounge in the backseat of the Hankmobile, but at six foot four and with self-described "enormous feet," he was finding lounging difficult. He had already earned a BA in geology and was pursuing a master's degree. "If all goes well, I should have the THING [My thesis on the origin of a gang of rather rowdy, confused metamorphic rocks located near Torrington, Connecticut] completed." He planned to study ecology and wildlife conservation after the Denali climb.

Settling down, though, didn't appear to be on the agenda. "Sometime in the next few years I intend to do some Peace Corpsing."

The vistas of wilderness adorned with ragged peaks that rolled past as Hank Janes steered his van through Northern Canada were a far cry from the inner-city school in Portland, Oregon, where he taught during the school year. Janes was small at five foot five, quiet, and introspective. He was a believer in the healing power of wilderness. His students suffered from myriad learning problems, which Janes attributed to their environment. During the summer he ran the mountaineering program at a camp for boys in Colorado where, he said, "some of the greatest moments of my life have been shared with these kids." He was a member of Mountain Rescue and Safety Council of Oregon and had climbed extensively in Colorado and in the Tetons.

Janes envisioned combining his love for the outdoors with teaching. "I feel that I can be of more help to kids by working with them in an outdoor situation rather than in an academic atmosphere—helping them to develop an awareness of others and of themselves—helping them develop a sensitivity to nature and to live—eventually I hope to start a camp of my own."

In the Green Bomb, Joe Wilcox, Steve Taylor, Walt Taylor, Anshel Schiff, and John Russell fought the monotony and dust of the long gravel road by learning about one another.

Steve Taylor—the Taylor who'd spoken up most heatedly against the merger with the Colorado trio back in Puyallup—was a tall, skinny physics major. Raised in Aurora, Colorado, Steve Taylor had spent his final two years of high school in Pittsburgh before heading west to Provo, Utah, and Brigham Young University. There he met Joe Wilcox, whose stories of mountain climbing piqued his interest. Soon he had joined the BYU Alpine Club and was spending his weekends camping, hiking, and climbing in the nearby mountains. He became a skilled rock climber who also had ice climbing and winter camping experience. He had worked with BYU's rescue team. Nevertheless, he had no real experience in alpine or high-altitude climbing. He had been the first one to sign on to the expedition, and that simple fact may go some way toward explaining his resistance to the latecomers from Colorado joining the group. He spoke of this adventure with all the exuberance of youth.

"My parents don't think it such a swinging idea, my jumping out of airplanes, etc., but I won't let life pass me by and when my tide comes I will be ready to take it at the flood."

The sarcastic exchange that had transpired between Wilcox and Brad Washburn was no secret to the expedition. Somewhere along the way, someone spelled out the words "Brad is a no gooder and a do badder" in the dust on the back of the Green Bomb and they remained there for the duration of the drive.

Jerry Clark was the reason the other Taylor, Walt Taylor, set out from Indiana for Alaska. "I first learned to water ski with Jerry Clark. I first learned to snow ski with Jerry Clark. I first learned spelunking with Jerry Clark. I first learned scuba diving with Jerry Clark," Walt said. "I learned to smoke and drink on my own."

The quick-witted medical student had climbed extensively in the Rockies and the Tetons and had worked as a technical climbing instructor for three summers at the Ashcrofters mountaineering school near Aspen, Colorado, where he got extensive experience between 11,000 and 14,000 feet. A few other lines in the bio he used to introduce himself to the other members of the Wilcox team, probably written off the cuff, carry a whiff of mortality: "I grew up in Indiana. I went to high school in Indiana. I went to college in Indiana. I have a burial plot reserved in Indiana. I plan to die elsewhere."

Anshel Schiff was, like Walt Taylor, a Clark acolyte and resided in Indiana. He had recently completed a PhD in engineering seismology and was working as an assistant professor in engineering sciences at Purdue University in Lafayette. The thirty-year-old's outdoor experience was limited to hiking, camping, and "scrambling as opposed to climbing." Bespectacled and serious, Schiff was an unlikely addition to the expedition, given his total lack of mountaineering experience, but his mission was to lead the scientific and support team, not to reach the summit.

It was the Summer of Love, the season of *Sgt. Pepper's Lonely Hearts Club Band*. The Doors released their first album and Jimi Hendrix used his wailing guitar to ask, "Are You Experienced?" But to the men headed north to climb Denali, the sounds of the era were little more than background noise. When I asked Howard Snyder what music he remembered from the trip, he said he sometimes sang tunes from the stage production of *Fiddler on the Roof.* Among the straitlaced young men who populated the expedition, only John Russell seemed to have embraced the zeitgeist of the '60s.

The stocky man with a shock of curly, reddish-blond hair and matching beard was the most enigmatic of the troop. Russell had led an unconventional life compared to the others. The variety of his work, study, and travel experience for a man of just twenty-three years was remarkable. He'd been a sheet-metal journeyman, electronics assembler, calculator and adding-machine repairman, cabdriver, gamekeeper, sandal maker, and logger. He had studied math, biology, chemistry, history, and philosophy but held no degrees. He had traveled in Europe and Central America.

"He was a fighter from conception," according to his mother, Jane Russell. "Precocious physically, extremely intelligent test-wise, but not too good in school."

Jane and John Russell Sr. had three children: two sons, both named John, and a daughter named Johnnie. After high school, Richie Russell, as he had been known since childhood, began calling himself John Russell and moved to Seattle, where he went to work at Boeing, attending night school at the University of Washington. Soon he left Boeing and spent a year at Idaho State University in Pocatello, "at which time," according to his mother, "he was a complete beatnik." Jane and John Sr. were separated by 1967 and neither had heard from their son in more than four years when he called on June 1 to say he was going to climb Denali. "He was pleased, and we were pleased for him," Jane said.

How Russell learned of the expedition is unclear, but when he did, he approached Clark and asked if he could join. His logging job had him in prime physical condition. "I have in the past carried load[s] of over 100 lbs, to over 10,000 ft. and I expect to be able to carry load[s] of up to 150 lbs. by June if necessary," he wrote. Though no one in the group had ever climbed with Russell, he had the experience, the fitness, and the desire.

Though driving duties were shared among the nine men in the Wilcox caravan, the dust and monotony began to take its toll. One night they were awakened by jolts and bounces that were more violent than normal for the gravel road. Wilcox was behind the wheel at the time and had meandered off of the road in his sleep. There was no apparent damage, so the drive resumed, but back on the road, Wilcox thought he noticed a new whine coming from the old engine.

When they crossed the US border into Alaska and left the gravel road behind, the quiet of the pavement revealed a disturbing noise emanating from under the hood. At Northway Junction, 40 miles inside Alaska, a mechanic confirmed Wilcox's suspicion. The engine bearings were shot. The car could no longer carry them forward. McKinley Park was still 500 miles away.

The Colorado men were flagged down and they agreed to take the trailer in tow. In return for the added fuel costs, Wilcox agreed to share more food during the climb, evening out the expenses both parties would incur. This was one expedition, not two, but they were still in the process of coming together. With the trailer attached to the Power Wagon by a hastily fabricated hitch, the three Colorado men continued on. The Green Bomb had bombed; the rest of the group would have to fit as best they could into the Hankmobile.

Nine unwashed young men counted off three days of nonstop driving. Weary, they tried to stake out comfortable spots in the van, which suddenly seemed much smaller. Behind the wheel Hank Janes drove on to the Moon Lake State Recreation Area, 15 miles past Tok, where they spent their first stationary night since leaving Washington State.

In the morning Walt, the Taylor from Indiana, approached Wilcox and told him he was too lax and needed to exert more authority. Half an hour later Clark pulled Wilcox aside and told him he was a little *too* authoritarian. These contrary reviews made Wilcox feel he must be doing something right. Everyone repacked themselves into the van and headed for Paxson and the junction of the Richardson and Denali Highways.

Peering out the windows of the Power Wagon, as he and his companions negotiated the Denali Highway with the poorly balanced trailer doing its best to send the vehicle off the shoulderless dirt road, Paul Schlichter looked up to see Denali for the first time. It was June 17, and the group was close to the boundary of Mount McKinley National Park. Still 100 miles distant, Denali dominated the horizon, its north side in full view. The scene evoked both awe and at least one second thought among the men seated side by side on the truck's bench seat.

"Gee, maybe I'd be happier just taking this time and spending it in Colorado, climbing some of the fourteeners there," Schlichter recalled thinking.

"Look there," Snyder said to the others, immediately picking out the route they'd follow, looking right up the maw of the Muldrow Glacier. Despite the distance and the haze that had lowered visibility that day, Snyder could identify the north and south peaks, Karstens Ridge, the Harper Glacier, Denali Pass, and Archdeacon's Tower. They arrived at Mount McKinley National Park that afternoon. Snyder soon discovered that the conflict between Washburn and Wilcox was not a secret to the park staff and that the details of Wilcox's letter had been blown out of proportion.

"The ranger at the Information Center told us that Wilcox made himself out to be 'God's gift to Mount McKinley' in the letter," Snyder recalled.

They checked in with Chief Ranger Art Hayes, with whom they'd been corresponding, and then set out on the 84-mile-long park road that led to Wonder Lake and the trail to McGonagall Pass.

The Hankmobile, packed with nine men, arrived in the park around 9:00 P.M. and drove on toward Wonder Lake. Wilcox felt a strange loneliness as he passed through the headquarters area, with the bright daylight of the midnight sun illuminating a scene of somber inactivity. Had the van turned into the small neighborhood adjacent to the headquarters area, he might have seen a large truck inner tube in the yard of the first house on the left, and even at that late hour one child bouncing on it: that would have been me. In our house, bedtimes were fluid, often forgotten during the long days of the Alaskan summer. On some nights my parents packed my sister and me into the car and drove along the park road to watch the wildlife that came alive as the midnight sun arced slowly toward its brief, midnight dip below the horizon. With no TV or radio, and a crank telephone system that connected only the residents of the park, we had to create our own entertainment. Mine was the inner tube. One of the maintenance men patched it up and inflated it, and when my dad rolled it down the hill from headquarters and set it up in our yard one night after work, I thought I was the luckiest kid in the park. I may well have been, since there were only a dozen of us.

▲▲

I spoke to Bradford Washburn's biographer and confidant Dr. Mike Sfraga about Washburn's scathing reaction to Joe Wilcox's letter over dinner at the Captain Cook Hotel in Anchorage one evening not long ago. Sfraga, a vice chancellor at the University of Alaska–Fairbanks, wrote his doctoral dissertation on Washburn and spent many dozens of hours with him. As we ate dinner we joked about our advancing age. Sfraga and I had lived in the same dormitory while attending the University of Alaska–Fairbanks in the early '80s and had both turned fifty recently. He suggested that Washburn's age and perhaps a little envy might have played into his reaction. Washburn was in his midfifties in 1967 and wasn't able to climb as he had in the past—as Wilcox and his team would be climbing that very summer.

CHAPTER 4

TROUBLE AT THE BASE

The climbers had driven the Alaska Highway through Canada to Alaska and traversed the interior on the 135-mile-long dirt road called the Denali Highway. Beyond park headquarters, they were on the 85-mile-long Park Road to its end at Wonder Lake. The gravel Park Road bridges small creeks and rivers and cuts through growths of spruce and birch trees kept small by the short summer season and the layer of permafrost that remains close to the surface year-round. Deeper in the park, the road climbs through a broad valley and the stunted trees give way to willows and tundra and then mineral-stained soil and rock. Caribou, moose, Dall sheep, and grizzly bears were a common sight near and even on the road.

Luchterhand heard the ancient, eerie call of a loon and they stopped the Hankmobile to listen for a moment. Then, just a few miles later, they saw Denali looming above the forest, bathed in pink alpenglow. They stopped, piled out of the vehicle, and stood transfixed.

They continued on as the road cut precariously along the side of the steep, rocky slope of the valley wall and stopped at Eielson Visitor Center. There they discussed communications with the summer season's rangers George Perkins and Gordon Haber. Eielson offers spectacular views of the mountain to park visitors, and its vantage point also meant it was the only manned facility in the park where radio communication with people on the mountain was possible. Neither the Wonder Lake Ranger Station nor headquarters are in line of sight of the Muldrow Route, line of sight being a requirement for radios of the day to work.

Eielson was a communication hub for the whole park. There were no phone lines beyond headquarters, so all communication with Wonder Lake was radioed via Eielson—including communications with climbers on the mountain. The idea of talking directly with climbers on the summit was new. Expeditions sometimes carried single-side-band two-way radios, but they were bulky and heavy, and messages from the mountain had to be relayed through Fairbanks to reach anyone in the park. It was an unreliable system, at best. However, in the late '60s, advances in electronics made small, light, and inexpensive Citizens Band (CB) two-way radios accessible to the general public and these were the kind that Jerry Clark had been tinkering with before meeting up with everyone back in Puyallup. The radios weren't compatible with the park's single-side-band, so when Clark wrote to Ranger Art Hayes suggesting their use, Hayes arranged to borrow a CB radio from George Robinson, a maintenance man at the park, and placed it at Eielson to try out during the Wilcox climb.

Jerry Clark had drawn up a map of the climbing route and marked the sites where he thought communications would be possible and the dates the party expected to be at each one. With the rough communications schedule mapped out and in the hands of park rangers Haber and Perkins, the Hankmobile rolled on.

It was late when they found the Colorado climbers at Wonder Lake and pitched the tents in the murky twilight that is midnight during summer in the far north. This was the first night the whole group camped together. The cool night air carried the tang of tundra plants, and the incessant hum of mosquitoes lulled them to sleep.

The next day, Wonder Lake District Ranger Wayne Merry stopped by to introduce himself and conduct a final equipment check. There was no official climbing ranger in 1967, but Merry filled that role. Though his climbing experience was not in alpine mountaineering and he had never climbed Denali, Merry was an accomplished rock climber, having made the first ascent of Yosemite's El Capitan with two other climbers in 1958.

Only a few weeks before, Ranger Merry sent a memo regarding the exchange between Washburn and Wilcox to my father, George Hall, who, just a couple of months earlier had become Merry's boss when he was named director of Alaska operations for the National Park Service and superintendent of both Mount McKinley and Katmai National Parks. My father happened to be in the National Park Service field office in Anchorage when Merry's missive arrived.

"After reading Brad Washburn's unusually hot letter, you will probably want some background on this group," Merry wrote to my father. He noted there were some marginal members but on the whole they were adequately qualified. "Basically, Wilcox ran afoul of Washburn's mountaineering ethics—and got well singed!"

Aware that Washburn had made his opinion of the expedition known in the park, Wilcox asked Merry what he thought of his preparations. "On paper," he replied, "you are the best organized party to ever assault the peak."

Later that morning, after Ranger Merry had left, their horse packer Berle Mercer stopped by the Wonder Lake campground and said he'd like to leave a day later. Wilcox thought an extra day of rest would do the expedition good. Everyone readily agreed.

Wilcox, still ruminating over the dissenting opinions of his authority during the drive up and maybe Washburn's letter, too, took advantage of the down day to call a meeting. He wanted to address leadership and organization concerns before they headed for McGonagall Pass and the Muldrow Glacier. "We seem to be a loose collection of individuals climbing the mountain separately," he told them. Success would depend on their ability to work together and he pointed out that little work was getting done to prepare for their imminent departure.

The response was notably muted. "No one even opens cans with gusto around here," Walt Taylor said, agreeing with Wilcox. In contrast to the late-night team meeting back in Puyallup at the foot of Mount Rainier, Steve Taylor said almost nothing.

They would be following the traditional route established by the Sourdough mountaineers fifty years before. But the Muldrow Glacier had surged a decade earlier and the sudden and swift—at least for a glacier—movement had left its surface a jumble of crevasses and ice blocks, making this route to the summit nearly impassable. The difficult passage forced climbers to seek alternate routes and subsequently, the West Buttress route on the other side of the mountain was becoming the preferred path to the summit. West Buttress climbers flew in from Talkeetna on the south side of the Alaska Range and landed at 7,400 feet. Though that route was easier, the cost of flying in a large expedition and all its gear was beyond the means of the young men who comprised the Wilcox Expedition.

Though the Muldrow Glacier's surge had slowed and its surface had smoothed itself out, the route remained longer, more difficult,

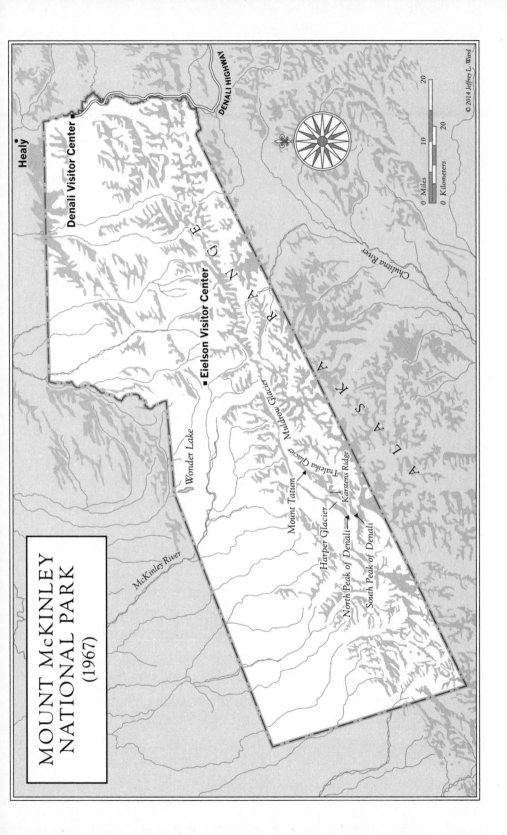

MOUNT McKINLEY NATIONAL PARK
(1967)

Healy

Denali Visitor Center

DENALI HIGHWAY

Eielson Visitor Center

A L A S K A   R A N G E

Chulitna River

Wonder Lake

Muldrow Glacier

McKinley River

Mount Tatum

Traleika Glacier

Harper Glacier

Karstens Ridge

North Peak of Denali

South Peak of Denali

0 Miles   10   20

0 Kilometers   20

© 2014 Jeffrey L. Ward

and more dangerous. Three of the four men who had died on Denali met their ends there: two in crevasse falls on the Muldrow and another from a fall while descending Karstens Ridge at the top of the Muldrow. This was the route the group would follow.

▲▲

Berle Mercer, a fixture in the region since he came into the country during World War II, arrived the next day with his sons, Kirk, age thirteen, and Baxter, age sixteen, with a string of eight packhorses. Brown-haired and fit, Mercer was neither tall nor short at five foot ten and wore a ready smile that belied an intense and opinionated personality. He had been packing hunters, miners, and climbers throughout the region for two decades and was renowned for his knowledge of local plant life. He and his boys made quick work of the expedition's gear, which weighed in at almost a ton, and set out for McGonagall Pass. Eight original Wilcox team members, along with Jerry Lewis from the Colorado group, headed out as well, each carrying 50-pound packs. Steve Taylor, for all his initial enthusiasm, was the last of the original Wilcox group to get to the mountain. He was sick to his stomach and waited with Snyder and Schlichter. They would hike in three days later when the Mercers returned for the rest of the gear.

Baxter Mercer, now in his early sixties, still lives in Healy, just 20 miles from the park. The climbers didn't seem much older than he was, but he didn't interact with them beyond a few short conversations. "Dad told us they weren't happy and to leave them alone. They all seemed to know what they were doing, but it was just like two groups of people that didn't really want anything to do with each other."

Snow stopped the horses about 1,200 feet short of the 5,720-foot

McGonagall Pass, so the loads were cached there and Wilcox and the other eight climbers began moving the food and gear up to Camp I on the edge of the Muldrow Glacier.

The Mercers returned to Wonder Lake for the Colorado group's supplies on June 22. Snyder described Steve Taylor's demeanor during the wait at Wonder Lake as that of a man "in a continual state of depression," and believes that Taylor was terrified by the sight of the mountain "and it was literally worrying him sick." Schlichter agreed, saying, "I think psychologically he just wasn't ready for this expedition and I'm not sure why he was there." Once the horses were loaded, Snyder, Schlichter, and Steve Taylor shouldered their own 50-pound packs.

The hike to McGonagall Pass did nothing to improve Taylor's attitude or his health. Snyder and Schlichter quickly outpaced him, stopping to wait for longer and longer periods as Taylor moseyed along the trail. At one point he got lost and followed a caribou path up another valley. After Snyder and Schlichter tracked him down and pointed him toward McGonagall Pass, Taylor needed to stop and rest. The two Coloradoans, eager to forge ahead, continued up the valley. Taylor had not caught up when they rolled out their sleeping bags, donned their head nets, and went to sleep beneath a sky that never got dark. In the morning, they went on to the pass without Taylor, believing he'd have no trouble finding his way.

"At a couple of places going up there these guys weren't even hiking together," Baxter Mercer recalled. "You had one on one side of the creek and one on the other. They wouldn't even talk to each other."

Wilcox, McLaughlin, and Janes were descending from the camp to the cache when Snyder and Schlichter passed them, still without the struggling Steve Taylor, on the way to Camp I at McGonagall Pass. When they returned to the cache to help carry supplies, Steve Taylor had just arrived and Joe Wilcox was seething.

Accounts of what had occurred along the trail differ dramatically. Snyder described waiting and at one point returning to search for Taylor, who dawdled incompetently along the trail. Wilcox said Taylor told him he had been goaded, ridiculed, insulted, and ultimately abandoned by his companions when he fell behind. A heated exchange ensued where Wilcox questioned their commitment to their fellow climbers. They, in turn, questioned Steve Taylor's competency and ability to climb without delaying the others. Ultimately, Wilcox threatened to send the Colorado climbers back, saying, "It seems you're still the Colorado Group." Then he turned and hurried to catch up with Taylor, who was climbing toward the pass.

The two Colorado men were again on the cusp of losing their opportunity to climb Denali, realizing Wilcox was more than a little upset. According to Snyder, "We both appreciated the position Wilcox was in as leader of the group," so they caught up with Wilcox and Taylor and apologized. Taylor said there were no ill feelings on his part.

Though Coloradan Jerry Lewis had no trouble hiking in with the Wilcox group, Steve Taylor's slow pace and the apparent impatience of Snyder and Schlichter was a distinctly sour episode that threatened the cohesiveness of the group. The Mercers turned for home, leaving the twelve young mountaineers on their own. The expedition was at last on the mountain, ready to begin the ascent, about to step onto Denali's unforgiving domain of ice and rock.

And wind.

▲▲

The expedition set up Camp I at the top of McGonagall Pass and there, at the margin between green earth and blue ice, they got their first close-up peek into the snowy interior. Before them the Muldrow

Glacier inched down the mountain to join the Traleika Glacier at the foot of Mount Tatum. Across the Muldrow, Tatum's icy flank rose steeply to a high ridge that paralleled the glacial valley all the way to the Harper Glacier and on to the summit.

Their initial ascent was right up the middle of the Muldrow Glacier, a monotonous stretch of slushy, featureless ice, with an elevation gain of just 850 feet over 4.5 miles. Relatively level and uncrevassed, the surface of the glacier is marked by rocky moraines and long, winding scars cut by flowing surface water. The walls rising on either side of the glacial valley are steep—the Muldrow's nickname is the Wall Street Glacier—and harbor snow, ice, and the occasional hanging glacier poking a blue tongue out of a high, hanging valley. In summer the cold isn't extreme but it is pervasive, and the confines of the valley give one the impression of walking through a giant chest freezer.

Shortly after the last three men reached Camp I, cool, wet weather arrived, settling in for five days. The rain, however, didn't put them off of their schedule. To reach the top, each man would climb the mountain multiple times, moving supplies higher and caching them before returning for more, methodically ascending with enough food and gear to support the team as it moved higher and higher.

The rain threw a pall over any excitement of finally being on the mountain and climbing. Clothes and sleeping bags became waterlogged, tent floors pooled with water, and when the sun made its brief appearances the men hustled to spread out their wet things, only to rush them back under cover when the rain returned. Walt Taylor, frustrated at the wetness, turned his face to the clouds and rain and called out, "C'mon, sun! Show us you haven't forgotten your chillun!" He also suggested they all walk around naked to show their faith in the Sun God. No one took him up on the proposition.

Jerry Clark led the foray up the glacier on June 24 with Luchterhand, Russell, and Walt Taylor on the rope team. While the others continued to move supplies from the horse cache to Camp I at the top of McGonagall Pass, the advance team checked their harnesses, clipped in to the rope at 50-foot intervals, and set out behind Clark, who led the way over the uneven terrain on skis. They established Camp II close to the base of the Lower Icefall at 6,500 feet.

The Lower Icefall was the first of several they would encounter on the route to Denali's summit. An icefall is the glacial equivalent of a waterfall. Like the water flowing over a cliff, a glacier moving over a steep or narrow part of its bed becomes broken and chaotic. Glacial ice is somewhat plastic and flexible, but where it bends sharply, its surface shatters and cracks, forming crevasses that vary widely in width and depth, some a few feet deep, others plunging all the way to bedrock. Intersecting crevasses form ice columns called seracs. Where the glacial bed flattens or widens out, the crevasses close and the surface of the glacier becomes smooth again. They would encounter six perilously crevassed icefalls on their route, three on the Muldrow Glacier and three on the Harper Glacier.

Jerry Clark and Mark McLaughlin had brought skis as well as plastic Snowtreads and snowshoes and were using the skis for glacier travel. This did not sit well with John Russell, who let it be known to whomever would listen that he thought skis were unsafe for mountaineering. Already he was gaining a reputation as the one who picked battles, and though he tried to keep calm, another appeared to be brewing just below the surface.

It didn't stay there long. On Sunday, June 25, only a couple of days after the conflict among Snyder, Schlichter, and Steve Taylor, Russell lost his cool. Clark, McLaughlin, Russell, and Janes were roped together, ferrying loads of gear from Camp I to Camp II. Russell and Janes walked while the other two skied. The slope on

that part of the glacier was slight, but one of the skiers—probably McLaughlin since Clark was leading—lost control and nearly pulled Russell and his overloaded pack to the slushy ground. The men exchanged words and Russell stewed in his juices all the way back. Upon reaching the McGonagall Pass camp, John Russell stormed up to Wilcox, face red with anger and said, "I want four days of food, a tube tent, and a stove. I'm leaving the expedition."

Wilcox listened and then convinced Russell to stay, promising to gather the team in the morning to work through the conflict.

The sun popped out briefly on June 26, quickly followed by sleet and then snow. Under the pall of wet snow, all twelve expedition members huddled under shared ponchos and rain gear. Wilcox began with an attempt at fostering teamwork but Russell quickly jumped in, complaining that skis were unsafe. McLaughlin and Clark had asked to form a rope team of two for trips down the glacier to take advantage of the speed of their skis. Wilcox refused, saying downhill skiing was forbidden. The skiers countered that the thousand-foot elevation change over 4.5 miles hardly constituted downhill skiing, and a long argument ensued. Both Clark and Mc-Laughlin had more experience skiing in the mountains than Joe Wilcox and contended that they were more qualified to say whether or not skis were safe.

Howard Snyder, the leader of the Colorado group, tried to end the quarrel: "Tell you what, Joe. You take one skier on your rope and I'll take all the rest of 'em on mine." His attempt at a joke (there were only two skiers) broke the atmosphere of growing hostility.

Wilcox had been lax in enforcing some of the expedition rules thus far, consciously abandoning the plan to rope up to cross the McKinley River and turning a blind eye to those risking giardia by drinking unfiltered water from tundra ponds during the hike in. They were low on the glacier, where crevasses were rare and those

oversights might not have serious consequences. Higher up, though, there was less margin for error.

"I know the rules are conservative," he said as the wet snow did its best to find a way through his rain gear, "but we have to be overly cautious on a climb of this magnitude." He continued, "I agreed to assume the responsibility of leading this expedition under a set of ground rules, and I am willing to continue only if I have your full support."

He asked if there were any other concerns, but the men grew quiet, then the ever-lighthearted Walt Taylor broke the silence. "I didn't have any until we called this meeting," he said. "Now I'm all wet." Rueful laughter along with nods of agreement broke out as the meeting adjourned.

Wilcox felt he had made it clear that he expected the men to follow the expedition rules, and then further established that the rules could be changed if the change made sense and didn't compromise safety. The gradient over the 4 miles between McGonagall Pass and the Lower Icefall is nearly imperceptible whether going up or down. McLaughlin and Clark kept using their skis following the morning meeting. Russell had been overruled.

The next day, still angry about the ski use, Russell refused to clip into a rope team that included Clark. When Wilcox heard about Russell's refusal, he put his foot down and in the heat of the moment told Russell that he might be better off leaving the expedition after all. This time Russell acquiesced, though he managed to avoid Clark's rope for the remainder of the climb. Russell was revealing himself to be a divisive force within the expedition, and Wilcox recognized it. Still, Wilcox wanted to get everyone up the mountain, and that included Russell despite his outburst.

The piles of gear amassing at the top of the pass had attracted Russell's ire two days earlier, and he suggested to Snyder and Wilcox

that they were carrying too much gear and should leave behind both of the Colorado team's stoves, one of the four stoves carried by the Wilcox team, and all the expedition's shovel handles, using their ice axes as handles when needed. Wilcox agreed to jettison a stove and the shovel handles, but Snyder refused. He kept his stoves and would carry the expedition's only complete shovel.

"Consequently, the Colorado group's shovel was in demand at every camp," Snyder observed.

John Russell's preoccupation with weight seemed out of character for the man who, upon joining the expedition, boasted of packing 100 pounds above 10,000 feet and promised to carry more on Denali. Indeed, just days earlier he had carried a pack weighing 115 pounds from the horse cache to McGonagall Pass.

Leaving the handles, shovels, and saws behind was a staggering mistake. Though their packs were lighter as a result, shovels and saws were essential for building walls and snow shelters to protect against deadly windstorms. More mundanely, they were needed daily to clear campsites, build tent platforms, collect snow for melting, and to keep tents from collapsing during heavy snowfalls. By leaving them behind they betrayed an ignorance of the power of Denali's storms, and left themselves vulnerable.

In the years since, snow saws and steel spades became mandatory equipment for Denali guides. Steel spades enable climbers to dig snow caves in the hard snow commonly found on the mountain's upper reaches. A snow cave can be dug with ice axes, but it is a dangerously slow process. Snow saws remain the only tools that work for cutting snow blocks for shelter building.

As is true for any group working together in a stressful environment, conflicts occurred, enemies were made, and friendships were forged. One conflict that has been overstated in various accounts of the story is the one between the original Wilcox team and the

Colorado group. Interviews with Paul Schlichter and Howard Snyder in 2013 revealed that in spite of the commonly held belief that the Colorado men sequestered themselves from the others, they understood themselves to be part of the Wilcox Expedition.

"I didn't see us as very separate at all," Schlichter said. "We had our own tent, our own meals, a cooking tent, and everything like that, so in that sense we were separate. But in terms of climbing, of the ropes that we were on, it was pretty well mixed around."

"We were three guys from Colorado who weren't an expedition. We were part of the Wilcox Expedition," Snyder said. He thought the Wilcox Expedition argument-prone, but Schlichter didn't find the group's behavior that unusual.

"Well, you take twelve people, put them on a mountain like that with the weather, the fatigue, all the things that go on," Paul Schlichter said, "you're going to have some bickering back and forth, but I don't think there were any major deals." Throughout those first weeks Wilcox held regular meetings that sometimes led to heated arguments.

"We had a couple of meetings where people aired out their grievances," said Wilcox. "There would be a discussion, not every day but at least every other day, on how things were going. Not on how to climb; the route, the camps . . . that was all worked out in advance." Still, some decisions fell to Wilcox alone. "I had the last word. But if all were opposed to something, there was no sense in doing it." Wilcox led by example, serving on both advance and relay teams, and with the exception of weather delays, the party advanced up the mountain at a moderate but consistent pace without prodding from the leader.

Joe Wilcox's leadership style sounds loose compared to most modern climbs in which a professional guide has the final word on all decisions—from where to camp to what to eat to evaluating a climber's fitness. Climbers can be sent back to Base Camp—with the assistance of a guide—for any number of reasons, including illness, attitude, and climbing in an unsafe manner. Professional guides are legally responsible for the well-being of their clients, who, even on Denali, are often novices who would not know what to do without a guide.

Wilcox, however, was not guiding the expedition; he was climbing an unfamiliar mountain with peers, some of whom were older and more experienced than he was.

"It's not like a military organization, where you've got the chain of command, or the corporate environment, where you have managers and subordinates," recalls Schlichter, a former Air Force cadet who would go on to see action in Vietnam. "It was a bunch of fairly young guys getting together to go for a climb, and there's a limit to how much control you have over the people who are up there."

CHAPTER 5

FROM A CREVASSE
TO BROTHERHOOD

B eyond Camp II, the Muldrow Glacier becomes heavily crevassed. The way through it exposes climbers to the danger of unseen
crevasses or that of avalanches, and sometimes to both at the same
time. They must negotiate two icefalls and a particularly treacherous feature called the Hill of Cracks. Here the glacier bulges as it
passes over an unseen mass, creating crevasses that radiate outward
and sometimes run at right angles to each other. Finding a safe route
is especially difficult.

To get through these crevasse fields, the Wilcox Expedition had
to either walk around, jump, or cross over the yawning fissures on
snow bridges, formed when snowfall covers and then builds up over
an open crevasse. Often the only sign of a hidden crevasse is a slight
depression in the snow caused when the heavy, overlying snow
droops into the opening below. With the lighter snowfall on the
north side of the mountain, the bridges on the Muldrow are often

thin and don't droop as obviously, making them hard to spot, even by experienced mountaineers. Another route through the icefalls requires climbers to hug the sides of the glacier, passing beneath the avalanche-prone snow and ice that collects on the steep canyon walls. Neither choice is without serious risk.

Brad Washburn warned of the hazards along the margins of the Muldrow in his unpublished climbing guide when he wrote, "I have often seen huge chunks of ice, which have fallen down the great gullies of Mount Carpe and rolled three-quarters of the way across the level floor of the valley amid a lethal cloud of flying ice and snow."

While Russell continued to avoid climbing with Clark, Wilcox shuffled the rope teams, giving everyone else a chance to work together and perform the different tasks required during the climb. This also built camaraderie, shoring up the team against the fractures that occasionally threatened to divide the expedition. The routine involved an advance team of four carrying half loads and breaking trail, followed by packers, carrying full loads. They would climb high, cache their loads, and descend again to camp low in order to better acclimate to the thin air at altitude. On a map, the distance from Wonder Lake to the south summit of Denali is 36.5 miles, but each man would travel many times that distance as he relayed load after load of food and gear up the mountain ascending and descending between camps or caches along the route.

After the ski meeting, Wilcox went to Snyder's tent and told him that he would lead the next push up the glacier, through the Lower Icefall to establish Camp III. Snyder's team would include Lewis, McLaughlin, and Steve Taylor. They gathered their personal gear and got ready to move to Camp II. Clark, Russell, Walt Taylor, and Anshel Schiff were also heading to Camp II carrying loads of food and supplies. A full load consisted of two one-day food packs, or a single two-day pack. Schiff was on his way out of camp when Walt Taylor noticed that a one-day food pack remained. Someone was carrying half a load and he knew who it was.

"Come back here, Anshel, you rascal!" he yelled.

Schiff returned and after a good-natured Walt Taylor–style scolding, he reluctantly added the second bag to his load and headed up the glacier.

Schiff was one of the least experienced climbers on the expedition, and given that he had joined to lead the scientific studies, no one was expecting him to reach the summit. Still, he was a member of the expedition and was expected to carry his share of the weight. Walt Taylor was in fact doing Schiff a favor by refusing to let him slack off where the climbing was relatively easy.

Charged with establishing a route through the Lower Icefall, Snyder had to choose between two dangerous options. The left side of the icefall had fewer crevasses, but the canyon wall on that side of the valley was a snow-covered slope, prone to avalanche. The right side was more heavily crevassed, but the slope above was more stable. Brad Washburn's advice was to skirt the crevasses by hugging the right side of the glacier and briefly moving through the less dangerous avalanche zone.

As Snyder considered his options on the morning of June 27, a thunderous boom issued from the left side of the valley, followed by an escalating roar. A massive avalanche shot down the valley wall, gathering rock and ice before surging far beyond the foot of the wall, well into the left side of the icefall. The men watched speechlessly as the thunder subsided and the snow billows drifted away to reveal a pile of rock, snow, and ice sprayed across the left side of the glacier. Their only option now was to go right.

Snyder led the way and put Lewis in the second rope position, figuring the big man would be able to handle it if he fell. A few hundred feet out, Snyder's snowshoe binding came loose. He paused to adjust it and told Lewis to carefully move up. Lewis was probing a small crevasse with his bamboo pole when he suddenly toppled into a larger one.

Snyder quickly drove his ax into the ice to arrest Lewis's fall but it penetrated just an inch or two, providing a tenuous purchase at best. Steve Taylor was third on the rope, and Snyder instructed him to carefully cross the crevasse and take over the ax belay. This was a test for the inexperienced Steve Taylor, whom Snyder and others had thought was not up to the psychological and physical challenges of mountaineering. At some level, it was the kind of test they had all come for. Taylor held fast.

Snyder placed two ice screws into the glacier and secured the rope to which Lewis was still attached. With McLaughlin anchoring the other end of the line by holding an edge on his skis, Snyder peered into the crevasse. Lewis dangled about nine feet below.

"Do you have me? Do you have me?"

"Are you all right?" asked Snyder

"Hell no, I'm not all right! Do you have me?"

He was wedged in horizontally, facing downward, staring down into the dark maw of the crevasse rather than up toward his rescuers. As his eyes adjusted to the darkness, Lewis found himself suspended above a gymnasium-size cavern with deep-blue walls and a lake at the bottom. Geared up and loaded down as he was, he knew a plunge into the dark lake would be a one-way trip.

They hoisted Lewis's pack out first, followed by his ax. Then they rigged a pulley system to bring Lewis up, with McLaughlin anchoring the pulley. In the thin, crusty snow over the hard ice, the long, sharp edge of McLaughlin's ski provided a solid grip—more reliable than the rounded edge of a snowshoe or a Bunny Boot without crampons. McLaughlin had proven the usefulness of skis, but Russell was not the kind of person to acknowledge such things.

As Lewis's nerves settled down, he described the scene inside the glacier. "I wish there was enough light down there to take pictures," he said. "It was all subtle shades of blue."

They pushed on and reached the top of the icefall but were halted by a large crevasse and whiteout conditions at about 7,300 feet. Shy of Camp III, they cached their loads, including their high-altitude boots and clothing, and returned to Camp II.

▲▲

That night, as Joe Wilcox prepared dinner, he overprimed the stove, spilling fuel onto the tent floor. When he lit the stove, the floor went up in flames, which he quickly smothered, leaving the tent unscathed. When the last rope team arrived in camp that night, Russell dutifully reported to them, "Our Fearless Leader tried to burn down the tent!"

McLaughlin demonstrated the practicality of skis while helping extract Lewis from the glacier while Clark showed how annoying they could be for others on the rope line. He stopped repeatedly during the passage between Camps II and I, adding wax, then removing wax; putting on climbing skins, then taking them off again. Each time he stopped, the others were forced to stop as well, and by the time they reached camp his companions were exasperated.

The rope team of Joe Wilcox, Hank Janes, John Russell, and Dennis Luchterhand pushed up to 8,100 feet the following day and established Camp III between the Muldrow's two major icefalls and then returned to Camp II. Snow whispered against the nylon walls of the tents throughout the night, piling up on the sides of the tents and muffling the snores and sounds of shifting movements made by the men sleeping inside. A sky opaque with falling snow greeted them when they awoke. Movement beyond the barely visible wands marking the boundaries of the camp would be risky, so they lounged in their tents rather than pushing their luck.

"The concealing snowfall had made the icefall a treacherous death trap," Wilcox wrote, "the valley walls echoed with the muffled rumble of distant avalanches." The whole group would wait until the risk of avalanche from the new snow had subsided.

They had spent four days on a nearly nonstop drive from Puyallup to Denali, hiked cross-country to McGonagall Pass, and then relayed gear up the glacier for five more days. The forced respite was welcome. Between sessions of clearing snow from the camp, snowball fights broke out. Wilcox and Steve Taylor played a marathon chess game. Luchterhand lamented the lack of women on the expedition. Janes read aloud from a book of Zen. Conversation soon moved to the Vietnam War and how each man had come to be hunkered down in a snowstorm on a remote Alaska mountain rather than wading through rice paddies in Southeast Asia.

Most of Joe Wilcox's original members had deferments; Jerry Lewis, who was thirty, had already served a stint in the Army. Schlichter, an Air Force cadet, would head to Vietnam at the end of the summer. A knee injury suffered when Wilcox played collegiate football had made him physically ineligible—a wonderful bureaucratic irony for the leader of an expedition to the alpine wilderness of Denali. Janes's teaching job kept him stateside, and McLaughlin had asthma that "became chronic whenever he got within two blocks of his draft board." It couldn't have been much of a surprise when Russell claimed that he had been declared unregimentable.

The snowfall subsided on the morning of June 30, and the men woke to three feet of powder. The dirty, jumbled surface of the glacier had been made smooth and immaculately white by the impossibly bright blanket of snow bathed in dazzling sunlight. The men were soon sweating in their tents as the temperature inside became unbearable, pushing them outside where it didn't feel much cooler.

A clear summer day on a glacier can be a contradictory experience. While the air temperature might be at or below freezing, the direct sunlight radiating from above and reflecting back from the ubiquitous snow can be uncomfortably warm. For those with fair complexions, the multiplied sunlight can be relentless, raising blisters on exposed skin and surreptitiously burning nostrils, lips, and—at least for mouth breathers—the roof of the mouth. Unprotected eyes can result in burned retinas and painful but temporary snow blindness. Still, it was hard to complain about after days of rain. They took advantage of the conditions by laying out all their soaked gear to dry in the sun while they comfortably moved around on the icy glacier dressed in just their long underwear or shorts.

The new snow clung to the steep walls of the valley with a tenuous grip and the heat of the sun was more than enough to break it free. The avalanche danger forced the expedition to sit tight during the warmth of the day and move only at night when the cold air hardened the snow and stilled the snow slides.

Near midnight, all twelve men set out for Camp III. Eight dropped their loads at Camp III and turned back to Camp II for more, while Wilcox led the advance team of Schiff, Janes, and Schlichter to establish a route beyond the Hill of Cracks and through the Upper Icefall. The first day of July dawned as they climbed, painting the valley once again with alpenglow—first a faint pink, then growing orange and finally gold with the ascent of the rising sun into a blue sky. By the time the packers deposited their loads and returned to Camp II, the blazing sunlight had returned, forcing them to shed their hats, gloves, and jackets.

Early the next morning, they packed up their tents and sleeping bags at Camp II and moved into Camp III, established at the top of the Hill of Cracks in a level spot between two large crevasses. One final carry would complete the move, but Snyder couldn't muster a full rope team to finish the job, so they settled in to wait for the stable conditions brought on by the cool of the evening.

This was the first camp without a pool of melted glacial water nearby, and soon stoves were hissing away, melting snow for cooking and drinking. As Snyder set a pan packed with clean white snow onto the burner he heard the whump of igniting gas and looked up to see Russell's stove engulfed in flames. He had apparently over-pumped the stove and gas burst through one of its gaskets and ignited. The fire was soon put out. No harm done.

The advance team returned around noon and reported that they had topped the Muldrow's second icefall, known as the Great Icefall, by going up the middle of the glacier and cached their gear at about 10,600 feet. Schlichter reported that he had taken some of Schiff's load when Schiff said he was having trouble carrying it.

"I didn't mind carrying it," Schlichter confided to Snyder, "except that he kept looking back at me with a big grin."

Wilcox said Schiff appeared to be the only man on the expedition who was not growing stronger as they progressed up the mountain. At one point he suspected that Schiff was dieting in an effort to lose weight. In reality Schiff suffered from acute heartburn and couldn't eat before or during strenuous activity. He was secretly consuming a dozen antacid tablets a day, but the medicine was doing little more than masking a growing problem.

Two rope teams set out for the final trip to Camp II near midnight on July 3 and by 1:25 A.M. on July 4 had reached the camp and packed up the last of the supplies to be carried up the mountain. McGonagall Pass, the escape hatch to the lowlands, was still in view, but once they moved up the glacier, it would disappear from sight and the expedition would be isolated and completely self-sufficient with no easy way back. Independence Day, indeed.

The Fourth of July dawned gray. Russell was nominated to lead the first rope team out of Camp II and up the glacier. At lower elevations and latitudes their friends and families were wearing T-shirts and shorts, preparing to celebrate the nation's birthday with parades, cookouts, and fireworks. To usher in the special occasion high on Denali, Russell lit a firecracker. The cavernous acoustics of the glacial valley made the pop sound like the demise of a party balloon. Before Russell led the way up, the expedition decided to take advantage of the sunny weather and take group photos. What proved to be a tedious process required each man to strap his camera to an ice ax, engage the self-timer, and hustle back in time to pose with the others. Luchterhand's camera wasn't working properly. He strapped it in place, pushed the release, jogged back to the line of men in his massive Bunny Boots, and waited the appropriate amount of time. Silence. He bowed his head, began to step forward, and heard the shutter click. Others waited to take their turn, so he decided he'd live with whatever image the camera captured. He removed his camera and asked who was next. After two hours had passed, the smiles began to turn wooden. Unhappy to be wasting good climbing weather, Russell began ducking behind Schiff just before the shutter clicked and finally retreated to a tent, refusing to leave until the cameras were put away. The group photo that ended up in the files at Mount McKinley National Park is one with Russell hiding—something that always bothered my father. More than once he mentioned the photo and the climber who ducked whenever a camera came out, and wondered what he was hiding from. Russell appears in at least two group photos, one taken by Snyder and the other by Luchterhand. (Denny Luchterhand cached his film on the ascent; Anshel Schiff retrieved it on his way down.) Those photos show a stocky young man wearing a plaid shirt and squinting in the bright sun. Curly hair and a thick beard frame his serious face.

Not a day was lost setting out for Camp IV. Luchterhand and McLaughlin chose to carry traditional wood-and-rawhide snowshoes rather than plastic Snowtreads. The others may have chided them about the extra weight but when the snow came, they ate their words. The big shoes were superior in the deep powder and invaluable in breaking trail through Great Icefall, to Camp IV at 11,000 feet, which was established by the evening of Tuesday, July 4. Many of the Snowtreads had been discarded between the Muldrow's Upper and Lower Icefalls.

▲▲

The group had reached the head of the Muldrow Glacier and entered the great cirque beneath the spectacular Harper Icefall, a jumble of snow and blue ice that cascades down an increasingly steep 1,500-foot face before dropping off a vertical, 500-foot granite wall above the upper Muldrow Glacier. The dangling glacier nourishes the Muldrow with regular and spectacular avalanches that can cast enormous blocks of ice a half a mile beyond the Harper's overhanging snout. Here the expedition's route veered left off of the Muldrow Glacier and onto Karstens Ridge, a 1.8-mile-long spine of snow-covered ice that circumvents the Harper Icefall and culminates at Browne Tower, an outcropping of pink granite at 14,600 feet. Though the wind remained calm, here the climb entered a new level of difficulty.

The advance team of Wilcox, Russell, Snyder, and Walt Taylor gained the ridge a few hundred yards past a feature known as

Karstens Notch early on July 5. The recent snowstorms had not missed the narrow ridge, and as the four men ascended, the snow grew deeper, reaching knees, then hips, then shoulders. In these conditions snowshoes were no help; moving through it was more like swimming in loose sand, and gaining enough traction to move uphill was nearly impossible. That they made any progress at all is a testament to their strength and tenacity. Whiteout conditions prevailed during the arduous slog, and the 4,000-foot drop to the Traleika Glacier on one side and the lesser but equally deadly fall off to the Muldrow on the other side exacerbated the risk. A narrow but level 50-by-30-foot notch in the ridgeline at 12,100 feet was the only viable camping spot on the ridge, so when the advance team reached it, they dropped their loads and established Camp V.

The expedition would battle their way to the top of the ridge over the next five days, each man making multiple trips, either breaking trail or relaying supplies up from the lower camp while the advance teams installed fixed lines on the steep slope. Unlike the ropes that link climbers as they move through crevasse fields or up lesser slopes, these lines would remain in place. Climbers ascending and descending the steep ridge could clip their harnesses to the line to prevent falls and use it as a handhold when needed.

The fixed line was anchored to the ridge by driving aluminum stakes, called pickets, into the snow and attaching them with carabiners.

The climbers used polypropylene water ski rope, a seemingly odd choice but cheap, light, and black in color, so it would stand out against the snow. Unlike manila rope—which had fallen out of use by climbers after World War II—braided nylon, and sheathed climbing rope, polypropylene doesn't absorb water, has very little elasticity, and doesn't give when tugged on, offering solid support when used as a handline. The downside to using it in mountaineering is its rare but potentially lethal tendency to shatter in extreme cold.

Elsewhere on the mountain, where fixed lines weren't necessary, the Colorado group climbed with gold-colored three-strand twisted nylon rope. The Wilcox ropes were kern-mantle construction, with a red, braided outer sheath.

Wind and snow halted all travel on Saturday, July 8, and filled the trail between Camp IV and Camp V, requiring it to be broken all over again. The following day, the advance team gained just 600 vertical feet beyond Camp V. As they turned for the descent after the frustratingly slow day, they saw the eight packers unloading and settling into the tight real estate of Camp V. Suddenly twin avalanches sprouted from either side of the ridge beneath the camp and rumbled down the slope. The men in camp felt the entire ledge slump when the snow let loose.

The ascent of Karstens Ridge was the most arduous part of the route, rising 4,000 feet over 2 miles, and whether breaking trail, placing the fixed lines, or relaying supplies from lower on the ridge, no task was easy. At 12,800 feet the climbers overcame the steepest pitch on the entire route, a 40-foot-long, 50-degree-steep stretch of white ice. This was where the ranger Elton Thayer had fallen 1,000 feet to his death while descending with three companions after reaching the summit via the South Buttress back in 1954.

The strenuous effort was tempering the bonds between group members.

Early in the assault on Karstens, Russell had challenged Schiff in front of the others. "Anshel, there's a rumor that you are only carrying half loads," he said. Schiff hadn't been one of the stronger climbers and had continued his efforts to carry less weight until Russell's accusations rang in the cold air. Schiff, an introvert who rarely spoke during the group debates, kept silent. He preferred to present his opinion to Wilcox one-on-one. But Clark didn't, defending Schiff, who had joined to conduct scientific studies and had never intended to climb that high, telling Russell that he shouldn't expect others to match his physical abilities.

What had set off the "unregimentable," volatile John Russell probably had more to do with his own demons than Schiff's physical abilities. Russell's childhood friend and early climbing companion Dave Cooley said Russell hated weakness, especially his own. Cooley grew up with "Richie" Russell and learned to climb at his side. Richie began going by his first name, John, after leaving home. One thing he couldn't change was the weakness that plagued him at high altitude. "Richie was worthless over ten thousand feet," Cooley says. "He could barely function, and it made him angry." Though Russell knew he would get sick, he climbed to altitude time and time again, trying to beat the sickness. Cooley said Russell never did beat it. When I asked why a man who knew he suffered from altitude sickness would attempt to climb the highest mountain in North America, Cooley said, "He wanted to beat it, proving he could go to the top of McKinley; that was the way he'd want to prove it to himself. That was Richie Russell."

Paul Schlichter recalled that later in the day it was Walt Taylor who smoothed things over with Schiff. "In my mind [Walt] was the most mature, had the best leadership qualities," Schlichter said. "He was a really good guy, he was a very straightforward guy. He said, 'Anshel, you're not carrying the loads like the rest of us are. Don't try to fake it and pretend like you are. If you can't do it, that's OK, we understand that, we can help out.'"

Schiff had started the climb in poor shape and continued to suffer from chronic indigestion in secret. The inability to digest food, or even simply a reluctance to eat, can deplete the body of energy anywhere, but at high altitude, low oxygen content and temperature add to the physical demands, making adequate nourishment critically important. Modern-day climbers often lose weight during guided Denali climbs despite consuming 3,000 to 5,000 calories per day. The Wilcox Expedition meals averaged 4,505 calories per day—plenty to sustain the climber in the conditions they faced, but only if the meals were consumed.

Walt Taylor probably calmed Russell down as well. The two men had bonded when rangers busted them while scaling the wall inside the Mount Rainier Visitor Center and the friendship flourished on the climb in spite of their contrasting personalities. Walt was a "witty humorist, tactful conciliator and lubricator of organizational gears," Joe Wilcox wrote in his memoir. Russell was confrontational and "wanted to be viewed as independent," according to Wilcox. Physically, the two men were well matched, and until they reached the upper mountain, both were among the strongest climbers in the group.

Jerry Clark and Mark McLaughlin had been friends before the climb, and that bond continued. They climbed together when they could and often tented together. Mark was in superior physical condition but was happy to slow down and let his slower-moving friend set the pace. Short and unassuming Hank Janes gravitated to tall and outgoing Denny Luchterhand. Neither their personalities nor their frames matched, but they spent as much time as they could together both climbing and relaxing in camp. Luchterhand also befriended Walt Taylor, and the two men developed the habit of calling out when they spotted each other. Calls of "Muthah" often echoed back and forth across the icy expanses as the two men maintained this inscrutable dialogue all the way up the mountain.

Though Steve Taylor had a less promising start, his calm handling of Lewis's topple into the crevasse revealed unexpected reservoirs of strength and presence of mind. In Wilcox's opinion, "As the trip progressed he gained confidence and strength. By the time we got to Karstens he was leading many rope teams. On Karstens Ridge I can honestly say that Steve was a stronger climber than I." He was affected by the altitude but had a strong summit drive.

But as the ascent quickened on Karstens Ridge the inescapable effects of altitude began to take their toll on everyone. One of the steepest parts of the ridge, known as the Coxcomb, was crusted with wind-packed snow slab and underlain with several feet of powder on July 10. Breaking trail was hellish, but John Russell led for five hours and reached Browne Tower at 14,600 feet before he and his team cached their loads and turned back for Camp V.

"John gave it all he had for twelve hundred vertical feet. He really burned himself out," Walt Taylor reported to Wilcox on the morning of July 11. And for several days, "John was not his usual overbearing self."

Among what was at times a discordant band of brothers had grown, as a result of their physical exertion in Denali's thin, remote air, a special kind of enduring bond. Some want no more from life.

CHAPTER 6

A RUN FOR IT

Luchterhand, Janes, Schlichter, and McLaughlin finished breaking trail past Browne Tower at the top of Karstens Ridge and traversed Parker Pass onto the lower Harper Glacier to establish Camp VI at 15,000 feet on Tuesday, July 11, and by the evening eight men had moved up. The team had started gaining altitude at a much faster rate and the resulting fatigue was an increasing factor in their decision making. Everyone rested on Wednesday, but by Thursday, July 13, the entire team had moved up to the 15,000-foot Camp VI. Several days of clear weather had prevailed, and that evening they began plotting where they would place their high camp and how they would make their summit bid. Along with a fellowship born of arduous mutual endeavor, a sense of urgency grew.

From Camp VI, the 20,320-foot south summit was visible, just 5,000 feet higher and 5 miles distant. The goal was within striking distance, but here the mountain could be its most vicious. If the weather changed, if whiteout conditions arose, if the wind came howling, the human body had far fewer resources to cope. Obvious symptoms of acute mountain sickness (AMS) were becoming evident in some of the climbers. Wilcox thought Steve Taylor and Schiff were the most likely to be affected, but altitude is the great equalizer in the mountains, treating the strong and weak with equal disdain. Headaches and vomiting are the most recognizable signs; the other symptoms are less obvious, including insomnia, dehydration, lack of appetite, and swollen hands and feet. Though the team had been on the mountain for nearly a month and had been careful to climb high and sleep low to aid acclimatization, inadvertent mistakes may have countered those precautions and fostered AMS.

Everyone going to high altitude experiences brain swelling, but some are affected more than others. Thin air means less oxygen is available to be absorbed into the bloodstream. The natural way the body copes with hypoxia (inadequate oxygen levels) is for capillaries and other blood vessels in the brain to expand, causing the brain itself to swell, hence the headaches many sufferers describe.

For most people, the symptoms ease as they become acclimatized to the altitude. For an unfortunate few, AMS can lead to two potentially fatal conditions: high-altitude pulmonary edema (HAPE), in which leaky capillaries fill the lungs with fluid; and high-altitude cerebral edema (HACE), where brain capillaries leak, causing dramatic brain swelling. HAPE symptoms include coughing, breathlessness, and the inability to walk uphill and usually appear two to four days after climbing above 10,000 feet. Those suffering from HACE have trouble walking, appear drunk, and suffer extreme exhaustion, drowsiness, and weakness. Both conditions can kill if left untreated, the best treatment being a quick descent below 10,000 feet.

It had taken four separate advance teams five days to top

Karstens Ridge, and most of the difficult work was done above 12,000 feet. Not surprisingly, strenuous activity is a contributor to AMS; so too is carbon monoxide poisoning. The Wilcox team had been cooking in a tent, probably the most common way climbers inadvertently poison themselves. The combination of hard work and cooking inside the tent may have contributed to the symptoms that were becoming apparent in some of the climbers.

Russell in particular had exhausted himself on the final push up the Coxcomb. He also had been sleeping in the cook tent. Schiff's indigestion was causing noticeable weight loss, but Jerry Lewis was also clearly losing weight. Jerry Clark and Joe Wilcox both exhibited extreme exhaustion climbing above Camp V on Karstens Ridge. The known remedy for altitude sickness is to descend. However, more than one climber has beaten it, or tried to, by summiting quickly and then retreating to a safe altitude before the symptoms become life threatening.

▲▲

The idea of ascending quickly made increasing sense to Wilcox. On Thursday, July 13, he gathered the original members of the Wilcox team in the cook tent after dinner to discuss plans for the summit assault. Light from the late-evening sun filtered through the orange nylon, casting everyone in an orange glow as they let their dinner settle. Heat from the stoves and the men gathered in such close quarters made the tent cozy in spite of the chilly air outside. Clark had been in radio contact with Eielson Visitor Center.

"The next two days will be perfect," he reported.

"Then what?" asked Wilcox.

"They only have a two-day forecast. I guess they're just getting it from a radio station."

The edge of the southern high-pressure system had arrived, bringing cold, thin air that settled over the mountain and the surrounding area. Highs tend to be big and stationary, often repelling weak lows that try to move in. This one was holding over the range with clear, cool, and almost windless weather beckoning the climbers to make their move.

Joe Wilcox considered the condition of the men and the weather prediction. It had been mostly clear and moderate since July 10, and it was predicted to hold for two more days. Such conditions don't last on Denali, and sooner or later the pendulum would swing the other way. If they were going to reach the summit, they had to move quickly.

"My feeling is that we should make a run for it," Wilcox announced. "All of us pack up five days of food to eighteen thousand feet and climb to the summit the following day."

One of those boisterous discussions followed during which holes were punched in Wilcox's plan. McLaughlin worried that they were climbing too fast and argued for an intermediate camp at 16,500 to allow for more acclimatization. Luchterhand said rushing to the summit before bringing more supplies up from the Coxcomb cache would leave them without enough food and fuel if they were halted by a bad storm. The expedition members pushed this way and that against Wilcox's ascent strategy. He was neither defensive nor dismissive, allowing the discussion to continue.

A consensus was reached: the two Taylors, Schiff, and Russell would remain low for another day and pack enough food to feed ten men for six days from the Coxcomb cache to Camp VI. The other eight men would move up to 18,000 feet, each carrying four days' worth of food, and go on to the summit on July 15. The other four would move up to the high camp on the fifteenth with three more days of food and make their summit attempt on Sunday, July 16.

The Colorado men ate in their own tent and had not been part of the meeting. But when Wilcox relayed the plan through the wall of their tent they agreed. Howard Snyder was "a bit apprehensive about depending on the Wilcox group's food and stoves, since both left a great deal to be desired," but he decided they could handle it for the two or three days it would take to get to the summit and back to Camp VI. Soon the camp was alive with preparations. They began paring down their gear to the essentials needed for a fast summit turnaround. The cook tent would remain there at 15,000 feet along with other unnecessary gear. They would carry a few pots, two stoves with full fuel tanks, two shovel scoops minus their handles, trail-marking wands, a first aid kit, two gallons of Blazo fuel, and the five-watt CB radio. Each man had a small amount of emergency food and his own personal gear and sleeping bag.

On the morning of July 14, eight men prepared to ascend the Harper Glacier and establish high camp around 18,000 feet. After the five-day Karstens Ridge ordeal, it looked like a cakewalk: a 3,000-foot ascent spread over 3 miles of hard-packed snow punctuated by two large icefalls. It would be easier going but not without danger, according to Washburn's guide: "There are a number of treacherous crevasses in this upper section of Harper Glacier, just where one would expect the going to be the best," he wrote. "The high winds up here often form smooth but very flimsy bridges of soft snow across many of the smaller cracks."

The route up the Harper also was rich in history. At 16,000 feet it passed beneath the Sourdough Gully, which Pete Anderson, Billy Taylor, and Charlie McGonagall ascended to reach the top of the north peak in 1910. At 16,400 feet it traversed the plateau separating the Upper and Lower Icefalls, passing through the site of Belmore Browne's high camp from which he staged his unsuccessful summit bids. Around 17,500 feet, in the middle of the valley, Stuck and

Karstens had pitched the final camp from which they conquered the peak in 1913.

They had arrived. This was it.

▲▲

Then flames erupted into the cold mountain air.

There are two versions of what happened and the ensuing tent fire that nearly halted the expedition. Snyder described it this way: "The men in the tent had been using two stoves simultaneously, a hazardous practice at best. One had almost burned dry, and W. Taylor decided to refill it. Instead of taking the stove outside, he opened the filler cap while the stove was sitting right beside the still-burning second stove. As the cap was unscrewed the pressurized fumes from the fuel tank filled the tent, and were immediately ignited by the second stove."

Wilcox, who was in the tent when the explosion occurred, drew a slightly different picture. "At 8:00 A.M. Hank, Walt, Steve, John, Dennis, and I were in the cook tent, when one of the cook stoves began to malfunction. When Walt inspected the gas tank release [relief] valve, it popped off, permitting fumes to escape, which were ignited by the second stove."

The Wilcox Expedition carried Optimus 111B stoves, popular among climbers of the day and known to be both durable and reliable. I owned one myself in the 1970s when I hiked and canoed around Alaska as a member of Boy Scout Troop 211. My parents tossed mine out sometime after I left home. During an interview with Frank Nosek, the former president of the Mountaineering Club of Alaska, I mentioned the fire and Wilcox's description of a relief valve. "I think I've still got my 111B," he said, "and I don't think it has a relief valve either." A few days later Nosek forwarded images of a well-used 111B. The blue metal box, five inches square, was open, revealing the brass fuel tank and steel heat shield. Tucked inside was the key that slid into the hole beneath the brass burner to open the fuel valve. There was no relief valve.

The Logan tent was suddenly engulfed in flame. The six men caught inside scrambled for the door, but the tent vaporized almost instantaneously. Walt Taylor, who had been at the epicenter of the conflagration, dove toward the wall of the tent, "but by the time he got there the wall was gone." By some miracle no one was injured save singed eyebrows and beards, minor burns, and a bruise or two.

All that was left of the tent was its smoldering floor and metal zippers. Walt Taylor's down parka and Russell's sleeping bag had been reduced to stinking piles of melted nylon and singed feathers. Observing the devastation, Russell delivered a swift kick to the offending stove and launched it, still spewing burning fuel, into the remaining Logan tent. Before the flames could catch, several men pounced and extinguished the fire.

Schiff was able to pay Walt Taylor back for his kindness by loaning him an extra parka, and McLaughlin, in spite of their conflict over the skis, gave Russell half of his double sleeping bag. As they cleaned up, Russell discovered a bundle of unburned matches among the smoldering wreckage.

"There's one thing that didn't burn," he pointed out. "The company matches."

The cook tent was a luxury and its loss wouldn't stop them; they had planned to leave it standing at the 15,000-foot camp rather than packing it higher anyway. The only irreplaceable loss was the odd stocking hat knitted by Luchterhand's girlfriend. They sifted through the wreckage and surrounding snow but never found it.

The fire had rattled them but the summit still called. The advance team got ready to leave. The exuberant mood of the night before had dissipated and a shroud of mist and fog settled in as they set out up the Harper Glacier.

Wilcox, McLaughlin, Luchterhand, and Janes clipped into their rope and headed out first but were quickly overtaken by Snyder, Schlichter, Lewis, and Clark. Jerry Clark wasn't happy about the pace set by the three big men on his rope and made it known as they took over trail breaking. Later on, as Wilcox's rope approached the base of the Harper's Upper Icefall, they heard Clark's angry words drift down from the top, where Snyder's team charged on: "God dammit, slow down!"

McLaughlin also complained about the fast pace, even though he, Wilcox, Luchterhand, and Janes had been overtaken. Luchterhand had been sick all day, so Wilcox slowed down. Snyder established high camp at 17,900 feet near the base of the north peak's highest buttress. The spot offered almost no wind protection, but little was to be had anywhere nearby. "Seeking shelter here was like trying to hide in the cracks of a sidewalk," observed Wilcox, but the snowless buttress overhead meant avalanche hazard was small. The second rope team finally arrived, and Luchterhand vomited again before retiring to his sleeping bag.

Snyder, Schlichter, Lewis, Wilcox, Luchterhand, McLaughlin, Janes, and Clark settled into camp for the night just a mile and a half from, and 2,500 feet below, their goal, the summit of the south peak. At this point, the miles meant nothing. As the crow flies, they were only 16.5 miles from McGonagall Pass, but each man had walked or skied many times that distance, making multiple climbs and descents to break trail and haul gear. Not only had they successfully threaded the needle between crevasse fall and avalanche hazard, but they also had pushed themselves to their physical limits to reach this point.

Now at altitude, the hazards became less obvious. Their bodies were much less able to absorb oxygen, and the air held half the oxygen they were accustomed to in the first place. The resulting short-age in the bloodstream meant an increase in heart rate as their bodies worked harder to deliver oxygen to crucial organs. At the same time, their bodies demanded twice the calories needed at sea level, but the fats and proteins that best provide those calories are scarce because the digestive system is suppressed in favor of cardio-vascular efficiency. In fact, eating fats and proteins above 14,000 feet can hinder acclimatization when the body has to trade cardiovas-cular efficiency in order to digest rich foods. Even resting at this altitude takes a toll. Their best bet was to get to the summit as quickly as they could.

The weather continued to guide their movement. The light fog had cleared away as they traversed the Harper Glacier. The high-pressure system that had arisen over the Bering Sea, far to the southwest, continued to hold its ground as predicted, but the low-pressure system was moving from the north, building strength as it approached. Still, there was no reason to think a meteorological event of epic proportions was coming. Clear skies prevailed; there were no surprising wind shifts, no dramatic changes in tempera-ture. The eight men at high camp settled into their sleeping bags for the night.

Before Wilcox's advance party fell asleep at high camp on the night of July 14, snow began to fall. Nevertheless, a radio conversa-tion gave them further hope that the window of good weather would stay open long enough for them to go for the summit in the morning. At the 15,000-foot Camp VI, John Russell, who was in contact with his teammates above and rangers at the Eielson Center below, asked the latter for a weather report.

"I'm afraid we don't have any new weather reports for you," the ranger replied to Russell. "We couldn't get headquarters very well today. About the best we can do is give you the barometer reading and tendency. Surprisingly enough, it's up a tenth from yesterday, 30.35."

It was surprising because although the two-day forecast they had heard the day before predicted a couple of good days, everyone was expecting conditions to start deteriorating, not improve, as increasing barometer pressure typically indicates. But Russell didn't know that.

"Fine. I'm not very familiar with what barometer readings mean," Russell responded. "Can you interpret?"

"Well, generally a rising barometer is a good sign," the ranger said. "That's about all you can go by without a lot of other data also. If you're going to want a schedule in the morning, why, we can try to get some information for you by then, but we couldn't get it this evening."

"Does that barometer reading mean it's going to stop snowing pretty soon?"

"I won't commit myself to that, but what is the weather like up there? The weather was considerably worse down here late morning."

"Well, it was snowing about five minutes ago and now it's clear for ten miles."

The radio conversation went on for almost half an hour, during which the climbers at the upper and lower camps talked with one another and rangers at Eielson, discussing food and the weather conditions in the park and on the mountain. They also had a brief exchange with a radio operator from Sitka, who, by some fluke of meteorological conditions, was able to communicate with them even though he was hundreds of miles to the south. Before signing off, Wilcox told the rangers that he planned to make a summit attempt in the morning, though he wasn't sure how many would be in the party.

▲▲

Since reliable communication between the park and the mountain was almost nonexistent prior to the Wilcox Expedition, there had been little demand for the park to provide weather forecasts for climbers. When forecasts were requested, rangers at Eielson could pass on only their own observations and weather reports picked up from Anchorage radio stations.

At the time, the National Weather Service collected information on atmospheric conditions like temperature, wind, and precipitation via balloons launched daily from Anchorage, McGrath, and Fairbanks, locations that roughly triangulate around Denali. However, that information would have been hard to translate into mountain-specific weather forecasts, according to Ted Fathauer, who worked as a National Weather Service meteorologist in Alaska from 1970 until his death in January 2013.

"It was primitive then," Fathauer said. "I remember getting a call that first year I was in Alaska. They wanted to know what was going to happen on McKinley. I had no clue. That was like asking someone's seven-year-old daughter what was going to happen on the stock market. I understood charts and all of this stuff, but I didn't understand the meteorology up there." Fathauer would go on to develop reliable weather forecasting for Denali, but it would be more than a decade in the making.

In 1967, according to Frank Nosek, president of the MCA that year, climbers relied on their own weather observations and reports from fellow climbers and mountain pilots like Don Sheldon and Cliff Hudson.

"They could look at the mountain and look at the clouds and, just from their experience, know," Nosek said. "I can remember flying in with Sheldon a couple of times and having to turn around and come back simply because while it looked good to go, it wasn't good when you got there."

None of the men on the Wilcox Expedition had been on Denali before, and while some, like Snyder, Schlichter, Clark, and Wilcox, had enough experience to recognize the signs of deteriorating weather, none had Denali-specific knowledge.

A juggernaut was bearing down on the mountain. The meteorological forces that would clash were powerful but unremarkable individually. Only when they came together would their potential be released. The counterclockwise-spinning low-pressure system was approaching from the north with its warm, moisture-laden winds. The big high-pressure system was still parked over the Alaska Range, its cold, dry air naturally rotating in the opposite direction. Soon, they would touch, rotating in tandem like cogs in a great weather machine, the air pouring from high to low and generating winds at the summit beyond imagining.

CHAPTER 7

FOUR MONTHS BEFORE AND 15,000 FEET BELOW

Four months earlier, while Joe Wilcox was still planning his expedition, Art Davidson, Dave Johnston, and Ray Genet became the first men to conquer Denali in winter when they stepped onto the summit late in the day on February 28. They clutched one another in a three-way hug and looked out into the night. There were no spectacular views of Mounts Foraker and Silverthrone; no thunderheads boiling up into the dark-blue sky; no lowlands stretching off toward the sea: it was dark. A faint glimmer of lights marked the city of Anchorage far to the south on the shores of Cook Inlet.

It was the culmination of an ascent fraught with cold and hardship. Eight men began the journey together; one died early in the climb and four others set aside their summit aspirations to support the three strongest climbers who reached the summit. It would go down in the annals of mountaineering history, but only if they returned home to tell the tale. Standing there, alone in the dark on the highest summit in North America, they had no idea that the hardest part of their journey was yet to come.

That night they bivouacked beneath a parachute 2,000 feet below the summit at Denali Pass and woke in the heart of a ferocious windstorm. As Davidson and Genet huddled under the flimsy shelter, Johnston sought refuge from the wind that threatened to peel them off the mountain. Neither Johnston nor Davidson can recall why they were using a parachute. Johnston says it was light and didn't require any setup, so convenience might have been the main reason. He thought they might have found the chute among supplies left by a prior expedition. Such caches were often left on purpose and were fair game for those in need. In any case, the wind soon carried the parachute away.

Johnston dug a snow cave just large enough to fit his two companions and his own six-foot-seven frame, and there the three men weathered the storm for a week. They had little food and almost no fuel to melt snow for water. When it ran out, Genet made a desperate dash into the storm to retrieve a fuel can cached by Johnston when he traversed Denali in 1963. The wind pinned Genet to the ground, so he made his way to the cache on his belly, crawling forward with the aide of two ice axes. He returned with precious fuel that kept the stove melting water, allowing them to survive in the icy cavity for a few more days in hopes of outlasting the wind.

Most of the climbers were Alaskans, and their bid to be the first to reach the summit in winter was big news in Alaska. When Jacques "Farine" Batkin fell into a crevasse and died just a few days into the climb, interest in the expedition only intensified. They climbed on, despite Batkin's death, tracked by local newspapers and radio stations. But late in the month, as the climbers neared the summit, a storm rolled in and the summit team went silent.

Other team members who waited below could see the stricken

men and tried to reach Denali Pass but were pushed back by the howling wind. It was March 5 when a civilian aircraft spotted their distress signal and notified the Alaska Rescue Group (ARG), a civilian search and rescue organization under contract with the Air Force and the Park Service to perform mountain rescues. Since 1956, when President Dwight Eisenhower signed the National Search and Rescue Plan, the US Air Force—specifically the Alaska Air Command—had sole responsibility for search and rescue on inland regions of Alaska. Search and rescue was (and still is) coordinated by the Rescue Coordination Center (RCC) at Elmendorf Air Force Base (now Joint Base Elmendorf-Richardson) in Anchorage. The ARG stood by to execute ground rescues and the Mount McKinley National Park superintendent or his representative coordinated any rescue effort that did not require assistance from the RCC. Soon word was out that the three men had disappeared into a ferocious storm that continued to hammer the upper mountain. Rescuers from the ARG and the Seattle-based Mountain Rescue Council, Air Force representatives, rangers from Mount McKinley National Park, and several reporters gathered in Talkeetna. But all they could do was wait for the weather to break.

"Nothing moved," said Gary Hansen, who was chairman of the ARG that year. "There was no overflight, or attempt to search for or rescue the winter group until the storm was over."

The one exception was Talkeetna pilot Don Sheldon. He had ferried the expedition in to the Kahiltna Glacier, brought out Batkin's body, and had been checking on them throughout the climb.

Sheldon was known to routinely risk his life when flying rescue missions on Denali and throughout the region. His son, Robert, told me his father had been a tail gunner in a B-17 during World War II and was the sole survivor when his aircraft crashed during a bombing run.

"He had a great guilt that he had survived when the others didn't," Robert said. "He believed all lives were precious and if he could help save one, he would."

When Sheldon heard his three friends were lost, he launched his plane, but even he couldn't get close to the peak and found himself running in place on a midair treadmill: "Yeah, I was hucklebuck'n on up there to take a look at ma boys, when I look out the window . . . Whoa . . . I seen this ridge just standin' still. I look down at my speedometer and it says 140 miles per hour. Yowza, I had to fly 140 just to keep even with that ol' wind."

Gary Hansen visited the Rescue Coordination Center at Elmendorf Air Force Base on the evening of March 6, to ask the commander to launch an observation flight. The commander agreed to send up a plane, weather permitting, and told Hansen he had to go along as an observer.

"His parting comment was, 'OK, you've got the flight at sunrise tomorrow morning. But you will be on the flight and if anything goes wrong, the crew will have orders to open the big flap in back and kick you out,'" Hansen recalls with a laugh.

The storm broke on March 7, and Johnston, Genet, and Davidson emerged from their cave frostbitten and weak with hunger. The wind had died, but a whiteout enveloped the upper mountain. Davidson dug into an ancient supply cache with his ice ax and unearthed food that looked to be at least fifteen years old but still edible. Thus nourished they descended into the whiteout. With skies clear above the whiteout and the winds diminished, both military and civilian aircraft took off and headed for the mountain. Around noon, Paul Crews of the Alaska Rescue Group, riding as an observer aboard an Air Force C-130, spotted three men descending near 18,000 feet. Sheldon took his Cessna 180 in for a closer look and recognized his friends. Though he couldn't land, he dropped a bag of oranges and a radio before heading back to report their position.

Though Talkeetna had been crowded with would-be rescuers and the Air Force stood ready, neither contributed to the climbers' survival. Only after the storm broke did the Air Force fly, and by then Genet, Davidson, and Johnston were out of the cave and well on their way to Sheldon's Kahiltna Glacier airstrip. They had survived because of their experience and strength in alpine arctic conditions. It was only after some debate that the three agreed to board the military helicopter sent to evacuate them.

Frank Nosek was president of the Mountaineering Club of Alaska and an officer in the ARG in 1967. He helped organize the ARG's rescue preparations and said that the winter storm's ability to ground all the people and the extensive resources gathered in Talkeetna was a wake-up call for the Alaska Rescue Group.

"That one set us back on our heels," Nosek said. "We didn't do anything in particular to help out. We tried, but we found out that we weren't able to help them because they were in an environment where help was very difficult to get to them."

He said that after the incident the ARG took a hard look at how it could improve its effectiveness. The group established better and more regular communications with the RCC and put greater attention on climbing application reviews, realizing that an expedition's ability to self-rescue was still paramount.

Ranger Wayne Merry said the ARG's stringent requirements were effective in that pursuit. "The club had fairly high requirements for whom they granted permits, and the result of that process was that if climbers were able to get a club permit, then they probably wouldn't need a rescue."

Nosek says concerns brought to light by the Winter Ascent, as it came to be called, were still fresh when Joe Wilcox's application reached the ARG. Around that time George Hall, the new superintendent of Mount McKinley National Park, reached out to the Alaska Rescue Group. My father's effort was probably motivated by concerns about the Wilcox Expedition raised by rangers Wayne Merry and Art Hayes, rather than Washburn's diatribe, which arrived long after Wilcox had been approved to climb. Whatever the reason, my father asked to meet with the leaders of the Alaska Rescue Group to discuss the Wilcox Expedition.

"When it came to the summertime and Wilcox went up, it didn't seem like anything extraordinary, just a long Muldrow slog," Nosek said. "But your dad had this idea that it would be good if there was a backup plan in place if Wilcox's party got in trouble. It wasn't just picking out Wilcox's party, it was any party, and Wilcox just happened to be one of the first parties after your dad had that idea."

▲▲

The Mountaineering Club of Alaska had planned a Muldrow Glacier ascent of Denali for late June 1967 to be led by Bill Babcock, a twenty-nine-year-old climber who had recently moved to Alaska after spending several years working for the Peace Corps in South America. A veteran of several high-altitude ascents in the Andes, Babcock was a careful climber, fanatical about safety, and a taskmaster when it came to preparing his team.

The Alaska Rescue Group formed a plan around that fortuitous coincidence of the two climbs. Nosek said Babcock and several members of his team were also ARG rescuers who could be activated if the Wilcox party got into trouble. "We thought that for the Wilcox party we had a good plan in place because ARG members were on their own climb, going up maybe a week behind the Wilcox party. That was a lot of our membership in the ARG on that single climb, so it was considered as the onsite backup for Wilcox." If the Wilcox Expedition ran into trouble and couldn't rescue itself like the Winter Ascent party had, a team of rescuers who were already on the mountain and acclimated was the next best thing.

With the exception of Bill's nineteen-year-old brother, Jeff Babcock, who was attending college in Maine, the MCA Expedition members all lived in Alaska. Leo Hannan was the coleader; anesthesiologist Grace Jansen-Hoeman provided medical support; and Gayle Nienhueser, Chet Hackney, John Ireton, Barney Seiler, and Don Haglund rounded out the team of nine.

Their training began in September of 1966 and they climbed together every other weekend throughout the winter and spring of 1967. Bill Babcock put an emphasis on mountaineering techniques and shelter-building on those training climbs. Six outings were conducted on glaciers "where the climbers ascended one-hundred-foot ice walls, ascended forty-foot prussicks, and spent hours cutting steps and placing ice screws."

He also kept a close eye on the group dynamics and didn't hesitate to act when he saw problems. "Each member of the group has come to know the others and there are no serious personality conflicts. Others, who initially joined the group, were eliminated because of personality conflicts that they were responsible for."

During their training they endured temperatures as low as minus 25 degrees Fahrenheit and winds in excess of 50 miles per hour. On two trips, one in January and one in February, they went out without their sleeping bags.

Based on his experiences in the Andes, Bill Babcock knew that tents were vulnerable to wind unless fortified by sturdy snow walls. At high altitude he preferred snow caves, which offered unparalleled protection from mountain storms. So, cave and igloo construction was an integral part of their training.

"You have to practice and practice to get good at digging caves and building walls and igloos," Babcock said. "It's the kind of thing that you have to do a lot of to feel comfortable that you can actually whip one out in an hour or so."

Though the MCA Expedition was better trained and more experienced in alpine arctic conditions than the Wilcox Expedition, it was not immune from hardship, conflict, and discord. Babcock planned to traverse the mountain, ascending the Muldrow and descending the West Buttress and flying out from the Kahiltna Glacier. They did not have the luxury of Berle Mercer's packhorses to get them to the McGonagall Pass, so on June 29 they gathered at Wonder Lake, shouldered their packs, and headed toward the mountain on foot under a ceiling of moisture-laden clouds piled up on the north side of the Alaska Range. High on the Muldrow Glacier, heavy snows pinned down the Wilcox team for a day. Down on the tundra the clouds loosed rain, sleet, and fog. It was the beginning of a wet, miserable, and meandering march for Babcock's team.

"Our first seven days were absolutely miserable, rainy, cold, zero visibility," Babcock said. "It made the going very, very difficult."

The McKinley River was high, making the multiple crossings difficult. Chet Hackney fell in twice, first losing his ice ax and later his camera. Don Haglund and Barney Seiler were spooked after running into a bear on the trail and grew more and more morose as the gloomy weather persisted.

"Don moody and fearful of just about everything bears, river, etc.," Bill Babcock wrote in his journal. "Also, despite months of having time to prepare he was not yet ready for the climb."

Seiler also began having second thoughts. "Barney took off on his own—had to talk to him, as result he got angry, decided to pull out." Haglund had been moody but hadn't quit the expedition. A

conflict over who would carry loads across one of the swollen
creeks was the last straw for Haglund, who gathered his personal
gear and left with Seiler.

I spoke with Don Haglund just a few days before he succumbed
to cancer at his home in South Anchorage in August 2012. He told
me he was in poor physical condition when he left for the climb,
and the incessant rain made him feel all the worse. He was an experienced mountaineer who had climbed extensively in the Alaska and
Chugach Ranges and knew the going wasn't going to get any easier.
He said he'd already had it in his head that he wasn't going to make
it to the summit when Seiler told him he was thinking of leaving.
Haglund said he thought about his wife and two young daughters
at home and made a split-second decision to go with Seiler. He gathered his gear and left without even telling the others.

I asked if he followed events on the mountain as the Wilcox tragedy unfolded in newspapers across Alaska a few weeks later. "I
didn't pay much attention to it," he said. "I had moved on, I was just
glad I left when I did."

Later that day Babcock realized he had mistaken Carlson Creek
for Cache Creek. He had led the expedition up the wrong valley and
it would take days to backtrack. His journal notes his matter-of-fact
realization of the mistake: "The map and book obviously told me
so, but [I was] too engrossed to fully realize it."

In spite of the weather and the conflicts, the remaining climbers
were committed to the expedition and persevered. Bill Babcock and
John Ireton found a shortcut between the Carlson and Cache Creek
drainages, redistributed the group's supplies, and headed for Mc-
Gonagall Pass.

It was July 9 before the sun returned and the expedition reached
the edge of the Muldrow Glacier. "Everything was soaked when we

got to McGonagall Pass. Everything," recalled Gayle Nienhueser. "Every piece of clothing we had was laying out in the sun. It looked like a Chinese laundry."

After days of cold, wind, and rain, the sun quickly became too much, as Babcock noted in his journal: "Hot weather made relays from eleven A.M. to three thirty P.M. unbearable."

Before leaving McGonagall Pass behind, Babcock made a surprising discovery.

"There were some halfway decent snow shovels and a couple of saws left by them [the Wilcox Expedition] at McGonagall Pass, which we couldn't really figure out," he recalled.

The MCA Expedition had pared down its own gear after Haglund and Seiler left, but shovels were not among the items discarded. In his July 9 journal entry Babcock noted, "Mistake to leave big shovel, each tent or cave team needs shovels for caves 2 or three man is about maximum."

By Tuesday, July 11, all their supplies were at the top of the pass and a rope team had already established a cache at the Lower Icefall. Buoyed by clear weather and improved morale, the pace quickened and they began moving up the glacier.

But a few days later the expedition lost another man, this time to a close call with an avalanche. "It was Gayle and Leo who made a relay," Bill Babcock said. "Right after they completed the relay a huge slide came down literally ten or fifteen minutes later. Had they been anywhere on that path they would have been killed. After that Leo came up to me and said he just couldn't go—with kids at home, he couldn't do it." Though it was a sixteen-mile round-trip, Gayle walked Leo back to McGonagall Pass and made sure he got off the glacier safely before returning.

Though Babcock's expedition had barely reached the mountain, it was already down three members. Yet Babcock's journal entries reflect no angst about the losses. I asked him about it.

"Early in the game, when I first started climbing, I had people going with me say they wanted to leave and I always tried to talk them out of it," he said. "It never worked out. I found that trying to push someone to go along who doesn't want to go along is senseless."

Though Don Haglund said he had abandoned the expedition, Babcock recalls it differently.

"Don and Barney just came to me and said they wanted to go back and I said fine. If you don't want to be here, you're not part of the team anymore." The two men were experienced climbers; they had their reasons for leaving the expedition and that was good enough for him. Babcock said coercing them to continue might have put the entire expedition at risk if the men weren't committed or prepared, which seemed to be the case. His attitude is in sharp contrast to that of Wilcox, who was intent on keeping his expedition together in spite of the obvious disparities in skill and, at least at times, commitment.

Between the Muldrow Glacier's Upper and Lower Icefalls, the MCA group camped at a site previously occupied by the Wilcox Expedition and found "several pair of broke plastic snowshoes, a considerable amount of miscellaneous equipment, and food and fuel." Discarding the impractical Snowtreads made sense, but Babcock thought leaving the food and fuel behind was foolish.

So the five men and one woman continued to make their way up the Muldrow Glacier under mostly fair skies, moving quickly along the trail broken by the Wilcox team several days before. The rainy weather and lost trail below McGonagall Pass had slowed their progress early on, and that delay of several days proved to be fateful.

While the Wilcox Expedition's eight-man advance team settled in to the 17,900-foot high camp, Babcock's MCA team was still negotiating the avalanche zones and crevasse fields of the Muldrow Glacier.

"I think the smartest thing I ever did was take everybody up the wrong valley," Babcock said. "It saved our lives. If we hadn't gotten lost, we would have been up on the Harper when the storm hit."

CHAPTER 8

HOWLING

A 40-mile-per-hour wind pulled and plucked at the fabric of the tents tucked into Camp VII at 17,900 feet and the noisy snapping made for a restless night. When Howard Snyder awoke on the morning of July 15, the sky was dark and clouds and wind-driven snow obscured the view across the Harper Glacier. A few feet away, in the tent he shared with Denny Luchterhand, Joe Wilcox listened to the wind and wondered if they would be denied the chance to stand on the summit. He knew many climbers had come this far only to be turned back by punishing wind and snow that can come with little warning and settle in with impunity. With the gusts still lapping at his tent, Joe Wilcox dozed off again.

Though the day seemed less than promising, Snyder began filling his small backpack with the essentials he would carry to the summit. By late morning on July 15, the ranger's interpretation of the rising barometer was proving accurate. The wind dropped to 5 miles per hour and clouds gave way to a deep-blue sky. In the Colorado tent, Snyder, Lewis, and Schlichter began dressing for the extreme conditions that can occur on the summit ridge. Over their long underwear and ski pants, they pulled on down pants and shirts and wind shell parkas. Feet were tucked into silk socks, then wool socks, then down booties, felt booties, felt overboot insulation, and finally nylon overboots. Thick silk gloves, followed by down mittens, covered their hands.

When they emerged from their tent around 11:30 A.M., Joe Wilcox was the only other climber who was ready to go. None of the others had budged from their tents. "Here we are, Jerry Lewis, Paul Schlichter, myself, and Joe Wilcox," Howard Snyder said. "We're out of our tents, we're ready to go, nobody's stirring in the two tents where these guys were. So I went over to Jerry Clark, the deputy leader, and said, 'Jerry aren't you guys going up?' 'Nah,' he said, 'we're just going to sit and watch the snow blow.'"

A different decision by Jerry Clark at this point might have changed the Wilcox Expedition's place in history from tragedy to a climbing footnote. Had those healthy enough to climb gone to the top they might have avoided the storm and left the weaker climbers with no choice but to descend.

Snyder said he was surprised at the time, but he's had a lot of years to think about why they decided not to go that day and now believes that Jerry Clark was looking out for the weaker climbers when he chose to wait.

"Well, they knew, at least Jerry Clark knew, of the correspondence with the park wherein they were forbidden to divide the group into the most experienced and the least experienced, and that's exactly what they had done," Snyder said. "So, he probably said to Hank Janes and to Denny Luchterhand and to Mark McLaughlin, he probably said, 'Look, we have been forbidden to divide our group like this. Denny can't go to the summit today. So we're going to stay here, we're going to wait for those guys to come up from 15,000 feet so we will not have violated the prohibition of the park. So, we will go together tomorrow, just like we have done all these years in the Cascades. We will go together as a group. Let Wilcox and these Colorado guys go on, what the heck do we care? We'll go tomorrow.'"

Comradeship, Wilcox believes, motivated their decision to stay behind. "I thought it strange at the time," he said. "In retrospect, I think that they might have wanted to climb with friends. That was probably the reason. Resting at 18,000 feet wasn't going to help much."

Paul Schlichter believes that strong leadership at that point in the climb might have changed the course of events that followed. "I think that was where Joe or somebody should have said, 'You know the weather is good, you're not going to get any rest by staying here at almost 18,000 feet for another day. You've got to decide whether you're going to come with us now, or it's probably smart to turn around and go back.'"

Over the decades since the four-man team went on to the summit, much has been read into their decision to go on without their companions. However, the decision had been discussed on the radio with the Eielson rangers and it followed the same routine the expedition had followed since it first set foot on the Muldrow Glacier at McGonagall Pass: an advance team led, followed by the support team a day later.

Wilcox also has been accused of abandoning his team at this point in the climb, but it is Howard Snyder, his oft-supposed adversary, who has long challenged that contention.

"In Joe's defense, if it is a defense, we were part of his group," Snyder said. "Just like the other guys. Well, not like the other guys, but part of his group . . . I don't think he is guilty of any wrongdoing in that. But it makes it very convenient for people to dump on him for it, to say he should have done otherwise. Here's what I tell people: We *were* his group. We were no longer an independent group. We were part of the Joseph F. Wilcox Mount McKinley Expedition."

So, while John Russell, Walt Taylor, Anshel Schiff, and Steve Taylor began their trek up the Harper Glacier toward Camp VII at 17,900 feet, Jerry Clark, Mark McLaughlin, Denny Luchterhand, and Hank Janes waited for them. Joe Wilcox, Howard Snyder, Paul Schlichter, and Jerry Lewis set out for the summit.

As they prepared to leave, Wilcox discovered that they had only fifty wands to mark the trail. "What a blunder, I thought. How could John have sent us barely half the wands needed to mark the route from high camp to the summit?"

Rather than waste the good weather waiting for more wands to arrive with the men coming up from Camp VI, they decided to go on and mark the route by breaking the four-foot wands in half. Howard Snyder led the rope out of camp; Paul Schlichter and Jerry Lewis followed, with Joe Wilcox bringing up the rear.

The summit team placed wands at 110-foot rope-length intervals, sometimes in as little as 6 inches of snow. The wands marked the trail both for their own return and for those who would follow in a day or two. When visibility is so poor that the trail and the next wand can't be distinguished, the team waits at the last wand and the leader walks to the end of his rope and then fans back and forth like a human radar beam until he finds the next wand. Once it is found, the rope team moves forward and the process is repeated.

They took fifty minutes to reach Denali Pass, and although that first half mile was nearly level, the going was difficult due to weak, crusty snow underlain by soft powder. At the pass, they found several caches from prior expeditions. "We did not inspect any of them," Wilcox reported. "Although we did notice one cache in wooden crates had been broken into—possibly by the winter expedition."

At Denali Pass, they attempted to hail Eielson using their hand-held radio but had no luck. At 2:00 P.M. near 18,500 feet, they made "loud and clear contact" with Eielson, which continued all the way to the summit.

"At Denali Pass we encountered wands leading up toward the summit, which apparently belonged to a recent West Buttress group," said Wilcox. "We chose to follow these wands, saving ours in case we needed them later. On the ridge behind Archdeacon's Tower we could see that the rest of the route to the summit was well wanded, so we cached the rest of our wands—about fifty."

Snyder disagrees. "It was not well wanded," he said. "I was leading all day long from the high camp to the summit. There were some wands; we saw about a half dozen before the summit. Two were at an ice cliff, near the side of Archdeacon's Tower Ridge. Otherwise there weren't very many and some were blown away by the time we returned."

On the featureless terrain between Denali Pass and the summit ridge, hard snow made the climbing easier. At 20,100 feet the trail narrowed as they gained the quarter-mile-long ridge that leads to the summit.

"I remember we got on that summit ridge and the weather was just beautiful," Paul Schlichter said. "We were in shirtsleeves going to the summit."

"On this day the summit ridge was a thing of rare beauty," Howard Snyder recalled, "purest white against the deep-blue sky, rippling and curling like a frozen wave. We climbed just to the left of the actual crest, because the right side dropped off 8,500 very sudden feet to the Kahiltna Glacier."

At 6:30 P.M., as the top came into view, Wilcox keyed the mike on his radio so Gordon Haber could record the broadcast on a tape recorder at Eielson Visitor Center.

Wilcox's quick, shallow breaths are the first sounds that can be heard, followed by his call to one of his rope-mates: "How far now to the summit? Sixty feet to the summit?"

A few more minutes of heavy breathing and scattered conversation follows, then Ranger Haber's voice breaks in: "Are you on the summit right now?"

"Roger, roger, all four of us."

The tinny voices on the recording are reminiscent of the sound of astronauts broadcasting from the moon, and both climbers and rangers are clearly excited. Though unable to communicate directly with the climbers from Wonder Lake, Ranger Wayne Merry stood by on the single-side-band and offered his congratulations, which Ranger Haber repeated to the summit team.

By coincidence, Ethel Worthington, Jerry Lewis's next-door neighbor, was at the Eielson Visitor Center when they called from the summit and she let Haber know that she wanted to talk to the six-foot five-inch Lewis standing on top of the highest peak in North America.

"This is Ethel, should I wire your mother that you reached the top?" she asks.

"Yeah would you do that? I'd really appreciate it," Lewis answers without a hint of embarrassment in his voice.

Haber asked for a description of the view, and Howard Snyder responded, "Foraker is completely out of the clouds; the clouds are down about 11,000 feet, and it looks beautiful. All of the peaks off, to, uh, let's see what would this be, to the southeast. The peaks to the southeast are visible; the clouds are lying low in the valleys. It's just a beautiful view up here."

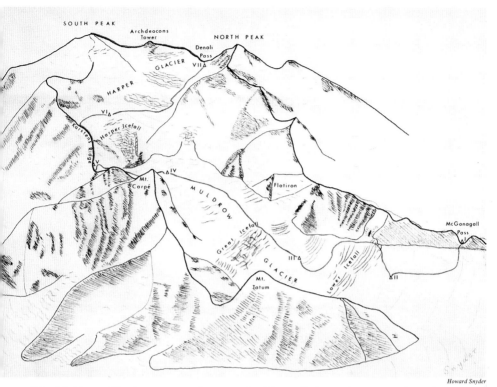

The Muldrow Glacier route to the summit of Denali drawn by Howard Snyder.

Sunshine filled the Muldrow Glacier valley on the Fourth of July, and the Wilcox Expedition took advantage of it, posing for a group photo. From left to right, Steve Taylor, Joe Wilcox, Howard Snyder, Dennis Luchterhand, Mark McLaughlin, Paul Schlichter, Jerry Clark, Jerry Lewis, Anshel Schiff, Hank Janes, John Russell, and Walt Taylor.

Paul Schlichter, left, and Jerry Lewis alongside Lewis's Dodge Power Wagon near the intersection of the Richardson and Denali Highways on the way to Mount McKinley National Park.

Howard Sn

Howard Snyder

Jerry Lewis pauses while following John Russell across the first flowing channel of the McKinley River. The men are using bamboo probe poles to aid in the river crossing.

Below: Camp I pitched at McGonagall Pass at the edge of the Muldrow Glacier. The relatively level glacier would be their path into the heart of the Denali massif.

Howard Sn

Mark McLaughlin /Howard Snyder Collection

Jerry Lewis peers into a crevasse after being hauled out of it. While waiting for rescue he saw a huge blue-walled cavern and an icy lake beneath him.

Jerry Clark crossing a snow bridge over one of the huge crevasses in the Great Icefall on the Harper Glacier.

Jerry Lewis /Howard Snyder Collection

Howard Sn

Joe Wilcox ascends
the crest of Karstens
Ridge at 11,500 feet.
Orange-flagged
bamboo wands for
trail marking are
strapped to the top of
his pack. He also
carries a reel of black
polypropylene
waterski rope to be
used as a fixed line
higher on the ridge.

Howard Snyder

Wind peels snow from
the crest of Karstens
Ridge on July 10 as the
advance team of Janes,
McLaughlin, Schlichter,
and Luchterhand near
12,850 feet. Just visible
as four dots on the
upper ridge.

Walt Taylor, Steve Taylor, Jerry Lewis, and John Russell leaving Camp VI at 15,000 feet on the Harper Glacier. Archdeacon's Tower is on the skyline, to the left of center.

The tent fire at Camp VI destroyed one tent and left Walt Taylor, seated, with a singed beard. On the left, Wilcox surveys the damage, McLaughlin stands behind Taylor, and Russell is on the right.

Paul Schlichter, Joe Wilcox, and Jerry Lewis leave Camp VI at 17,900 feet for the summit on July 15, 1967. Lewis carries wands for trail marking strapped to his pack.

The summit team takes a break on the summit ridge at an elevation of 20,150 feet. Jerry Lewis is lying down, Paul Schlichter stands, and Joe Wilcox is seated. Mount Foraker is in the background.

Jerry Lewis / Howard Snyder Collection

Howard Snyder

Joe Wilcox on the summit of Denali on July 15, 1967, holding a pennant from his alma mater, Kansas State College of Pittsburg.

Howard Snyder on Denali's summit. The team carried a CB radio and with it held one of the first direct radio conversations between the summit and the rangers in the park.

Howard Snyder

Jerry Lewis on the summit. During his radio conversation with rangers at Eielson Visitor Center he spoke with his neighbor from Colorado who happened to be visiting the park.

Right: Paul Schlichter sets off a smoke flare on the summit of Denali while rangers and visitors at Eielson Visitor Center in the park below observed the smoke.

Leaving Camp VII at noon on
July 17, 1967. Paul Schlichter
is closest to photographer
Howard Snyder. Behind him
from left to right, Anshel
Schiff, Mark McLaughlin,
Hank Janes, and Walt Taylor.

Right: John Russell's bamboo
staff, flagged with the remains
of the burned tent, stood alone
in the snow a few hundred
yards below Camp VII after the
storm. A sleeping bag and shell
containing wool socks and a pair
of down booties was wrapped
around the shaft. The pack that
can be seen in the image belongs
to the MCA rescue team.

Denali National Park and Preserve Museum Collection. Dena 13611 Folder

Gayle Nienhueser

The storm-blasted high camp as
encountered by the MCA team
on the morning of July 28.
Rather than survivors they
found a corpse gripping a tent
pole, wrapped in the wind-
shattered yellow tent. The gear
bags in the foreground appeared
to be propping up the tent.

"Well, it sounds fabulous. I hope you're taking lots of pictures."

"We are," Snyder replied. "All kinds of them."

They spent an hour and a half on the summit, dictating postcards to Haber, setting off smoke flares, taking photos, and sharing a Coca-Cola that Wilcox had secreted all the way to the top.

A skein of high cirrus clouds obscured the sun during their descent, and by the time they reached Denali Pass, the wind picked up. Both Joe Wilcox and Jerry Lewis were out of breath for most of the ascent, according to Howard Snyder, and both began to show signs of fatigue on the way down. Wilcox led the rope team off of the trail more than once but, with occasional guidance from the others, had no trouble getting back to camp in just two hours.

As the summit party reached the high camp at 17,900 feet, Anshel Schiff, Steve Taylor, Walt Taylor, and John Russell were just approaching from below and it was apparent that they needed help. Howard Snyder described the scene in a letter, written a month after he returned home.

> When the party Russell was with arrived at Camp VII on the evening of the 15th, he was so weak with sickness that the returning summit party descended to him without stopping in camp so as to take his pack. Russell had been sick on almost the entire trip from 15,000' to 17,900' and had redistributed much of his load to the others on his rope. As sick as he was, and having to divide up his load, he nonetheless was carrying his "flag" on his packframe. The wind had been blowing about 25 to 30 mph for an hour, and the "flag" added at least ten pounds to the load in the form of wind resistance. I took Russell's pack from him, and carried it the last 200' into camp.

Walt Taylor and Steve Taylor refused help, but Schiff relin-
quished his pack for the final 200-foot walk into camp.

John Russell's "flag" was made from one of the ten-foot bamboo
crevasse probes picked up in Seattle on the way to Alaska. He had
intended to plant it on the summit.

After watching Russell make the flag the day before, Howard
Snyder probably wasn't excited to be carrying it even the short distance into camp. He wrote in his journal:

> While the first party of eight moved from 15,000' to 17,900'
> on the 14th, Russell busied himself by opening the Colo-
> rado Group 1st aid kit, and using the entire supply of ad-
> hesive tape to make a "flag" from the scraps of the burned
> tent. In the process he also lost the scissors, razor blade,
> needle, and Band-Aids from the kit.

Even in his debilitated state, Russell found a way to be ex-
asperating.

The sixteenth was supposed to be the second summit day, but the
winds continued to build, bringing clouds and blowing snow. By
midnight gusts of 70 miles per hour buffeted the tents and continued
through the following day and dusklike darkness that is night in mid-
July. The entire party was pinned down in their tents, unable to
climb or descend. Luchterhand and Wilcox took turns shoveling
drifting snow away from their two-man tent, allowing neither man
to get a good night's sleep.

Luchterhand appeared to be improving, but Russell remained
unable to hold down his food. Schiff and Steve Taylor were feeling
the effects of altitude but kept their condition to themselves. Walt
Taylor, on the other hand, had been one of the strongest climbers
on the expedition, and his energy didn't flag at altitude. Without a

cook tent where the men could gather, they had to eat in their tents, so Walt moved through the camp delivering food and filling water bottles. On the evening of the sixteenth, Clark told Wilcox he was considering abandoning his summit aspirations and heading toward lower elevations as soon as the weather broke.

Despite the bad weather, altitude sickness, and Russell's flag, humor was alive and well. Late that night, as they lay in their sleeping bags, with the wind roaring and the nylon tents snapping in the breeze, Luchterhand let out a long, lonely howl and soon the entire camp was howling along in lupine unison.

When Jerry Clark peeked out of his tent on Monday, July 17, he was greeted by much better weather—much like it had been two days earlier on Saturday morning when the first group summited. Clark made two calls to Eielson to get weather advice, but no reports were available. It left the decision in the climbers' hands, and from their vantage point high on the mountain, conditions were looking good.

"I think we'll just wait and see what the weather does," Clark told Wilcox.

As the morning progressed, the wind died and the skies continued to clear. Wilcox and the Colorado group prepared to leave for Camp VI at 15,000 feet, where they would await the second summit team. Fewer people at the high camp meant more food and fuel for those who remained. Moreover, Jerry Lewis's condition continued to worsen, so getting him to a lower altitude was a priority.

And he wasn't the only one who was suffering. While Dennis Luchterhand had recovered after falling ill during the ascent to high camp, neither Steve Taylor nor Anshel Schiff felt any better despite having remained at Camp VI for an additional day. Altitude sickness wracked John Russell's body more severely—whenever he'd try to eat, he'd throw up.

Howard Snyder tried to convince John Russell to head down. "I knew John was sick; I knew he was suffering from altitude sickness," Snyder said. "I went over to the tent he was in and, knowing his prickly character, I didn't say, 'John, you're sick and I think, really, you should go down with us.' That wouldn't have worked. I went over to his tent and said, 'John, any of you guys want to go down with us?' Well, that veiled attempt was too obvious for him, and it made him angry. He said, 'No, no one wants to go down.' Moments later, Anshel Schiff exploded out of that tent as though he had to escape. I mean, he didn't just throw open the door and crawl. He exploded out of the tent and said, 'I'm going down with you,' which saved his life."

Wilcox didn't find out Schiff had digestive problems until much later, and his perspective was less dramatic. "Anshel had a realistic view of his own abilities when he got to high camp. He had come along to do the science stuff; he was in good physical shape but didn't need or want to go to the top."

What of Steve Taylor, the young man who felt sick as soon as he got to the foot of the mountain? He had been the first one to sign up with Wilcox and had appeared to some to be the weakest man on the team, even back in Puyallup. The altitude began to affect Taylor when he topped 12,000 feet on Karstens Ridge, and he'd showed no signs of bouncing back. This is from one of Snyder's letters written just after the climb:

> Lewis asked specifically if [Steve] Taylor wanted to come down with us, and he replied that he would stay with the party at camp VII. Schiff said that he is almost certain that S. Taylor knew he was not going on to the summit. If this is so, Taylor was either playing a bluff to the last

minute to avoid having "backed out"; or he had decided to rest a day at 17,900', going neither up nor down.

One other man on the expedition who may have been feeling the effects of altitude: Joe Wilcox. Both Howard Snyder and Paul Schlichter claim he appeared to be suffering. "He was so damn sick before we came down that he didn't pack his own pack," Snyder said. "His guys packed it for him."

"I was tired after staying up shoveling; other than that, I felt fine," says Wilcox. He planned to wait at the high camp and told Jerry Clark, "I'll stay here while you guys try the peak."

"That really won't be necessary," Clark replied. "We have the majority of the strongest climbers with us, and besides it would further conserve our fuel for you to descend to Camp Six."

Wilcox decided to go down. "I felt that I should stay with the high group; however, this would mean sending only four people down [two of them very weak]. I didn't feel that I could ask any of the other climbers to give up their summit aspirations, so I accompanied the weak group myself."

Jerry Lewis, Howard Snyder, Paul Schlichter, Anshel Schiff, and Joe Wilcox were ready to leave camp at 1:00 P.M., but the second ascent team was still walking around the camp, packing, excavating gear buried by snow during the windstorm, and searching for two one-liter bottles of fuel that had been left outside and lost. Wilcox found Clark, reminded him that food had been cached at 16,500 feet between Camp VI and Camp VII, and said, "Don't take any chances, Jerry; it's not worth it."

"Don't worry," Jerry replied. "If we can't climb today, we'll probably go down tomorrow."

They shared a mittened handshake and parted. Joe Wilcox tied into the 270-foot rope Howard Snyder had strung together, and they headed down. Along with their personal gear they carried the Colorado team's four-man McKinley tent, a two-man yellow Mountaineer tent, and the expedition's only complete shovel.

"We could see the camp as we moved down," Paul Schlichter told me. "It seemed like a couple of hours after we left, they were still milling around getting ready to go to the top, taking forever."

It was 3:00 P.M., about the same time that Wilcox and the four others arrived at Camp VI, that the summit team finally left Camp VII with Walt Taylor breaking trail up the Harper Glacier toward Denali Pass.

It was late to be leaving on a climb that in ideal conditions would require six hours to get to the top, and at least two to return. But on Denali in mid-July there is no shortage of daylight, with the sun setting at midnight and rising before 4:00 A.M.

Joe Wilcox believes that when the summit party finally left, each man packed a sleeping bag, down pants, insulated overboots, a face mask, and two to three days' worth of emergency food. Distributed among the seven men were one handle-less shovel, a stove, two ropes, a five-watt handheld radio with an extra set of batteries, and 150 wands for trail marking.

Howard Snyder, however, says the only food they carried was lunch.

"It is possible that some had carried sleeping bags as a precaution," he adds, "as Dennis Luchterhand had said he intended to do."

Two tents remained at 17,900 feet: Mark McLaughlin's homemade, two-man Cascade—which could hold three in a pinch—and the surviving four-man Logan. Inside the Logan, Steve Taylor stretched out his long frame, swallowed back the nausea, and listened to his companions as they moved up the glacier, their voices fading until all was silent and he was alone.

Around 8:30 P.M., Jerry Clark's voice crackled through the radio at Eielson Visitor Center. Ranger Gordon Haber answered the call and then started the tape recorder.

Clark's voice is clear and unhurried and free of the heavy breathing notable during Wilcox's call two days prior.

Clark: ETA is approximately forty-five minutes to one hour, Gordy.
Haber: Forty-five minutes to an hour?
Clark: [Garbled affirmative response]
Haber: OK, I'll tell you what. When you get to within about a hundred to a hundred and fifty feet of the top, why don't you give me a call. I imagine that'd be somewhere between a half an hour and forty-five minutes or so and, uh, maybe if you've got enough battery power, we can monitor you up the last few feet and I can record like I did for the first four guys that went up.
Clark: Way cool. We'll see what happens, Gordy. [Chuckles] We'll try to give you a call. KHD6990 Unit One clear.

Haber said he'd be downstairs but would leave the volume high so he could hear their call and then he signed off: "If I don't answer the first time, don't get too shocked. I'll be right up."

Due to the geography of the peak, Camp VI at 15,000 feet is not in line of sight with Denali Pass. While Haber could speak with both groups, they could not communicate with each other.

Moments after Clark signs off, Joe Wilcox breaks in but his voice is faint.

Haber: I thought I heard you say, I may be wrong on this, but did you want to know what was going on up there? Is that what you asked?

Wilcox: Roger, roger.

Haber: Yeah, they figure their ETA right now is about forty-five minutes to an hour from the top. They wanted to know, originally from you, whether or not there was a large cornice on the summit. Of course you answered affirmative to that, but that's about all I know right now. They just told me they'd be up there about forty-five minutes to an hour from now. I can check on more if you'd like to know.

Wilcox: Is everyone there in the party. Are there seven in the party?

Haber: I understood there were only six in the party, but I'll check on that again. Unit One, are you reading me?

[After repeated calls he gives up.]

Haber: I guess they shut the transmitter off, John [apparently Haber momentarily forgot Joe's name]. They had told me originally, Jerry told me that, uh, they had fifteen-knot winds and he estimated the temperatures of zero to ten degrees. But the last I talked to them at four forty, he said there were six climbers, six of them in that group.

Wilcox: OK, thanks a lot.

Haber: OK, they're going to call back again in about a half an hour, forty-five minutes or so, when they get close to the top. Maybe we'll get a hold of you then. Are you going to be listening in or turn it off now?

Wilcox: We'll probably listen in. It depends on what's going on.

Haber: Whereabouts are you right now, Joe?

Wilcox: We're at the 15,000-foot camp on the Harper.

Haber: OK then. When you first came on I couldn't read you but you're coming in real clear now. Maybe we should let well enough alone. Do you have anything further?

Wilcox: Uh, no, I uh, you said some climbers didn't go to the summit. I was just wondering who it was.

Haber: You were wondering who was up there? Is that what you said?

Wilcox: Yes, I was wondering who was up there. Who did not go to the summit? There were seven at high camp.

Haber: Yeah, the way I understood it, there was one of the seven that got a little sick I guess and couldn't quite make it so I guess he went back down with some of the others that were going back down to the 15,000-foot camp. That's the way I understood it. Right now I assume there are six.

Wilcox: There is no one here, uh, Anshel Schiff did not attempt the summit. But there should be one other climber at the 17,900 camp who did not attempt the summit today. I was just wondering who it was.

Haber: Oh, I see. OK. No, they didn't mention to me who it was. Next time I talk to them I could ask them.

Wilcox: OK. We'll listen in, in about a half an hour.

Haber: OK then, Joe. We'll see what we can do then.

Fifteen-knot winds at 5 degrees Fahrenheit would have produced a wind chill factor of about 15 below zero. Hardly extraordinary conditions, and certainly nothing to be concerned about. An hour passed before Clark called again, around 9:30 P.M. and Haber starts the recorder before answering.

Haber: This is KHD 6990 Eielson. Go ahead, Unit One.

Clark: Gordy, we've got real problems up here. Do you have any arrangements to contact Unit Two?

Haber: I tried to call them just a little while ago and I couldn't get an answer. Why don't you let me try again; stand by.

[Haber calls Unit 2 but gets no response.]

Haber: Uh, I don't get an answer [from] Unit One, Jerry. Uh, I originally had told them we would, you'd probably be calling about a quarter to nine and so they said they'd be listening in. I imagine they had their radio on and shut it off. But they might, they might turn it on periodically, uh, although I don't know when. I don't imagine they'll leave it on the whole time because of the batteries. What's the problem?

Clark: Well, this route is not well wanded at all. We've lost the wands. We're just floundering around. We don't know whether we're on the summit ridge or not. We don't know whether the summit ridge is supposed to be wanded or not, and uh, we just thought we'd check it out. We think we're pretty close to the summit, but uh, we can't tell. We're just floundering around on the flat here. Visibility is about three hundred feet.

Haber: Ah, I didn't understand all of that, Jerry. I got, I think I got the gist of it. You think you're up near the summit but you can't be sure if you're at the summit or not, you're just sort of floundering around; you're not sure where you are. Is that correct?

Clark: We're not even sure we're on the summit ridge yet. We don't know whether the summit ridge is supposed to be wanded, and we've lost the wands. The wands are set too far apart, can't find out where they left the ridge.

Haber: OK, we're still a little fuzzy there, but I think I understood you to say that you don't know where the summit ridge is and you have lost the wands because they are too far apart. Is that correct?

Clark: Roger. We're at the summit ridge. We have followed the wands to what we think may be the summit ridge. I'll say that over again. We have followed the wands to what we think may be the summit ridge. And if we find one more wand, one more wand, it'd probably be enough, uh, to tell us which way to go on the ridge. That would be enough for, to tell us which way to go on the ridge.

Haber: Uh, Jerry, uh, I don't know if your batteries are warm enough or not or what, but I couldn't get too much of that. I understood you to say you followed the wands up to the summit ridge and then you lost them. Is this correct? Let's try this again.

Clark: [Garbled] We have cold batteries. We have cold batteries.

Haber: You have cold batteries. Is that what you said?

Clark: The rest are at camp.

Haber: OK. Is there any chance that you can let them warm up a little bit and then we can try again?

Clark: Roger.

Haber: OK. Let me stand by here for a few minutes then because I can't really understand what you're saying. Eielson standing by. . . .

Around 11:00 P.M., Jerry Clark hailed Eielson. Haber responded but nothing followed. Just over twelve hours later, at 11:30 A.M. on July 18, Clark's calm voice again hails Eielson. After Haber's response, Clark's voice breaks in, midsentence.

Clark: . . . blowing, seven degrees.

Haber: What happened last night? You called about quarter to eleven, I guess. I heard you and I answered but you didn't, you didn't acknowledge. I thought maybe you had radio trouble.

Clark: We probably didn't copy you. We had some weak batteries; in fact, they're still weak right now. We ended up bivouacking, as a matter of fact. It got so fogged in that we couldn't go up and we couldn't go down.

Haber: Well, you're coming in loud and clear right here now. How long do you plan on staying on the top?

Clark: Well, five or ten more minutes, Gordy. It's kind of cold up here. Hank wants to read something for you, stand by.

[Mark McLaughlin, not Hank Janes comes on.]

McLaughlin: Hey, Gordy, you still sending postcards from the summit?

Haber: Yeah, go ahead.

McLaughlin: I'd like to send one to my parents. Do you have a pencil and paper there?

Haber: Go right ahead.

McLaughlin: Mr. and Mrs. S. P. McLaughlin.

Haber: Mr. and Mrs. S. P. McLaughlin . . .

McLaughlin: Dear Mom and Dad, Radio from the summit. A-OK. See you in a week or two. Love, Mark.

Haber: OK, got that. How about giving us a little description of what you can see up there? Tell us how the view is right now.

McLaughlin: The view consists of four other guys at the moment. That's all. It's completely whited out. We're sitting just below the summit; you can see the wands on the summit, that's all. Over.

Haber: Boy, you didn't luck out like the last four, I guess. They got a real good view when they were up there. Do you mind naming off the people that are up there right now?

McLaughlin: Ah, sitting on the summit: Jerry Clark, Hank Janes, Dennis Luchterhand, ah, Mark McLaughlin—oh, and Walt Taylor. Wouldn't want to forget him—he led all the way up.

Haber: OK. Say, when I talked to Joe last night, Wilcox, um, he was wondering what happened to the seventh man. He thought seven were going to try for the peak and I told him there were only six. He'd like to know what happened to the seventh man. He doesn't know where he is. Do you?

McLaughlin: Ah, seventh man is Steve Taylor, and he didn't feel good at all so he stayed in camp at seventeen-nine. He's probably wondering where we are at the moment.

Haber: I imagine he is. What was his name again? Can you repeat it once more real slowly?

McLaughlin: Steve Taylor.

Haber: OK, when I get back in contact with Unit Two, I'll tell him that. He was wondering. Anything else you want to say?

[A voice can be heard speaking in the background and then McLaughlin speaks again.]

McLaughlin: Jerry says to say all five of us got the summit at exactly the same time.

Haber: All of you got up there at the same time. Is that what you said?

McLaughlin: Roger, roger.

[After clarifying the address for his postcard, Mark continues.]

McLaughlin: Well, I guess that's about all the talking we can do, especially since you're not copying us.

[His words grow garbled and then halt.]

Haber: OK. Thanks for the call. Yeah, I can't read you very well at all anymore. You're fading out. Well, not fading out but very indistinct. I think your batteries are going down too. We better clear for now. Just before you do cut out: What time do you want us to stand by here for the next call? Do you have any schedule that you want to maintain?

McLaughlin: Just eight o'clock, I guess.

Haber: OK, eight P.M. We'll have someone here then. Be lookin' forward to talking with you. Congratulations again. If nothing further then this is KHD6990 Eielson Base clear.

McLaughlin: Thanks very much. KHD6990 Unit One clear.

The 8:00 call would never be made. These were the last words heard from any of the seven young men at or above the high camp.

After a long climb and what must have been a bitter and sleepless bivouac, the young mountaineers had made the summit and quickly turned for home, or the next best thing: the tents of high camp, where Steve Taylor waited alone. Five thousand feet below him, near the bitter end of the Harper Glacier, Joe Wilcox, Anshel Schiff, and the Colorado team waited in their tents.

One man, however, remained unaccounted for. Overlooked by ranger Haber and unmentioned by the summit team is the "unregimentable" flag-carrying John Russell. True to form, the group's maverick had again ducked out of sight.

Six men had headed for the summit at 3:00 P.M. the day before. At 4:40 P.M. that day Haber's radio log notes six men climbing to the summit. But at 11:30 the following morning, sitting just below the summit, Mark McLaughlin named only four companions: Jerry Clark, Hank Janes, Denny Luchterhand, and Walt Taylor. When Haber asked who remained at 17,900 feet, McLaughlin explained that Steve Taylor had felt too sick and never left the high camp. So what happened to Russell?

"I could imagine him turning back on his own," Joe Wilcox says. "He had exhausted himself on Karstens Ridge, and he wasn't as strong on the upper mountain. At some point he might have left the summit group. The disposition of the group would have been against it, but he would not have wanted anyone else to forfeit their summit attempt."

Given Russell's personality, there could have been a disagreement. Or, he might have stayed behind at the bivouac site while the others climbed to the summit, which they thought was close at hand. He could have fallen into a crevasse; the first summit team had crossed one that was narrow but apparently bottomless two days prior near 20,000 feet. In any case, and for whatever reasons, John Russell and Steve Taylor, in some ways the most perfect opposites in the Wilcox Expedition, both chose to break off from the group. The seams of the expedition had come apart and would never be put back together.

CHAPTER 9

SPLIT APART

Depending on where you were on Denali on the day of that last radio call from Mark McLaughlin, conditions were cold, warm, clear, cloudy, calm, and blowing from the northwest or blowing from the southwest. Each of these conditions was reported on the same day, some at the same time, and each is accurate to the location and elevation or vantage point where it was recorded. Rarely does the mountain host the same weather across its vast height and girth.

Joe Wilcox's journal entry for that day, Tuesday, July 18, simply notes, "Radio contact with Eielson reveals six made summit at 11:30 A.M. Strong winds from S.W. all day."

Five thousand feet lower, on the Muldrow Glacier, the Mountaineering Club of Alaska team pushed up from the top of the great icefall to the foot of Karstens Ridge. Expedition leader Bill Babcock's journal describes whiteout conditions throughout the day, interrupted by periodic clear skies and hot weather.

On the west side of the mountain, at 17,200 feet on the West Buttress route, the Western States Expedition, comprised of several highly experienced mountaineers, waited for a break in the weather to make a dash for the summit. Expedition member Louis Reichardt's journal entry of the day reports bad weather had hit the night before:

> As feared, the weather turned foul last night. Snow has steadily been falling on us throughout the day, and we have been constantly buffeted with gusty winds with estimated velocities of up to 60 m.p.h. The combination has kept us in a consistent whiteout, dangerous even to go over to the ice caves without wands.

At Wonder Lake, 35 miles north of the mountain, the rangers' logbook notes: "Mountain clear from 6:30 until 9 A.M. Clouds blowing in directly from Northwest."

Such disparate same-day conditions are not unusual for Denali. The weather on the north side of the Alaska Range often differs from that on the south side. The mountain itself is so big and its features so distinct, a single system rarely prevails. But the variation goes much further than that; the twin summits, exposed ridges, gaps between peaks, and deep glacial valleys can give rise to unique microenvironments, each harboring very different conditions simultaneously.

The fog that had shrouded the summit ridge through the night dissipated early on July 18, but by midmorning Snyder noticed from his vantage point at 15,000 feet that a saucerlike lenticular cloud had formed over the summit.

McLaughlin finished the postcard to his parents, ended the radio call with Ranger Haber, and, along with Walt Taylor, Luchterhand, Janes, and Clark, headed down the summit ridge.

A phenomenon called orographic lift had formed a cloud cap over the summit as warm, moist air moved into the cold, stable air near the mountain. This was the result of the low-pressure system's approach. Around noon, about a half an hour after the Unit 2 summit team began its descent, the two systems began to interact violently. At the same time Wilcox reported that a strong, snow-laden wind rolled down Browne Tower ridge and clapped into the broad sides of the tents at Unit 1's 15,000-foot camp. On the south face, another expedition, the A-67 Expedition led by Boyd Everett Jr., also logged a sharp wind increase. "Light snow and fog all day— wind increases at noon and becomes quite violent . . ."

On the exposed summit ridge, inside the otherworldly cloud cap and blind to the atmospheric forces building around them, the summit team caught the brunt of it. Though they carried one sleeping bag for every two men, they had no place to seek shelter—both tents remained at high camp—and they had limited ability to make one, since they carried no intact shovels. Whether or not they had food and stoves is a matter of contention, but with no way to escape the wind, it was impossible to light a stove and to melt water, let alone cook.

At high camp on the north side, where Steve Taylor waited, the wind may have been less intense, but not by much. He had shelter, a stove, and enough food to sustain himself for several days. Fuel, however, would have been limited if the two one-liter bottles had not been located before the summit team left. It is possible Steve Taylor and John Russell reunited at high camp, but there is no clear evidence either way.

High wind and blowing snow kept Wilcox, Schiff, Snyder,

Schlichter, and Lewis at the 15,000-foot camp, confined to their tents, waiting for the 8:00 P.M. radio check, when they expected to hear that their friends were back at high camp. When the summit team did not call in at the appointed time, no one was particularly worried. The radio checks had been inconsistent, and given the exhausting climb and exposed bivouac, who could blame them if they collapsed into their tents after returning from the summit without bothering to call?

Late that night Schiff interrupted the rambling discussion he and Wilcox had been holding inside the bucking and snapping nylon tent.

"Listen," he said. "I hear voices." Wilcox poked his head out of the tent and into the driving snow but, real or imagined, the faint sound was gone.

Constant wind and heavy snow continued through the night and into the next day. In his journal, Joe Wilcox tried to stay measured:

> Wed. July 19. Strong winds all [last] night until noon— Northern storm moves in and dumps a foot of snow during afternoon and night. No contact with High Camp at 8:00 P.M. Becoming a little concerned.

When breaks in the snowstorm allowed glimpses up the Harper Glacier, Wilcox looked toward Camp VII in vain hoping to see a line of seven forms moving down through the swirling snow. Instead he saw a pale landscape devoid of detail save the spindrift dancing on the wind.

At 17,200 feet on the West Buttress, the Western States Expedition realized something unusual was occurring. Louis Reichardt's journal entry on Tuesday night says:

The wind picked up and began blowing steadily from the north. The clouds were whistling by our tent and Lloyd's prognosis was favorable. "South winds bring moisture from the ocean. North winds blow it away!" We retired, planning a summit attempt this morning. However, when we awoke, the weather remained the same. The wind continued to be fast and from the north. The clouds continued to blow by. We were soon in a blizzard and there has been no sign of a break since. Lloyd's prognosis has been grim. "When the north wind does not clear out the clouds, you are really in for it!"

On the Muldrow, the MCA team relayed supplies to the base of Karstens Ridge and, in spite of the whiteout, moved up the ridge to establish a campsite at 11,550 feet.

The Wonder Lake Ranger Station's log's July 19 entry notes, "Denali visible briefly to 17,000'."

In a narrative report written immediately after leaving the mountain, Wilcox stated, "The failure to establish radio contact at 8:00 P.M. with the upper group led me to believe that their radio was damaged or lost (seldom had we missed scheduled radio contacts for two consecutive days.)" Though it was 8:00 P.M., Wilcox argued for heading to the high camp immediately, but Howard Snyder dissuaded him. The sun wouldn't set until midnight and would be up again by 4:00 A.M., but heavy overcast and fog cast a gray pall over the Harper Glacier, and the wind had dislodged many of the wands, making the trail hard to follow. He suggested they wait for better weather, and Wilcox reluctantly agreed.

"We knew they got to the top," Schlichter recalled. "We thought, Well, they're at the high camp and they're hunkered down. We kept thinking, We'll hear them, we'll see them in a few hours, at the end of the day, the next morning."

At 5:30 the following morning, Thursday, July 20, two days since they saw their teammates, Snyder, Schlichter, and Wilcox prepared to return to high camp in search of them. Each man carried basic supplies, including a sleeping bag, along with three gallons of fuel and a stove to resupply the high camp. Schiff and Lewis were weak but not dangerously ill, and stayed behind. As Wilcox prepared to leave, Schiff asked, "How long should we wait for you?"

"Two days," Wilcox answered.

The response must have caused Schiff some concern. They had food and fuel and an intact tent but the altitude continued to affect them. They'd been above 12,000 feet for six days already and Lewis's condition continued to worsen. Neither of them had any experience at high altitude, and if they had to descend alone, they faced a treacherous descent down Karstens Ridge and passage through the crevasse-filled Muldrow Glacier icefalls.

Joe Wilcox led the rope team, breaking trail through foot-deep powder and a 40-mile-per-hour headwind. The storm had dislodged or buried many of the wands, and they had none to replace them. "With our trail obliterated as soon as we broke it," he wrote in his memoir, "we were in danger of cutting off our retreat."

Progress was painfully slow, according to Snyder. "We stood still for minutes at a time, straining to see the wands ahead. When the wands came into view during momentary lulls, first one, then two, then three, we memorized their positions and plodded onward."

After four hours they had covered only three-quarters of a mile and the wind was increasing. A radio call to Eielson yielded no weather forecast, so Wilcox made the decision to turn back. He and Snyder exchanged heated words when Wilcox decided to leave the fuel there on the trail rather than pack it down and then back up again when they returned in better weather. "I thought he shouldn't have left it but didn't say it," Snyder recalled. "He announced the decision wordlessly by putting down the gas can on the trail."

The weather cleared not long after the three men returned to camp, but the wind did not relent. Thin, wispy clouds raked the peak but still no climbers came into view.

▲▲

My father, the park superintendent, is conspicuously absent from the dialogue during the early days of the incident. Early in July he had left the park at the request of National Park Service director George Hartzog to guide US Congresswoman Julia Butler Hansen on a tour of parklands in Alaska. She was chair of the House Appropriations subcommittee that funded the Department of the Interior, and Hartzog wanted to make sure she was well taken care of.

"He said I was not to leave her out of my sight for one minute when she was in Alaska. So I just packed up and followed her around in just that exact way."

Superintendent Hall was away for nearly three weeks showing the congresswoman and her entourage the national parks at Katmai, Glacier Bay, and Sitka, as well as sites that were under consideration for new parks. He had been concerned about the Wilcox Expedition since Washburn sent his fiery letter, and soon after he returned home he asked Chief Ranger Art Hayes for an update.

"The ranger said to me, 'Well, we've got good news. The first party consisting of the two leaders and a few others went to the top and came down. The second party, meaning the rest of the people, all relatively inexperienced, were now up and they radioed they were on the top and on their way down . . . Unfortunately that was the last we heard from them.'"

▲▲▲

The Wonder Lake log describes Wilcox's midday radio call on Thursday, one that would set in motion a chain of events that would involve dozens of people desperate, but impotent, to help.

> At about noon, Wilcox exp. called from 15,000' camp expressing concern for 7 men at 17,900' camp who were out of contact for 2 days and requested ARG overflight if no contact made by 8 P.M. Merry to Eielson to talk with them at 4 P.M. contact and to get further info.

Mount McKinley National Park headquarters, however, didn't wait for another missed radio check. At 2:15 P.M. Chief Ranger Hayes called Gary Hansen, the chairman of the Alaska Rescue Group, the civilian organization that provided mountaineering rescue support for the National Park Service and the Air Force.

By 4:30 P.M., Hansen had received his briefing.

By 5:00 P.M., Hansen was on the phone with the Rescue Coordination Center at Elmendorf Air Force Base in Anchorage. He had worked with the RCC during the Winter Ascent operation a few months earlier and knew they could be slow to launch rescue flights. No rescue had been called, but the sooner the RCC was made aware of a potential rescue situation, the better.

Hansen says, "The same spirit of preparation for such a contingency that Art Hayes had exhibited in contacting me, prompted me to contact Capt. Flanik at the RCC, understanding that the RCC had the greatest capacity to make high-altitude overflights, and to make drops, of any party that could be reasonably called upon to participate in a search of the upper mountain."

Meanwhile, desperate to do something, *anything,* to assist,

Wayne Merry had driven from Wonder Lake to Eielson so he could speak directly with Joe Wilcox. Wonder Lake was not in line of sight with the Harper Glacier and thus out of direct radio contact. Once he got there, he told Wilcox by radio that "the ARG had been alerted." Merry asked "if he understood that they would probably be billed for the flight, as there was no certainty that an emergency existed." Wilcox replied with a "Roger." Merry asked if he wanted to have Don Sheldon chartered if the Alaska Rescue Group could not fly, and again Wilcox replied simply "Roger." He was then told that a "go-ahead" on the flight would be transmitted to ARG as requested at 8:00 P.M. if the upper camp had not been heard from.

At 5:30 P.M., Chief Ranger Art Hayes and ARG's Gary Hansen were on the phone outlining the situation on the mountain and already discussing an airdrop if one was deemed necessary. "If a flight is required upper party (17,900) requires: White gas, 5 gals. Citizen's band radio, channel 10. Lower party (15,000) requires: Pen light batteries, alkaline, size AA."

When the climbers failed to make the scheduled radio check at 8:00 P.M., Eielson called headquarters:

> Word passed to H.Q. (Hayes) at 8:30 P.M. that flight was requested for soonest possible time—airdrop of fuel and radio to high camp and batteries to 15,000 camp.

At 9:15 P.M., Art Hayes called Gary Hansen again to tell him that ranger Wayne Merry had spoken with Wilcox, "who requested an air drop to both parties (8:00 P.M.) of items above as soon as weather permits. Wilcox party will reimburse ARG costs." Hayes requested that "GH (Gary Hansen) advise him when the drop is to be made, and after, how many people can be seen at each elevation."

At 9:30 P.M., Hansen called ARG member and pilot Paul Crews

with no luck. Five minutes later he was talking with Lowell Thomas Jr., a well-known glacier pilot, seeking advice on what type of aircraft would be best suited to make the high-altitude airdrop. Thomas recommended contacting Ward Gay, who flew a turboprop Beaver.

At 9:40 P.M., Gary Hansen called Sea Airmotive, Gay's flight service: No answer. Two minutes after that, he rang Gay's residence: Again, no luck.

At 9:50 P.M., Hansen was ringing a radio-supply store seeking Citizens Band radios for the drop. When he learned none were available, he asked if anyone could check out the three the Alaska Rescue Group's sets that night. He was told to call back in the morning.

All these would-be rescuers knew how dangerous the situation was. They had the first of many restless nights. Unable to act, immobilized by a storm that continued to rage, waiting for it to break. The next morning, Chairman Hansen went straight back to work.

At 8:15 A.M. on Friday, July 21, Hansen and Hayes were on the phone, going over weather conditions on the mountain. "Report from the mountain: Broken clouds, 50–60 mph winds @16,000 ft. (Wilcox) Estimated winds @17,900 ft. 80 mph. Hayes standing by for news of attempt @ overflight by Sheldon." For context, winds at 74 miles per hour are considered hurricane force.

While pilot Don Sheldon prepared to go up in his stripped-down bare aluminum Cessna 180, Hansen continued his search for an aircraft that could withstand the high winds and make the airdrop if Sheldon could not.

At 8:40 A.M., he was on the phone with ARG pilot Crews, and the two men identified three aircraft that might be suitable: a Cessna 310 operated by Alaska Aeronautical, a Pilatus Porter operated by Wien Air Alaska, and Ward Gay's Turbo Beaver. Hansen had reached Gay ten minutes prior to calling Crews—notes taken on that call say only that Gay will call back.

By 8:50 A.M., Hansen was on the line with Sheldon, who reported poor weather. Indeed, Wilcox had called Eielson an hour earlier and reported winds at his elevation were steady at 50 miles per hour with gusts to 65.

▲▲

Snyder estimated the winds he and Wilcox were experiencing on Friday to be in excess of 70 miles per hour. "The storm, which had been battering the party at 15,000' for two days reached the peak of its fury on 21 July. A man could not stand outside the tents, and the wind made inhaling very difficult, giving the sensation of suffocation."

On the West Buttress, the Western States Expedition awoke at 4:30 A.M. to a very different picture. "The day was cold and clear, not too windy with only a few clouds high above," Louis Reichardt's July 21 journal entry reads. Stove problems delayed breakfast and kept them in camp until 7:30. By then the weather had started to change: "Those few high clouds turned into a cloud cap and the wind began to whisper." Hoping the clouds would dissipate, they set out across the basin that separated their camp from Denali Pass.

"Unfortunately, the weather did not break," Reichardt wrote. "Instead, as we labored across the basin, the mists sank lower and lower. By the time we had reached the other side and begun our angling ascent to the pass, we were in a whiteout."

The men ultimately turned back to the shelter of the West Buttress camp.

▲▲

At 11,500 feet, on Karstens Ridge, Babcock's MCA Expedition was up at 1:30 A.M. on Friday, July 21, under cold but clear and windless conditions. So much snow had powdered the ridge that they deemed it too dangerous to ascend after climbing just 100 feet.

Working in two-hour shifts they spent the next eight hours clearing the ridge with snow shovels, reaching 12,100 feet around noon, just ahead of the rising wind.

"Storm appears to be roaring off the Harper glacier. Hit us about 12:30," Babcock's journal reads.

By 1:30 P.M., they all were back in camp. "We build huge snow walls all around our tents plus an igloo in case of emergency. It looks real bad and may be with us for several days." The storm had battered the mountain for days, but these experienced climbers suspected that they hadn't seen the worst of it.

The team hunkered down in their fortified camp while the storm raged around them. "When visibility improved, winds coming off Browne Tower and Harper Glacier were frightening and appeared to have velocities in excess of 100 miles an hour. Early this morning, a dark mass of clouds came in from the north. The prevailing winds, however, were from the southwest."

The high- and low-pressure systems continued to vie for dominance over Denali, and the chaotic, incongruent conditions experienced by those on the mountain offer only a hint of what was happening in the violent, turbulent air swirling around the peak. It's no wonder that neither Don Sheldon nor any of the pilots Hansen contacted were willing to fly.

Though they had not been contacted yet, Babcock and his team, most of whom were members of the Alaska Rescue Group, knew the Wilcox team was in trouble.

"I knew there was a problem up high when that storm hit, just having experienced big storms elsewhere," Babcock said. "Winds were easily a hundred miles an hour plus."

The Mountaineering Club of Alaska team carried enough food to wait out the long storms, and with the camp reinforced, they settled in. Bill Babcock said the vantage point high on Karstens Ridge offered a spectacular and sometimes frightening view of the storm's power.

At one point when the snow and fog cleared, an extraordinary sight was revealed high over the Harper Icefall, a few thousand feet above camp.

"I didn't know what it was at first, but with binoculars I could see the crust—it was just being picked right up and thrown down," he said. "It was a half mile, three-quarters of a mile away. They were fifteen-to-twenty-foot slabs of ice being picked up and thrown around like kites. When I realized what it was, I said to myself, My God, those are slabs of ice just being picked up and carried away."

At 15,000 feet, the snow continued to pile up, threatening to bury the tent Wilcox shared with Schiff. They took turns getting up and clearing it away to keep the tent from collapsing. Between snow-removal duties, Schiff queried Wilcox about the summit and summit ridge and asked if the upper team could have fallen. Wilcox said it was possible but not likely.

The conversation must have sparked a revelation in Schiff. "You know," he said to Wilcox, "I think to not try the summit with the second team was the most important decision I have ever made in my life."

▲▲

Strong winds continued through the night of Friday, July 21. The Colorado team was jarred from their fitful sleep by voices outside their tent calling for help. They opened the tent door and Schiff and Wilcox squeezed in. Their tent had collapsed under the weight of the relentless snow. Now five men were crowded head to foot inside the four-man tent.

Soon, Jerry Lewis quit eating altogether, the others munched on candy, crackers, and anything else that didn't require cooking. With no room to operate the stove, they relied on body heat to melt snow-filled water bottles for drinking water.

Conversation was impossible inside the bucking shelter. The wind outside sounded like a jet engine, with huge gusts announcing their approach with thunderous roars. Schlichter said the words of the Animals' recent hit song "We Gotta Get Out of This Place" was stuck in his head. He said he couldn't keep his eyes off of the tent seams that strained under the onslaught of the wind. "I remember thinking, It's only a matter of time before those things split apart," he said. "I thought, If it happens, I'm going to dig down through the floor of the tent and dig my own little foxhole and see what happens."

The sky cleared in the morning on Saturday, July 22. It had been a week since Joe Wilcox stood on the summit. Despite the clear sky, the wind was unrelenting, stirring up a ground blizzard that obscured visibility even though the fog was gone. The blizzard ended only when the wind carried away the last of the loose snow around noon. Late in the day it began to ease, and Wilcox started talking about making another attempt to reach the high camp. Schlichter and Snyder were incredulous. Lewis was deteriorating quickly, Schiff and Wilcox were weak, and to make matters worse, Wilcox was having difficulty moving his hands. The two Colorado men hadn't been affected by the altitude and might have been able to make it, but they were unwilling to leave behind three sick men who couldn't care for themselves. Just getting the party down Karstens Ridge looked as if it was going to be dangerous, and while the wind in camp had diminished, they had no idea what conditions were like up high.

Later that evening, when the rangers at Eielson asked if anyone was willing to go up, they shook their heads no. Wilcox, operating the radio, said, "Not more than one of us would feel like going up," implying that he was willing and able to go but the others weren't.

They spoke with Eielson again later that night and an odd stand-off occurred. Snyder asked Wilcox to tell Eielson that they had three sick men and couldn't go up again. Wilcox refused, saying it wasn't true.

Howard Snyder, believing Wilcox was unwilling to admit he was ill, took the radio and tried to tell Eielson himself. The connection was poor and after five attempts finally got a "roger" from Eielson after saying, "We have three people pretty sick up here. This is why we could not go up. We have to get these people down."

The Wonder Lake log notes the condition of the men as reported by Snyder and that they would descend in the morning: "They understand that they were the closest team to upper camp but felt they could not stay or go up."

Had they gone, they likely would have been forced back, or been pinned down by winds that were not apparent from anywhere other than near the top of the mountain. Earlier that day, the wind dropped abruptly at 17,200 feet on the West Buttress, prompting the Western States Expedition to take advantage of what they thought was a break in the weather to try for the summit. Even though they could see Denali Pass and the summit, they had no idea how strong the wind there was until it was too late.

"It was such a surprise," expedition member Louis Reichardt told me in 2013. "Suddenly, when we got in line of sight, it was more than you could deal with."

His journal describes what happened as they approached Denali Pass:

> A few hundred yards from the pass, we walked into a steady breeze blowing up from the Peter's Glacier Basin. We con-

tinued onwards and soon it was accelerating us up the slopes. This was an aid, not a problem, though, and we moved at an accelerating pace towards the pass. Soon we were practically running uphill and the moment we crossed the lip, the wind literally picked us up and hurled us on through. For a few moments my pack became a sail and I was blowing above the ground with my feet no longer touching. We were moving rapidly through the pass towards some rocks. Behind them, the terrain dropped off for an uncertain distance and, for an instant, I thought we were all going over a cliff. I could not remember any cliffs on our photos or maps, but then even 20 feet would be quite a bounce. Fortunately, I reached a low boulder first and stopped by lying down in the snow and bracing against it with my feet . . . The wind was steady and had a terrific velocity, magnitudes greater than anything I had seen before. Our estimates ranged from 100 to 150 m.p.h. . . . . chunks of snow, sometimes entire snow hummocks, were being blown through with some large enough to be dangerous . . . .There was no visible limit to the wind on this side of the pass and it would have been dangerous to be blown further into its vortex.

They had to get out of the wind, and the only escape was back through the pass, so lying on their bellies, using ice axes and their crampons for traction, they crawled several hundred yards to escape the relentless blast.

By refusing to go high again Snyder and Schlichter had dodged another bullet. That Saturday evening they dug out the buried tent and moved in for their final night at 15,000 feet. Joe Wilcox lay awake in the tent he shared with Schiff and Lewis, considering whether to stay behind and try to reach the upper camp alone.

"Climbing alone unroped on the Harper would be a possibility, since no one had fallen completely into a crevasse since the Lower Icefall of the Muldrow, and I already had a trail to follow. I doubted that the others would force me to go down if I insisted on staying high alone." In the other tent, Schlichter lay awake massaging his feet to ward off frostbite. Snyder said he drifted off quickly and enjoyed a deep sleep.

Wilcox woke in the morning to find that his hands were numb. They didn't appear to be discolored or frostbitten, yet he had trouble moving them and though he packed his own gear, he needed help with his crampons. Schiff complained of dizziness when he emerged from the tent in the morning, and Lewis had trouble walking.

Still, the men realized they would only get weaker, and it was time to get to a lower elevation. They radioed in to Eielson with their plans, and then set out for the steep traverse across Parker Pass between the Harper Glacier and the base of Browne Tower, from which they would descend to Karstens Ridge. Lewis collapsed three times in the 150 yards between camp and the top of the traverse. "When Lewis would fall, Wilcox and Schiff would immediately sit down and slump over on the snow," Snyder wrote.

The descent was grueling, tedious work. The men encountered ice fields so dense their crampons wouldn't catch, spanned by soft, crumbling snow paths. Finally, on Karstens Ridge and approaching the steepest part of the descent, the Coxcomb, they spotted the tents of the Mountaineering Club of Alaska Expedition at 12,100 feet.

With refuge in sight, Jerry Lewis seemed to give up. "You'll just have to leave me behind," he said. But with gentle prodding from Snyder he stood up and continued down the steep slope.

When the MCA Expedition spotted the five men high on the ridge around noon, they weren't quite sure what to make of them. Dr. Grace Jansen Hoeman's journal describes the initial reaction.

We see a party of 5 coming down the cocks comb really slow. I watch them thru my binocs and make funny comments #3 sits down, #1 talks, what the hell is going on? Until it occurs to me that there is trouble. As one we go up and meet the five man group who are staggering down.

Hoeman, Bill Babcock, Jeff Babcock, Gayle Nienhueser, John Ireton, and Chet Hackney gathered food and drink and met the exhausted climbers at the top of the fixed line about 900 feet above their camp.

"They literally drank and drank," Babcock told me. "They drank everything we had and ate everything we had. We belayed them down the icy pitch and then fed them again. We were elated to see the climbers but then we wondered what the heck happened to the other ones."

CHAPTER 10

AN ICE AX
IN THE SNOW

When Bill Babcock realized that the seven remaining men had been incommunicado high on the Harper Glacier for nearly a week and might be running short on food and fuel, he urged Joe Wilcox to call an all-out rescue. "To me, it was blatantly obvious four days earlier that anyone up there was going to be having serious problems," Bill Babcock told me.

Grace Jansen Hoeman's journal reads, "Bill will go up in forced ascent if the decision is made."

The 4:45 P.M. entry on Sunday, July 23, in the Wonder Lake log notes, "Wilcox reached MCA group at 12,100 OK. Asks that rescue not be called until observation made, but should be ready to go immediately. Asked about a larger plane. Merry again recommended to HQ that overflight by large craft be made."

The Wonder Lake log was clear: do not launch a rescue until an observation flight is made. But as far as Joe Wilcox was concerned, there was no difference between calling for a rescue and calling for an overflight. "Somehow, there was the idea that Merry hadn't called an all-out rescue," said Wilcox. "I kept repeating 'I need an overflight.' I didn't see the distinction. You can't have an overflight without an emergency situation." He was asking for help.

At sea, when lives are at stake, the distress call is mayday, mayday, mayday. On a mountain it is not so simple; at least it wasn't then.

Neither the Park Service nor the Alaska Rescue Group had the authority to order the Air Force to launch a plane. That decision lay solely with the commander at the RCC. Given that National Weather Service wind charts showed high-velocity winds had been constant at 18,000 feet since July 18, any flight would have been dangerous, if not impossible, and visibility virtually nil anyway. Only the uninformed would have thought an overflight possible.

"I got the sense that Wilcox did not want to trigger a rescue unless he was absolutely sure it was necessary," recalled Frank Nosek. "I don't know what the thinking would be behind that. I've often thought to myself, Well, Wilcox viewed rescues like most of the climbers did in the early '60s; it's kind of a sign of weakness. You didn't want it to happen unless there was absolutely, positively no other way but to call a rescue."

Late that day, Gayle Nienhueser, one of the MCA climbers, overheard Joe Wilcox and Schiff arguing over whether to call a rescue. Schiff, Nienhueser recalled, was worried about the cost, a familiar concern. Though keeping costs down had been a factor when planning the expedition, Wilcox says he wasn't worried about the expense when it came to searching for the lost men. One way or another the matter was resolved between Schiff and Wilcox quickly.

"There's a full-scale rescue under way!" Schiff announced to Snyder and Schlichter at 10:30 P.M. "Do you want your parents notified?"

The Wonder Lake log on July 23 makes no mention of a formal

rescue call, only noting continued calls for an overflight: "Merry again recommended to H.Q. that overflight by large craft be made—decision apparently has been to wait until Sheldon can make it." The Alaska Rescue Group diary doesn't note a change in status either, but after all, with the mountain socked in, rescuers in Anchorage and Talkeetna could do no more than stand by.

"I remember we mobilized and were ready, but we didn't feel like we were in a better position for a rescue than Babcock's group was," Nosek said. "Sheldon couldn't go, and the RCC wouldn't."

How hard would it have been to do a flyover? Chuck Sassara flew in Alaska from 1951 to 2010, piloting more than 171 types of aircraft from a two-seater, 65-horsepower Luscombe to the four-engine, cargo-carrying Lockheed L-1049 Super Constellation. Sassara says effective search aircraft must be able to fly low and slow enough to allow for a visual search while maintaining maneuverability. "You have to be moving faster than your aircraft's maneuvering speed in the mountains. It's stall speed plus 50 percent because of downdrafts and other turbulence." For the small, single-engine Super Cub and slightly larger Cessna 180, that's 60 and 85 miles per hour respectively. The multiengine C-130 would have to maintain a speed of at least 200 miles per hour.

Because of their need for speed, large aircraft don't like small spaces. "You simply can't get it down in those cracks and crevices that have to be searched like you can a 180 or a Cub," Sassara said. "You need a lot of room to turn. If you're in the Mojave Desert: no problem. If you're in Denali Pass trying to get through a notch, you're going to be in a world of hurt."

The plan that Superintendent Hall and the ARG had made, calling on the MCA Expedition to become a rescue team, was the only option available. They were acclimated, in position, and ready to move as soon as the weather allowed.

That night Bill Babcock, along with his brother Jeff, Nienhueser, Ireton, and Hackney, made preparations to move up as quickly as they could. Grace Hoeman had been sick and Babcock felt that she would hinder their progress and told her she would have to descend with the Wilcox team. She was not happy about it but agreed.

Joe Wilcox expressed no interest in climbing back up the mountain with the MCA team. Babcock saw his anguish. "He just wanted to take off, and I wasn't in a position to stop him. It seemed like he should go out with his group. Joe was obviously very distraught. I mean, I can't even imagine what was going through his head."

Wilcox Expedition group one, accompanied by Dr. Hoeman, continued their descent at noon on Monday, July 24. Heavy snow and whiteout prevailed at the MCA camp on Karstens Ridge through the day. Babcock's journal notes that at 9:00 P.M., the high winds returned: "Winds began to pick up and by midnight were 50–60 mph and the tents all but blew away. The high winds lasted until early morning."

At 4:30 A.M. on July 25, Chet Hackney woke the camp. The skies had cleared and they readied to leave, packing warm clothes, sleeping bags, food, and their shovels and snow saws. The tents that had proven vulnerable to the wind and sapped their energy during the night were left behind. From here on they'd rely on snow caves for shelter.

Though there is no mention of it in Babcock's journal, the Wonder Lake log reads, "MCA report good flying weather."

That day, Don Sheldon flew for the first time since July 18. Though a standing cloud cap obscured the mountain above 15,000 feet and rose well above the summit, to 25,000 feet, he proved the versatility of his small plane by slipping in and dropping a radio and food 500 feet below Wilcox's 15,000-foot camp.

Higher on the mountain, at 17,200 feet on the West Buttress,

Louis Reichardt reported, "We awoke at 3:30 A.M., the familiar thin cloud had returned to the mountain, a harbinger of storm. Every one of us had seen that cloud before and knew what it implied." After playing cat and mouse in the clouds, the sun and the peak disappeared from view, and heavy snow resumed.

▲▲

The weeklong storm that hit those men on the mountain was a once-in-a-lifetime event, maybe once in a century. John Papineau, who's been a meteorologist with the National Oceanic and Atmospheric Administration (NOAA) for more than a decade, sits at his desk in the fall of 2011, studying a modern-day version of the 1967 storm on a computer screen. Even today, he says, if a storm of this magnitude hit, there'd be little we could do to save anyone unfortunate enough to be clinging to the side of Denali when it rolled in.

Under the fluorescent lights at his desk in the Anchorage Forecast Office, Papineau sits down in front of two side-by-side computer screens.

"Would you like to see the storm?" he asks, then without waiting for an answer clicks the mouse and makes a few keystrokes: a map of Alaska appears on the screens, overlain with concentric circles representing the weather systems that were moving across the skies of interior Alaska on July 18, 1967.

Since the 1930s, NOAA's National Weather Service has used weather balloons to collect information on atmospheric conditions, including temperature, moisture, pressure, and wind speed and direction. In Alaska, balloons are launched daily from thirteen locations, and data collected during their flights is used to create weather forecasts for the region. Three of those locations—McGrath, Fairbanks, and Anchorage—triangulate almost perfectly around

Denali. That data, from July 18 to July 25, 1967, is what Papineau has used to produce the model on his screen.

"This is where it began, in the Arctic," he says, pointing to the top of the Alaska map. "In the Beaufort Sea, we had an area of low pressure, and in that airflow the winds are going to be counterclockwise."

He grabs a white pad of paper and makes an inverted V in the center saying, "Denali is here." Then he draws a spiral swirling counterclockwise just north of the mountain. As the spiral grows, the lower part of the rings, representing wind direction, begins overlapping the mountain in a west-to-east direction.

"That's the low to the north," he says.

Beneath and slightly to the left of Denali he draws another spiral, this one swirling clockwise. As he widens it, the upper lines of the spiral overlap the mountain as well, also indicating west-to-east airflow.

"That's the high in the south."

Then he taps the overlapping lines.

"So anytime you get a low and a high and they get close together, you get strong winds," he says.

On the computer screen the weather systems were bigger and less distinct, but as Papineau advances the maps showing July 19, 20, 21, and 22, more and more lines appear, compressing tightly together over Denali. Those lines, he explains, represent unusually strong westerly winds.

The data Papineau is using tells a story of just how horrific those winds were, whipping at 60 to 70 miles per hour, nearly nonstop, from July 19 to July 25. Papineau shakes his head and exhales in a long, slow hiss, his eyes never leaving the screen.

"Those guys on the mountain just had the unfortunate timing—the wrong place at the wrong time."

Just a few weeks later, the late Ted Fathauer ran a similar model at the Weather Bureau office in Fairbanks and also marveled at the stack of lines indicating the winds over Denali during the weeklong July storm.

"They were where the wind is just like a river," he said, confirming Papineau's analysis. "It goes slightly upstream, but when it begins to flow with gravity, then it accelerates. I can see eighty miles an hour in Denali Pass, but the real change began on the nineteenth of July. They must have had gusts of eighty or ninety miles an hour."

Fathauer, advancing through the weather maps a day at a time, shakes his head.

"It's not the first time we've ever seen them act like this, but it's certainly the worst. Then, on the twentieth, there, it was even faster I'm sure. In the south pass they were getting west winds gusting to a hundred miles an hour. More of the same on the twenty-first; the twenty-second must have been a real scene. The twenty-third was only a little less terrible. I'd say this is the worst storm to hit the mountain, the worst when people were on it."

Then he explained a factor known as gap flow, where air movement through tight passes is accelerated like water through a fire hose, and that thereby the wind could have been three times as fierce as 100 miles per hour. It would have surpassed the highest wind gusts ever recorded on land by some 70 miles per hour, but a back-of-the-envelope calculation of gap-flow acceleration suggests maximum wind-gust velocities as high as 300 miles per hour could have raked the ridges and passes of the upper mountain on Wednesday, Thursday, and Friday—July 20, 21, and 22 of 1967.

▲▲

Though they were exhausted after a night spent wrestling with their tents in the high winds at the 12,100-foot camp, the MCA Expedition turned rescue party made swift work of the steep and treacherous Karstens Ridge, covering 2,400 feet in nine hours—a feat that had taken the Wilcox crew a full week to accomplish.

And the work wasn't over when they reached the top, as Babcock's journal notes: "Spent several hours digging cave and building igloo. VERY TIRED."

To be fair to the Wilcox team, part of the reason they'd taken so long was because they were relaying supplies, necessary when supporting a large team high on the mountain. The MCA team moved fast, intent on reaching the men they believed might be stranded without food and fuel.

"We were still planning to relay," Babcock said. "But then the park asked us if we would just go nonstop in hopes of getting up to where someone might be alive."

To move fast, they had to go light, discarding all unnecessary equipment, including their tents.

"I had been very happy with snow caves and igloos, and everyone had experience over the winter building them. Our tents were quite heavy; we had those big pyramidal tents, so I decided we would go just with entrenching tools and we would take more food and fuel and go on up without stopping, without relaying."

On the morning of July 26, the short traverse across Parker Pass to the Harper that Snyder and the others had found so treacherous and icy two days earlier was buried under two feet of new snow. "The going was extremely difficult with deep new snow from 14,500 to 15,000," Babcock recalled. "Gayle Nienhueser did an excellent job of leading all the way and breaking trail."

They reached 15,100 feet at 1:30 P.M. and spent the next two hours looking in vain for Don Sheldon's airdrop after getting bad directions from Eielson.

Later they found one of the packages containing three radios, including one Sheldon was supposed to keep for his own use, precisely on the trail. It had been so hard to find because it was wrapped in a white pillowcase. Babcock's anger over the incident is reflected in his log entry: "Never should have done it, wasted hours looking. Sheldon's reliability highly questionable due to the fact a pillowcase, unwanted drop at 15,100, his uncertainty of exact location of first drop after it could not be found, etc. BILL PISSED OFF!"

Looking back on it, Bill Babcock said he isn't surprised that communications were fouled up. They were unable to speak directly to Don Sheldon, or to the park for that matter.

"We had this crazy way of communicating," he said. "They could hear us in Fairbanks, and Fairbanks could reach Eielson, and Eielson could contact the headquarters. It was a back-and-forth thing; it took forever to communicate."

After the first foul-up, they asked to have Sheldon drop food and fuel at 17,900. If any of the seven men they still hoped to find were alive, they would need to feed them. Babcock's concern grew as his party, which included his nineteen-year-old brother, put itself at greater and greater risk, climbing higher without getting the supply drops that had been promised. They carried a fraction of the food and fuel he liked to have at high altitude to facilitate the quick ascent. Not enough to endure another extended storm if they were marooned, and certainly not enough to support survivors.

Even the scheduled radio calls were exhausting. "Today, you can have a conversation in thirty seconds," Babcock told me. "These conversations would take twenty, thirty, forty-five minutes the way communications were going. Gayle would say something; it would go to Fairbanks, to Eielson, and then to the park headquarters. Then the park would go to Eielson, then to Fairbanks, then to us. It took forever to get anything done, and you're sitting out there, totally exposed, out of the snow cave. I really think that got to Gayle. He started to get sick; then you get weak, you get dehydrated on top of it. It's only a matter of time before you're getting pulmonary or cerebral edema."

On Thursday, July 27, the summit of Denali stood white against the blue sky for the first time in more than a week. The shroud of clouds and blowing snow that had hidden it were gone and Don Sheldon wasted no time. He was at the mountain at 4:30 A.M., passing over the MCA's 15,100-foot camp at 4:45, and further angering Bill Babcock when no supplies were dropped. Sheldon spent two hours searching the upper mountain to 18,000 feet in his Cessna 180 but saw no sign of the missing climbers. Gary Hansen and Paul Crews of the Alaska Rescue Group followed a few hours later in a chartered Cessna 310, flying through Denali Pass several times but spotting only the Western States Expedition on its way to the summit.

The MCA climbers started up the Harper Glacier at 10:00 A.M., and after building an igloo at 16,500 feet, they settled in for another night. Stoves wouldn't start that night, and the Babcocks weren't able to cook dinner until 10:00 P.M. It was cold and windy on the Harper Glacier, but the igloo offered warm refuge, free of the rustle and snap of a nylon tent bucking in the wind. Babcock's journal reads, "Bill exhausted, shelter constructed fair, Gayle starting with cold, windy otherwise weather good and fair."

Clear skies and light winds reigned again on July 28, and the A-67 Expedition spotted Sheldon's shiny Cessna 180 at 10:00 A.M. and again at 12:30 P.M. searching the upper mountain.

The MCA party left for the Wilcox party's camp at 17,900 at 10:00 a.m. Ireton and Hackney, both unaffected by the altitude, moved too quickly for Nienhueser, so he tied on to the Babcock brothers' rope, which moved at a more moderate pace. Each man carried a 70-pound pack filled mostly with food and fuel. It was almost 5:00 P.M. when Ireton spotted a Stubai ice ax, the brand Steve

Taylor had carried, lying on top of the hard-packed snow a mile below the 17,900-foot camp.

"The snow was hard enough; it looked like it had been blown from camp," Ireton said. "So I picked it up and stuck it in the snow right where I had found it."

A quarter of a mile on, he and Hackney found John Russell's bamboo summit pole thrust in the snow, its top festooned with black strips of nylon from the burned tent. "Around that," Ireton described, "there was a sleeping bag, and over the sleeping bag was an alpine hut red shell. It was just wrapped around and we came up to it and I thought it was just a cache or something so I picked it up and there was nothing inside of it except a pair of wool socks and some down booties."

Next to the pole, Bill Babcock said, a crevasse yawned black against the bright, white snow. "We hollered, we looked into it, and it was one of those bottomless things. I certainly wasn't going to rappel into it. I have no idea what happened, but I would suspect someone is down at the bottom of that thing."

The worst was yet to be discovered. After several more minutes of trudging up through the wind-crusted snow, the Wilcox team's 17,900-foot-high Camp VII came into view.

There was no movement, no welcoming calls, and no survivors. Just silence.

Mark McLaughlin's homemade tent stood oddly taut in the light breeze. Next to it was, as Bill Babcock described in his journal, "a ghastly sight, a man sitting upright alongside a Logan tent. Face and hands are blue, green, white, frozen yet decomposing."

Ireton said the frozen man wore orange and his face was covered with snow.

"He was blown over, but during the storm he was holding the pole," he said. "The tent had probably ripped apart and the sleeping bag had blown away and he was there holding the pole and he obviously froze to death."

Gayle Nienhueser did not look closely at the body, though he took a photo of the tent-shrouded figure. The memory still haunts him forty-five years later.

"I was twenty-six," Nienhueser says. "I'd never seen a body before. The hand that was exposed was black, and it had frozen and thawed a couple of times. I wasn't feeling good, and the smell . . ." His voice became choked and tears erupted from his eyes as we spoke. He put his face into his hands, bowed his head forward, and didn't say anything for more than a minute.

The sight of the corpse was frightening for the climbers, suddenly bringing home the realization that on Denali, death is never far away for the careless and the unlucky. However, the gruesome condition of the climber's body didn't mean he had died a painful death. Freezing can be a peaceful and relatively painless way to go.

If there is any real pain, it comes at the beginning, when the cold begins to penetrate the skin and causes surface capillaries to constrict, shunting blood deeper into the body. Fingers, toes, the tip of the nose, earlobes, and other extremities are sacrificed in order to keep the vital organs warm. As the blood retreats to protect the core, feet and hands begin to ache, and the nose and ears sting. But the pain, rarely overwhelming, soon is eased by numbness settling in where the blood once flowed.

Hypothermia takes over when the body temperature slips below 95 degrees Fahrenheit. With it comes violent shivering as muscles contract involuntarily, trying to generate body heat. When warmth continues to flee, the shivering slows and then stops, leaving the muscles unnaturally tight and making simple tasks like donning a jacket or striking a match difficult. Loss of muscle coordination soon follows and walking becomes problematic.

Hands and feet are soon useless, nose and ears turn white, and lips turn blue, making clear speech impossible.

Feelings of detachment to the rapidly deteriorating situation soon cloud the mind. A lost glove or hat? No worries. A sleeping bag carried away by the wind: vaguely inconvenient.

When the body's core temperature drops into the 80s, complete apathy comes, and then stupor as the cold renders brain enzymes less efficient. The consciousness that still clings to the rapidly cooling body grows blissfully unaware of the catastrophic breakdown of physical function. As blood gathers around the organs most vital to life, the kidneys go into overdrive to deal with the excess fluids that have flooded inward. An overpowering need to urinate rises, followed by one last, sweet release and the fleeting feeling of warmth on the skin.

A degree or two lower and the pulse becomes irregular and erratic as chilled nerves lose their ability to carry the signals that cue the heart to beat. When the core temperature reaches 85 degrees, a sudden and inexplicable feeling of heat cascades across the body, so hot that victims often tear their clothes off seeking relief, unintentionally hastening their own end. One theory behind this paradoxical undressing suggests that the surface capillaries that constricted early on to push body heat into the core suddenly dilate, bringing a burning sensation as blood surges into the nearly frozen flesh. Whether it is the body's last-ditch effort to warm itself or a sudden failure of the muscles constricting the blood vessels is unknown. Unconsciousness and death usually follow close behind.

▲▲

Bill Babcock said the grisly discovery was disturbing for the entire team, him included.

"It was a nightmarish thing to run into," he said. "We tried to open the zipper on his parka but it was frozen. There was a terrible stench. I'd never seen anything like that before. We dug our snow caves quite a ways away."

Too traumatized by their discovery, the men avoided the body, not thinking to take more photos that might help identify him later. They reported the dead man and the ruined camp to Eielson, and the rangers asked if the expedition would continue searching, promising to drop radios, 180 man-days of food, sleeping bags, and heavy-duty tents.

Babcock said they'd go for the summit in the morning and search along the way, but as to staying on for an extended search, "We give negative as we must return to jobs if we make the peak."

Back in Anchorage, Gary Hansen was hard at work again. With the mountain finally clear for flying, he worked to coordinate the large airdrop that had been promised to Babcock. After confirming that Joe Wilcox had requested it and would cover the cost, Hansen tried to secure the use of an aircraft large enough to drop the load above 18,000 feet on Denali. The Air Force was the obvious choice.

At 3:25 P.M., he contacted Major Stevens at the RCC and asked if the Air Force could provide the food and supplies and make the drop. Stevens's response was curt: "Not likely."

At 4:30 Stevens called back and asked, "Can this be accomplished commercially?" Hansen responded, "All equipment required not commercially available. Civilian aircraft available but not experienced in making critical air drop such as required here." Then he added, "Timing most critical."

Stevens called back fifteen minutes later. The flight was on.

The next morning, at 7:06, a C-130 took off from Elmendorf Air Force Base in Anchorage with a crew of six, accompanied by a combat photographer and two Alaska Rescue Group observers:

Gary Hansen and Dave Johnston, one of the men who was part of the Winter Ascent of Denali earlier that year.

The upper mountain was clear and windless, and the bus-size prop plane thundered through Denali Pass ten times, varying its altitude with each passage. Johnston and Hansen rode in the cockpit and peered through the observation windows looking for the missing climbers.

Johnston was probably the most qualified man on the planet to be on the flight searching for the lost men. Just a few months earlier during the Winter Ascent, he himself had survived a similar weeklong storm in Denali Pass by digging a cave and holing up in it for a week with two companions. If anyone knew where to look, he did.

But on that day, though the sky was cloudless, the wind calm, and visibility about as good as it gets, they saw no sign of survivors. Johnston said while the military plane was perfect for dropping large amounts of supplies, it proved to be a poor platform for searching the upper mountain. "It's not the kind of rig you want to be looking for little dots from," he said. "Too fast an airplane."

On one run they dropped radios near a rope team of three men, probably Nienhueser and the Babcock brothers, who were climbing together that day. A few minutes later the plane made a west-to-east run through the pass and dropped 180 man-days of food in the form of forty-six cases of C rations, along with twelve double sleeping bags. On the return east-to-west run, they dropped five Gerry cans of stove fuel and nine two-man tents.

Bill Babcock said their accuracy left something to be desired. "Well, the plane flew over and dropped everything off the West Buttress, right over the edge—tons of stuff, and it didn't do us a bit of good."

High overhead, the plane circled the mountain twice and headed back to Anchorage. So much for the flyover.

The MCA team had risen at 2:30 A.M. after a fitful night, haunted by thoughts of the young man who sat in permanent repose so close by. They were on the way to the summit by 5:30 A.M. Bill Babcock broke trail to Denali Pass, and then Hackney and Ireton, on their own rope, took the lead. Around noon the five men were approaching Archdeacon's Tower at 19,650 feet. Nienhueser was suffering from a bad headache and Bill Babcock watched him closely, but the weather was holding and they all pushed on. Ireton and Hackney pulled ahead and reached the summit first. They were on the way down the summit ridge at 2:30 P.M. when they passed the other three heading up.

"By three fifteen we also reach the summit," Babcock's journal notes. "Somehow Gayle makes it. Weather definitely closing in so we take a few pictures and depart."

As Hackney and Ireton waited below, the sound of an aircraft engine filled the sky. It was Don Sheldon, this time in his Super Cub. The plane circled the slope below Archdeacon's Tower, dove at it once, and then flew close to the two climbers and dropped a message.

Scrawled on a piece of brown paper bag was a diagram and a note. Two marks indicated Ireton and Hackney; three others represented the men near the summit. Below a scrawl indicating Archdeacon's Tower was a note: "I see something red over on the slope."

Ireton started toward it, far enough to spot the patch of color on the icy slope, but Hackney blew his whistle to call him back, insisting they wait and discuss it with Babcock, the expedition leader.

Babcock could see the signs of an approaching storm and was eager to get back to the safety of their snow caves. He thought investigating the bodies would be too risky and time-consuming. "I really tried very hard to talk them out of going over there," he said. "But John was a very conscientious guy. They wanted to go over and check."

Nienhueser and the Babcock brothers continued on toward camp while Ireton and Hackney went to investigate. Hackney broke through a crevasse bridge as his partner belayed him down the 50-degree slope but continued until he could get a good look at the object. It was another frozen man, this one dressed in a red parka, orange wind pants, and green overboots.

"The body was in a sitting position facing downhill with one leg extended and the other leg in a sitting position underneath his body, in a semi-relaxed position," Hackney said. "I never seen an ice ax or a pack or a sleeping bag, anything. He was just in a very relaxed sitting position, just as if he had died in a very relaxed state."

Directly below they could see a second figure clad in darker clothes with a sleeping bag wrapped around its shoulders.

Ireton described this encounter. "He again was in a position where one leg was extended and the other one was put up," he said. "It wasn't quite as steep, but he was laying back. And around his body he had what looked like to me, an Eddie Bauer Karakorum [sleeping bag] in a green element cloth cover. And he had it wrapped around the upper part of his body. And I think he had blue wind pants, and I think he had light-colored hair."

The men were not roped together and neither wore gloves or packs. Both were sitting with one leg tucked underneath and one extended in front, as if bracing themselves. Whether it was against the wind at their backs, or to hold a rope that may have belayed others below them is unknown. There was no rope present when the MCA climbers inspected the bodies and no other gear was found. Below the bodies, the slope descended into a crevasse field, and beyond that lay the Harper Glacier and the Wilcox Expedition's high camp. In an interview with the Park Service, John Ireton speculated that they were trying to take a shortcut back to camp and concluded, "I don't recommend anyone use that again."

South Peak

Archdeacon's
Tower

**Second and
third bodies**

Camp VII

Denali Pass

First body

John Russell's flag

Steve Taylor's ax

WHAT THE MCA CLIMBERS FOUND

After viewing the bodies briefly, Hackney and Ireton continued on, traversing the slope to meet the trail that the other three had taken back to camp. On the way down they inspected a few of the airdrops but left the contents undisturbed. "We looked into the cans and there were radios, but we didn't think they were of any use to us," Ireton said. "Because we had found three of the seven bodies and it was pretty much an indication as to what happened to the rest of them."

The MCA party had done its part in the search; though they'd found only three bodies, they knew there would be no rescue for the lost Wilcox climbers.

Ireton and Hackney reached camp fifteen minutes behind the others, just ahead of the storm that Bill Babcock had seen coming. His journal describes its arrival: "Mysterious clouds spill over McKinley, streamer indicating high wind velocity, black billowing clouds have reached Denali Pass and winds increase and white out conditions prevail."

Babcock told me, "If we had dillydallied a half an hour, we wouldn't have found our camp. John and Chet, they got back and within a half an hour you couldn't see a hand in front of your face. A lot of it is just plain, dumb luck."

▲▲

By this time, Joe Wilcox had reached Wonder Lake and was safely recuperating with the Merry family. Wayne Merry shared his frustration over the rescue effort and the failure to launch an overflight with Wilcox, and asked him to read and initial a document outlining the rescue as Merry had interpreted it from Wonder Lake.

"I didn't have enough knowledge of the inner workings. I had a one-sided view," Wilcox says. "I saw Wayne Merry's rescue log;

I saw communication problems. I was surprised Wayne wanted me to read it and initial it to say it was accurate, but I did."

News of the first body reached Wilcox there and the impact of it felt like a sucker punch. The Merrys offered words of comfort, but they couldn't ease Wilcox's shock and sadness.

Early the next morning my father relayed a message to Wonder Lake asking Joe Wilcox to come to headquarters. Wilcox made the long drive alone in the Hankmobile, followed by a ranger driving a park vehicle. It was a lonely ride. A month before, the van had rung with the voices of excited young men on their way to the adventure of a lifetime. Now one was confirmed dead and six others lost. The silence must have been deafening. At headquarters, Wilcox met with my father and Chief Ranger Hayes, providing information on camp locations, caches, and various other details that might help with the search effort.

Later, Wilcox joined my father in the superintendent's office when he called Steve Taylor's parents. My father told the Taylors the worst news a parent can hear, that their son, the young man who had graduated from college just a month earlier, was dead. Wilcox took the phone and spoke about the climb, trying to answer their questions. Wilcox had mentored Steve Taylor on his first forays into climbing and convinced park rangers to let him climb when they questioned his qualifications. Now he had to try to make sense of the loss to his friend's parents.

That evening, Joe Wilcox had dinner at our house. He entered the front room and seemed to tower over my dad. He had a dark beard and spoke with a soft, melodic voice, and though he was only twenty-four, he seemed to me to carry himself like a much older man. Mom forbade discussing the accident, to give Mr. Wilcox just a few minutes of peace. I was intensely curious about what had happened but knew to hold my tongue. Though just a child, I could sense the sadness in the room, the somber feeling that had us eating dinner in silence.

After dinner, the old crank phone hanging on the kitchen wall rang short-long-short, the ring sequence that had been assigned to us on the party line that ran through the housing complex.

Dad lifted the earpiece from its cradle and spoke into the microphone extending from the front of the wooden box. He listened momentarily, then hung up and turned to Joe Wilcox.

"Let's go. They've found two more bodies."

They jogged across the road and up the short hill to the headquarters. There they listened in as the MCA party described the two bodies found near Archdeacon's Tower, and the worsening weather. It was becoming clear that the lost men were dead, the window of good weather was closing, and the MCA party was ready to leave.

Reporters already had gotten wind of the developing disaster, and the parents had to be notified. My father and Joe Wilcox stayed late at the headquarters building that night, calling the parents of the lost men. One by one, my father went down the phone list, telling the anguished parents on the other end of the line the words no one wants to hear. After each heart-wrenching conversation, he would hand the phone to Wilcox, who would try his best to console them.

My father told me that it was the longest night of his life.

After the calls, Joe Wilcox paced the building feeling hopeless and useless.

The storm kept the MCA party in their caves for another eighteen hours; when they emerged, it took a half an hour to dig their way out. Around noon on July 30, the wind subsided and they packed and left within forty minutes, leaving the body where it sat, still clutching the tent pole.

They wasted no time descending and that night settled into their fortified camp at 12,100 feet on Karstens Ridge. With food in their bellies and a secure shelter, spirits were high. Then, during a radio call, my father set Bill Babcock off again.

"Would you fellows consider going back up?" he asked.

Gayle Nienhueser, back on radio duty, relayed the question to Bill.

"I think I yelled at Gayle that whoever was asking that, it was the dumbest thing I'd ever heard of. That we were in really critical shape ourselves and needed to get down. That I wouldn't even think about doing something like that," he says. "I weighed one hundred and sixty when I got out; I normally weigh two hundred. Jeff was down to about one twenty-five. We'd been in the mountains for five weeks by then. The storm went on for, I don't know, seven or eight days; it took a lot out of us. It's a logical thing to ask, it's *the* logical thing to ask, especially if you have never been up there. Under those conditions, it was all we could do to get ourselves down."

That evening the Babcocks lay in their snow cave and discussed the seven lost men. They felt both relief and guilt and an inexplicable sense of animosity toward the dead men. As they discussed their feelings, the others weighed in. Bill Babcock wrote this account in his journal:

> We had no feeling toward him as we did not know him. I looked at him the first day. He was unreal, frozen, discolored and horribly cracked and swollen. I disliked him particularly on the summit day and had led a route 75 feet W. of where he sat watching us. I felt no compassion until I was at 12,100 and 8,100 where I was greatly disturbed by his plight and the other six, 2 of whom we saw at a distance. At that altitude it is all that one can do to meet his own needs. This poor fellow and his six companions made demands upon me and I resented it. It made me angry with my team, the park, Sheldon, anyone. Jeff discusses this

with me and has similar feelings. Gayle says he wished we had dug a hole and buried "him." Chet said he wanted nothing to do with any of them once he saw that they were dead. John, who is the most compassionate one of our group did the most and he and Chet descended a very steep slope checking the bodies of the two visible climbers below the Archdeacon's Tower.

After leaving the MCA camp on July 24, Grace Hoeman and the five survivors had moved quickly to escape the icy environs of Denali. Snyder's narrative, written in longhand at Dr. Hoeman's Anchorage home a few days later, chronicles their return to civilization.

24 July

The Colorado Party of three continued their descent. They moved non-stop to McGonagall Pass, where they repacked all gear for lowland travel. Dr. Jansen [Hoeman] suffering from migraine headache, decided to descend with Wilcox and Schiff.

25 July

Snyder, Schlichter and Lewis set up camp at the upper fork of Cache Creek to sleep for the first time in 30 hours. Wilcox, Schiff and Dr. Jansen passed them during the night, and continued on toward the Clearwater River. Upon reaching the Clearwater, Wilcox crossed at great risk, and went on alone toward Wonder Lake. The river could be forded only with great difficulty at best, and not at all by a man in Lewis' condition, therefore Dr. Jansen instructed Wilcox to get a helicopter in for Lewis. Lewis' frostbite was in need of immediate attention, and he could ill afford to wait for the river to recede.

26 July

After swimming the Clearwater, Wilcox continued on to the McKinley River where he had to swim three channels. He reached Wonder Lake and called for a helicopter. No military craft were made available, so a commercial helicopter was brought in. Lewis was taken to Wonder Lake, along with the rest of the party of five, which was at the Clearwater.

27 July

Lewis was flown to Farewell by helicopter, thence to Anchorage by the CAP, where he entered the Providence Hospital for treatment of his Frostbite.

Written at the end of Snyder's narrative is a note, printed in neat letters and signed by Dr. Hoeman's husband, mountaineer Vin Hoeman. "Grace says not true, they could have made it but Snyder & Schlichter refused. VH." It is a striking counterpoint. But what to make of it?

Snyder says the note is puzzling because neither he nor Schlichter were with Dr. Hoeman when she sent Joe to call for the helicopter. The five survivors and Dr. Hoeman had not remained together on the way out. When Snyder, Schlichter, and Lewis put up a tent and camped, Hoeman, Schiff, and Wilcox kept walking. When those three got to the banks of Clearwater Creek, Wilcox went on alone.

"We weren't there; they were several hours ahead of us," Snyder said. "The decision had been made before we got there. It was her order, but we didn't know anything about it until we got there. We thought Paul and I could cross it. Jerry was upset that a helicopter had been called . . . I think the doctors Jansen and Schiff wanted a ride."

Whether or not the helicopter was necessary is unclear, but if it hadn't come, the survivors would have had a long wait. The river had risen since Wilcox crossed its three rain-swollen channels.

"We had wanted to hike out that day; however, we would have gotten nowhere beyond the McKinley River," Howard said. "Once up in the helicopter, we got out over the river and it was a mile wide, with no divided channels."

On the other hand, Wilcox's physical drive and courage is plain.

▲▲

Late on the twenty-seventh, before leaving the park, Snyder met with my father and Chief Ranger Art Hayes at park headquarters. Snyder went over the route and the campsites used by the expedition and discussed whether or not there might be any survivors. Dad voiced the possibility that the climbers had descended the West Buttress and were holed up, waiting for the storm to pass.

Like Ranger Merry, neither he nor Hayes had set foot on Denali and were not familiar with the upper mountain. Snyder told them that mistaking the West Buttress for the Harper Glacier was unlikely since the terrain was very different and stated that if they were alive, they would already have shown themselves.

Snyder believed my father was out of touch with the severity of the situation at the time, but I, perhaps self-interestedly, believe he was trying to remain optimistic in the face of tragedy. He and Hayes had already notified the Air Force and the ARG and had activated the rescue plan, sending the MCA Expedition in search of survivors. In a 1999 interview he discussed the Wilcox tragedy and described his reaction when he learned that the two bodies had been found beneath the Archdeacon's Tower. "My question was, are they alive," he said. "I can hear myself saying it, but I knew damn well they weren't alive. I just wished they'd be alive."

CHAPTER 11

WHOSE SON?

Dennis Luchterhand's nineteen-year-old sister, Erika, learned of the crisis on Denali over the radio while driving in afternoon traffic near her home in Brooklyn, New York, on Saturday, July 29. She immediately called her father and he wasted no time, first calling my father and then turning to his neighbors for assistance.

"Further information came through efforts made possible by one of our neighbors, who happens to have the military rank of brigadier general, and who offered to call the post commander of Elmendorf Air Force," wrote Luchterhand's father, Elmer.

Only one body had been reported at this point, but after talking to my father, Luchterhand's dad made a flight reservation and headed for the airport.

Later that morning, the Rescue Coordination Center called Gary Hansen to tell him that Elmer Luchterhand, an assistant professor of sociology at Brooklyn College of the City University of New York, was on his way to Anchorage "and that he had contacted Senator Edward Kennedy asking for a humanitarian Air Force flight and had been denied it."

At 9:50 P.M., Captain Gordon of the RCC called Hansen to let him know of the two bodies that were found near Archdeacon's Tower, tentatively identified as Walt Taylor and Dennis Luchterhand. An hour later, he suggested the possible use of a civilian "turbo helicopter" for further operations. The journal Hansen kept during the operation notes, "Capt. Gordon has talked to Maj Stevens, and RCC would prefer to stay out of the body removal business."

On the morning of July 30, Elmer Luchterhand was at the Rescue Coordination Center at Elmendorf Air Force Base in Anchorage, where he was briefed on the airdrop that had been made the day before and, he wrote, "the generally slight prospects that any of the seven men might still be alive, and the inability of the Air Force to do anything further under their rules."

Later that day Hank Janes's father, Paul, arrived in Anchorage, and ARG member Vin Hoeman picked him up and drove both grieving fathers to the Alaska Railroad station in downtown Anchorage, where they boarded a train for Mount McKinley National Park. Steve Taylor's parents, Perry and Beth, also were on the train. Elmer's wife and daughter, along with his sister and brother-in-law, joined them at the park hotel a few days later.

The press had chartered a plane and flew to the park's small dirt airstrip as well. McKinley Park, as the community around the park entrance was known at the time, was small, and I'm not sure how he did it, but my father managed to keep the reporters separated from both Joe Wilcox and the families.

Perry Taylor and Elmer Luchterhand continued to push for the search and rescue efforts to continue even though it was becoming more and more apparent that all seven men had perished. Taylor called Hansen and told him to call the RCC and ask if Elmer "could be of any assistance in evacuating bodies." Later Perry asked my father and Chief Ranger Hayes if the MCA party would return to the upper mountain to continue searching, prompting my father's radio request that set off Bill Babcock.

After Babcock made it clear that the MCA team wouldn't be returning to the upper mountain again, Elmer Luchterhand, overcome with grief and a feeling of helpless desperation, demanded that my father find someone else to go. My father tried to reason with him, but he would have none of it.

"Send the Air Force!"

"I don't have that authority."

"Then send the Army."

"I can't do that."

"I don't care who you send. Send somebody—I want my son!"

Then my father asked a question that Elmer Luchterhand could not answer.

"Whose son should I send?"

▲▲

The MCA party boarded the train after meeting with the parents and headed home. They debriefed with their colleagues in the Alaska Rescue Group and went back to their jobs and were never recognized for their selfless efforts on behalf of the lost Wilcox Expedition climbers.

The families remained in the park for a few more days, hosted by the Park Service and looked after by Park Hotel Manager Wally Cole. Before they left, one of the hotel vans brought them to Eielson Visitor Center, where they held a memorial service for their lost sons.

The weather was clear that day, and the mountain dominated the horizon.

On August 4, Gary Hansen called my father and asked if the park would support an expedition to make one last search for clues to the lost climbers' fates before winter set in. Against the wishes of the regional director, my father approved $1,000 to assist in the cost of sending a team of climbers back to Denali.

Dubbed the Humanitarian Climb, the expedition's stated purpose was "to find and bury seven members of the Wilcox Party who perished on Mount McKinley in the storm of July 18–23 and learn the causes of their tragedy. Secondarily, to salvage what we could of their gear and airdropped material to cache on rock where it would benefit other parties or rescues in the future."

Vin Hoeman led the climb, which included his wife, Grace; Edward Boulton; Charles Crenshaw; Richard Springgate of the Seattle Mountain Rescue Council; and Ray Genet of the Alaska Rescue Group, who had been a member of the group that made the historic Winter Ascent back in February. On August 19, Don Sheldon delivered the six climbers to 9,800 feet on the Kahiltna Glacier. After making a few side climbs and collecting and repacking a number of food and gear caches, Vin Hoeman and Genet headed for Denali Pass on August 26, recovering some of the materials from the big airdrop and placing them where the material might remain accessible for future emergencies. Then they moved to the north side of the mountain and headed down the Harper Glacier.

They located the top six inches of John Russell's ten-foot flag decorated with ribbons cut from the remains of the cook tent and Snyder's "entire supply of adhesive tape." With so much new snow, probing and digging farther was pointless. They cut several of the ribbons to bring back as evidence of their find and continued down a little farther on the Harper Glacier, scanning the slopes all around, but found nothing.

The snow at 18,200 feet made for poor digging, but they managed to scour out individual snow caves—and one double—in temperatures of minus 25 degrees. Grace Hoeman had left the mountain earlier with Don Sheldon, and Boulton was ill, so Vin Hoeman, Genet, Springgate, and Crenshaw set out for the summit at 8:30 A.M. Vin Hoeman's journal reads:

> Ray and I on the first rope scout the steep slope of Archdeacon's Tower on the way, finding 3 Wilcox Party wands at the top of the steep slope NW of the Tower where no party would go if they could see to do better. We theorize that the shelf atop this slope may have been their 17–18 July bivouac site and/or a regrouping area on their descent.

From there they went on to the summit, giving Genet the distinction of making the earliest and latest successful climb in a single year. He had been on the summit on February 28 and repeated the feat on August 26.

They continued their search during the descent: "We belayed down the steep northern slope of Archdeacon's Tower but could find no trace of the two bodies that were seen there, though we must have passed within a few feet of them under the new snow," wrote Hoeman.

When the men returned to camp, they found Boulton suffering the effects of altitude sickness and made a hasty retreat down the

West Buttress. Along the way, they salvaged the sleeping bags and fuel that had overshot the pass by cutting shelves on the wall of a serac and stacking the supplies there in hopes it would be available in case of future emergencies.

In conclusion, Hoeman wrote, "Little was added to what is known of the fate of those who died in July, the deep new snow prevented accomplishment of the most important part of our mission. Some material was cached where it may be of possible use in the future."

Both my father and Vin Hoeman wrote to the family members to let them know that the expedition had found no further clues to the fate of their sons. Perry and Beth Taylor, Steve's parents, wrote back to thank the Hoemans for their efforts and to share information.

Dear Vin and Grace,

Thank you for you [sic] nice letter and expecially [sic] for the effort you both made to satisfy many of the questions involved in the tragedy. We are both quite aware that it was a considerable part that you involved yourselves in and will always feel indebted to you.

This past weekend, Mrs. Taylor and I visited with the parents of Walter Taylor and Hank Janes. They are both wonderful families. At the same time while in Indiana, we located Anshel Schiff and spent several hours with him. He gave us one bit of information that we have had a question about. He says that in his conversation with our Steve that Steve never intended to go to the top with the others and that he was in reasonably good health and made a rational decision to just wait at camp and descend with the others when they returned. In addition, Anshel in his correspondence with Joe Wilcox thinks that Joe has now come to believe that Steve was not the boy in camp. However, our speculation is leading to little satisfaction and I agree with your statement, that there is no valid answer to exactly what happened.

Sincerely,

Beth and Perry Taylor
Parents of Stephen
Arnold Taylor

S. P. McLaughlin wrote to my father in September to thank him for sending personal items his son Mark had left at the park and revealed that he still carried a spark of hope that the climbers might still be found.

I know that considerable effort has gone into this search and climb and yet both my wife and I, along with some of the climbers here that knew the fellows, have entertained the theory that maybe they came off the mountain between storms. Just a thought, but has any looking been done around the base of the mountain? True the majority of those involved hold the opinion that the party met with disaster near the summit. It is just a thought though, but sort of a "nagging" thought.

S. P. McLaughlin.

A few weeks later, Paul Janes wrote to my father with sad news. Helen Bellows, mother of the sensitive lover of wild places and inner-city schoolteacher Hank Janes, had died. She had been grief-stricken since learning of her son's death and had suffered a massive heart attack. She was forty-nine years old.

Unanswered questions, grief, and doubt lingered among family members, particularly Elmer Luchterhand. He continued to press for answers through the winter and into the summer of 1968. On June 17, he wrote to Vin Hoeman asking why the families hadn't been notified as soon as radio contact with the summit team was lost, saying the parents would have offered "naïve but unlimited determination" to the search effort had they known earlier.

Hoeman's response, written on June 20, offers insight into the challenges facing rescuers in the early days of radio use in mountaineering.

> Radio communication is a great thing, but it has definite limitations in mountaineering. Many things go wrong with radios and the use of them on Mount McKinley and we cannot start full-scale rescue operations when parties fail to make scheduled contact. In 1963, when Harvard climbers were reported "missing" on McKinley's Wickersham Wall we went to the expense of searching for them till we found them OK. There was bitter reproach later for the extra expense we caused them.
>
> Three other expeditions were on McKinley at the time of last year's July tragedy but there was radio contact only with the Wilcox Party. The Gerhardt party on West Buttress had no radio, the radios of the Everett party on the South Face and the Mountaineering Club of Alaska Party on Karstens Ridge were not working. Our best hope was the latter MCA party because it included 3 ARG members and was ascending the line of

descent of the 5 Wilcox party survivors. However, in a storm such as the one that had McKinley in its grip 18–25 July movement up or down is virtually impossible and it was not until the latter date that those survivors staggered down to the MCA Party . . . The remaining 5 MCA Party members started up to render what aid they could to those above. At this time it was assumed they'd have dug in but would be short of supplies. The MCA took the Wilcox Party radio with them, but soon it was only functioning well enough to click yes or no to questions from below.

There was actually nothing to cause a great deal of alarm until the MCA party reached the 17,900 camp 28 July and found a body in the remains of a tent there, at least nothing definite on which to base long distance phone calls, as the summit party would naturally have holed up for the duration of the storm, and anxiety was only really warranted when they failed to reappear as the storm slackened.

Elmer Luchterhand's belief that he might have been able to save his son and the others if he had known sooner is understandable, but it is incorrect. The rescue could have been conducted many different ways, but the result would not have changed. Once this superstorm caught the young men on the upper mountain, neither aircraft nor rescue climbers could be deployed to search for or assist them.

Snyder, Schlichter, and Wilcox were within 2 miles and 3,000 vertical feet and highly motivated to reach the upper camp when they set out to go back up from 15,000 feet, but they were halted after moving just a few hundred yards in four hours. Don Sheldon made flights around the lower part of the mountain during the storm but clouds and high winds repelled his attempts to get above 15,000 feet until July 27. The Air Force refused requests to launch an overflight while the storm raged. When it broke on July 27 and perfect conditions reigned, their large C-130 aircraft made ten runs through Denali Pass, but moved too quickly for observers to effectively search. Had a C-130 been able to get close enough to the mountain during the high winds and low visibility of the storm, they would have been even less effective and done little more than risk the lives of the flight crew.

Certainly mistakes were made both by rescuers and climbers, but as is often the case in a catastrophe, no one action can be singled out as the cause. In this case, however, one element had an overriding effect on every human player in this story: the storm.

Had there not been a storm of such endurance and overwhelming power, the Wilcox Expedition would not have ended in tragedy. Had the storm been less intense, the climbers might have made it to shelter. Had it been shorter in duration, they might have outlasted it, or rescuers might have reached them before they succumbed. But such analysis is just as pointless as trying to place blame for the tragedy on action or lack of action by any one person, whether rescuer, ranger, pilot, or climber. In the end, seven young men died probably before anyone else even suspected they were in trouble.

The records and recollections of the survivors and the people who took part in the rescue effort have shed light on their actions. Reconstructing how the last hours and minutes of the lost climbers' lives played out on the mountain is more difficult. The observations of those who knew the climbers, who were on the mountain during the storm, who saw the bodies, and who climbed in search of answers offer a perspective of unique authority. In a letter to Vin Hoeman written later in the fall of 1967, Joe Wilcox outlined what he thought might have happened on their last night.

> On the 17th and 18th their radio contacts reported using cold batteries. Using cold batteries was considered almost an unforgivable sin on the expedition and was definite evidence of their fatigue. They apparently underestimated the energy drain from spending a night in the open. They stated their reason for bivouacking was not being able to go up or down in the whiteout. They had been wanding and I do not really believe that they couldn't go *down*. In any event they should have come down at the first weather break. It's easy for us to say that from a sea level observation point—it is quite another thing for them to come to this conclusion when they find themselves so close to the summit of a mountain, which they had spent the last month climbing.

Bill Babcock penned a likely scenario of what happened while resting in his snow cave high on Karstens Ridge when thoughts of the dead men he and his team had seen were still fresh in his mind.

> The six climbers made the push sometime early in the morning, completely exhausted, probably cold and miserable. The storm hit with violence only a climber of McKinley can appreciate; you cannot see! Your face and hands begin to freeze and you start to think of camp, even though it may be totally out of the question, camp it is. The two climbers found on the slopes of Archdeacons

Tower were not even roped! The slope is 45 to 50 degrees! . . . the climbers panicked several thousand feet above camp each trying his own way to get down.

These scenarios do make sense. However, a very persuasive explanation of the sequence of events comes from none other than Brad Washburn. He knew the mountain more intimately than anyone else at the time, and he shared his thoughts on what might have happened in a letter to Perry Taylor.

It would appear to me that these fellows got into difficulties crossing the long flat area between the summit and the Archdeacon's Tower. As they approached the Tower they had to be walking directly into the gathering storm. When they reached the end of the flat, they had to go uphill a couple of hundred yards (perhaps 100 vertical feet) on the way down. At this point it appears as if someone may have said, "I simply can go no farther" and the group may have retreated to the right, (N) into the semblance of shelter offered by the Archdeacon's Tower—mighty little shelter, but at least a bit better than being out in the full storm. As the storm gathered intensity, they may have decided to dig in somewhere on the east side of the Tower (they are supposed not to have had a tent or stove). This would have been an extremely dangerous move without any fuel and, therefore, with no means of making warmth or hot liquids. Two members of this group were either dispatched or volunteered to try to get from this spot back to camp. Whether they did this on the first day or later will probably never be known. The location of their bodies on the NW side of the lower part of the Tower would certainly indicate to me that they were endeavoring to take a short cut to their high camp by cutting around the flank of the Tower rather than by descending directly from the regular climbing route. These two men appear to have simply been overcome by the storm right in the trail. It was, evidently, an "every man for himself" crisis, as these men were unroped and two or three hundred yards apart. If they had succeeded in getting much farther, they would have gone right over a 60 or 70-foot ice cliff which would have been utterly invisible in the storm and lay directly between them and their camp.

The fact that this high camp tent was completely destroyed by the storm is no surprise either, as it requires continual work by climbers in a tent at that altitude, both inside and out, to keep a tent standing in a McKinley blizzard—and these efforts will succeed only if the tent is extremely strong and pitched and protected in precisely the right way . . . it would have been virtually impossible for a single sick man in a tent at that altitude to keep it standing . . .

Vin Hoeman's letter to the grieving Elmer Luchterhand describes what their son's final moments may have been like.

. . . you have to dig a snow cave, which is not easy in wind hardened snow by a party already exhausted as the party on McKinley undoubtedly was. I think they made a fatal decision not to do so, to try to make it down through worsening conditions and those conditions got so bad the afternoon of their summit day that they were literally frozen in their tracks, unable to help themselves. I would not have you think this is painful, for it is not, the blowing snow is what stops you, you can't see to even take a step. Unless you have a good drift and a shovel you can't even dig a hole for it drifts in as fast as you can dig. You huddle down in a fetal position and the circulation system shunts off less essential extremities until the spark goes out, I don't believe one can even think clearly what's happening, you just sort of go to sleep.

The most puzzling enigma is the whereabouts of John Russell during all of this. He was not with Walt Taylor, Clark, Janes, Luchterhand, and McLaughlin when they reached the summit on July 18 and he had not stayed at the 17,900-foot camp with Steve Taylor. Joe Wilcox believes the body found in the collapsed tent was Russell, based partly on the description given by the MCA party of its frozen and matted hair. He said Steve Taylor wore his hair short, as required by Brigham Young University, where he had been attending school. Russell's hair was thick and curly and more likely to be described as "matted."

Joe Wilcox also says Steve Taylor had small hands. The MCA climbers described a small body with big hands. However, after giving that description, Ireton pointed out that the exposed hand had frozen and thawed more than once and may have been swollen. No one looked closely at the dead man's face, which was snow-covered. And after the initial discovery, they avoided it altogether.

The strongest evidence that Russell returned to high camp is the presence of his bamboo flag 200 yards below the high camp. He had decorated it and carried it all the way from 15,000 feet at Camp VI to 17,900 feet at Camp VII while suffering from altitude sickness. He still planned to plant it on the summit and it was in camp when Wilcox, Schiff, and the Colorado climbers began their descent.

Steve Taylor remained at high camp when the second summit team left and probably died early in the storm when the wind was most intense, trying to hold his tent upright in the "blowhole," as Bill Babcock described the location of the high camp in his journal.

The tent's failure was probably a sudden and catastrophic event for its occupant, whomever it was. A breach in the fabric that allows a violent influx of wind can burst a tent like an overinflated balloon. Mountain guide Blaine Smith described the scenario: "As soon as there is any kind of infarction in the tent, the wind can get in and it's almost like being in an explosion," he said. "It happens so fast and then, boom, suddenly you're in the middle of this huge fucking storm, and you're in your underwear and all of your shit has just gone everywhere. You're scrambling to get your boots on, things are freezing, you're racing as fast as you can to get prepared before you lose the ability to use your hands. It is desperate."

Steve Taylor had more than enough food and fuel to support one man, and the MCA party's description of food lying around camp could indicate such an explosive event, which would have tossed food and gear into the snow around the tent. With no walls to hide behind and no cave to retreat into, the man in the tent would have little choice but to cling to the meager protection offered by the flapping nylon or to try to make a run for the camp at 15,000 feet. If two men were in the tent when it failed, one may have stayed while the other went for help.

If Russell was returning from his summit attempt when the storm hit, he may have holed up somewhere along the way. If the wind eased briefly on July 19, he may have reached Camp VII and found

Taylor's frozen body. From there he might have taken the sleeping bag from the corpse and continued down toward Camp VI at 15,000 feet, only to fall into a crevasse on the way.

Snyder put forth a similar scenario, suggesting Russell may have returned to camp and endured the early part of the storm in the tent with Taylor. If one of the men died where he sat, supporting the tent pole, the other may have taken the sleeping bag and ventured down the Harper toward the 15,000-foot camp, carrying the bamboo pole as a signal to call for help. Whether he fell into a crevasse, was carried away by the winds sweeping down the Harper Glacier, or had lain down and was buried by blowing snow is a puzzle that is not likely to be solved.

The bodies found up high were frozen and showed no signs of decomposition, while the body in the tent was black and green, and stinking of decay. Wayne Merry speculated that the more pristine condition of the bodies higher up means they had lived through much of the storm, holed up in a cave, and died in a desperate bid to reach the 17,900-foot camp after several days of waiting for help. He may be right. However, the very different conditions of the dead bodies don't necessarily mean one was dead any longer than another, according to Dave McMahan, who retired in 2013 as Alaska's state archaeologist. During his three-decade career, he worked on numerous crime-scene investigations, applying forensic archaeology techniques to help determine the time of death and other factors when studying human remains found in Alaska's cold climate. When I described the bodies and their conditions as reported by the MCA climbers, he immediately asked if the decomposed body was subject to varying temperatures due to sun and shade. If so, he said, decomposition would be accelerated dramatically compared to the others.

To answer his question I turned to longtime guide Brian Okonek, whose mountaineering expertise is regularly tapped by the Park Service to assist in rescues and in accident investigations. Okonek said the slopes below Archdeacon's Tower and high camp on the Harper Glacier get about fourteen hours of direct sunlight in late July.

"The big difference between the bodies would be whether they were on the surface of the snow, buried in snow, or in a tent," Okonek said. "In midsummer the interior of a tent warms up considerably when sun is shining on it. Even at high camp it can get outright hot inside a tent, even when it is cold and windy outside."

He speculated that the upper bodies' lack of decomposition could mean they died early and remained frozen with no tent to capture the heat and thaw them out.

"I have had the unfortunate duty of burying three people over the years high on Denali," he said. "Two people were at 19,300 feet and the third was at 18,000 feet. The two at 19,300 feet had been on the surface for about a month and looked like white marble. The person at 18,000 feet had been on the mountain for a year and also looked like white marble; all we could see of any of these people were their faces."

When I discussed Okonek's thoughts and observations with archaeologist McMahan, he agreed that heat in the collapsed tent could have accelerated the decomposition of that body.

All this, regardless of the expertise of those I consulted, is speculation. Only the discovery of a body could reveal the identity of the corpse in the tent at 17,900 feet and possibly shed light on how Russell's flag and a sleeping bag came to be thrust in the snow below high camp.

After half a century the mountain is unlikely to give up its secrets. Climate change continues to melt away many of Alaska's glaciers, and Denali's annual snowline—the delineation between permanent and seasonal snow—is much higher than it was four decades ago. But the upper mountain where the young men's bodies rest is still one of the coldest places on the planet and, as my father described it to me so many years ago, remains a place where the snow never melts.

CHAPTER 12

WHAT CHANGED

T he Humanitarian Climb had yielded no additional clues to the fate of the lost climbers. The only trace of the Wilcox Expedition that remained was the top six inches of Russell's bamboo summit flag protruding from the heavy snow that blanketed the upper Harper Glacier. Vin Hoeman retrieved some of the strips of tent cloth that Russell had used to decorate the top of the pole and brought them to the park, where they were filed away in a small envelope.

In September 1967 the National Park Service convened a "critique" meeting in Anchorage to examine the tragedy in an effort to determine what may have caused the tremendous loss of life and evaluate the rescue efforts in hopes of avoiding similar incidents in the future.

Art Hayes, Wayne Merry, and my father represented the Park Service; Brad Washburn and his wife, Barbara, came from Boston; and several members of Alaska's climbing community attended.

Most were members of the Mountaineering Club of Alaska and the Alaska Rescue Group, including Vin Hoeman, Frank Nosek, and Gary Hansen, as well as the veterans of the Winter Ascent, the Babcock party, and Don Sheldon, who had done most of the flying during the Wilcox rescue efforts. Notably absent from the meeting were Joe Wilcox and the survivors of his expedition.

The meeting began with questions about the Wilcox party. Hansen said the combined group's lack of leadership and experience contributed to the accident. John Ireton, who had inspected the two bodies near Archdeacon's Tower, defended Jerry Clark's Antarctic experience. None had *expedition* experience, clarified Hansen. "What is expedition experience?" replied Merry. Hoeman said the amalgamation of the Wilcox and Colorado parties compromised the personal connection necessary for a successful expedition. Art Davidson, who had led the Winter Ascent earlier that year, said the party's large size made the team weaker. Brad Washburn agreed. Bill Babcock countered that group strength is not measurable. "Was it Steve Taylor who was found in the tent?" asked Alaska Rescue Group member Paul Crews.

It was an unfettered discussion among a group of men and women who comprised what was probably the greatest concentration of Denali climbing experience and rescue knowledge ever gathered in one place. Early in the meeting discussion dwelled on what might have gone wrong within the Wilcox Expedition, but it went on to cover myriad topics, including the use of handheld radios; requiring climbers to wear dog tags for body identification; construction of a rescue shelter at Denali Pass; climbing fees; insurance for climbers to cover potential rescue costs; and the development of a climbing brochure to inform climbers of Denali's extreme weather.

There also were criticisms of the rescue efforts. Bill Babcock finally had a chance to let the Air Force, the Park Service, and Don

Sheldon know what he thought of their airdrop capabilities, politely describing them as "not always as described." Sheldon described his own communication challenges and his method for making air-drops on the upper mountain and in other conditions encountered on Denali.

Wayne Merry, perhaps more than anyone else, remained convinced that a rescue could have been pulled off. It didn't matter that everyone else involved maintained that the weather was too bad; Merry simply disagreed.

To this day, Merry still believes not enough was done. When I visited Wayne and Cindy Merry in their small house on a hill looking out over Atlin Lake in northern British Columbia, Wayne was waiting for me in the driveway. He is a small man with thick, white hair, smooth skin, and thoughtful eyes that give him more than a passing resemblance to Spencer Tracy; talking to him and watching him move nimbly around the house, it was hard to believe he was eighty years old.

We sat at a dining table in the large, book-lined room that over-looked the lake and talked about the park and the Wilcox tragedy. But the conversation returned again and again to the failure to launch an overflight.

"Whether we could do anything for them or not remained to be seen," he said. "We couldn't say until we could find out what the situation was. Chances are good that we couldn't do much for them directly, but we were legally and morally obligated to try to help these people and we didn't even try."

When I described radio logs, journal entries, and weather reports that consistently indicate that weather kept aircraft from flying near the upper mountain until Sheldon flew on July 25, Merry dis-missed them.

"This I don't know, but I do know that I requested it and Wilcox requested it and I radioed this to headquarters. Where it went from there, I haven't the slightest idea. The radio communication was so poor and so irregular that it is hard to say exactly what the sequence was. A number of times I was told by [Chief Ranger] Hayes that things were being taken care of, or they were thinking about this or discussing that. But I couldn't seem to get a solid answer."

When I asked Merry if he continued to ask questions when he returned to headquarters in the fall of 1967, he replied, "No."

At the end of the daylong critique meeting, three "proposed needs" were identified: improved radio communications, designation of a climbing ranger with authority to deal directly with the Alaska Rescue Group, and construction of a mountain refuge at Denali Pass. After dinner, those needs were debated and critiqued and narrowed to two resolutions noted simply as "Radio system funding and Climbing personnel." Whether or not they agreed with one another, all the participants were motivated to learn from the events of July 1967 in order to avoid repeating a similar tragedy in the future.

My father wrote to the families of the victims on September 21 to describe the findings of the meeting.

> The critique meeting . . . became more of a discussion of proposals for future protection and, of course, contained positive proposals to check for traces next spring since nature is known to do unexpected things on McKinley. This is not expected to be productive. Every person at the meeting must have wished for a different result and, in fact, probably wished that the meeting did not have to be held at all. Some of these people knew your sons personally, and it was obviously a sensitive matter. No speculation as to the cause of the accident was made that could hold up against the known facts. We know the winds

were intense, we know there was a "white-out"—we still don't know why they did not continue down or dig into snow caves. We therefore have to assume there was an extraordinary factor over which there was no control, one we may never understand completely.

During the critique meeting Don Sheldon brought up the idea of requiring climbers to be bonded (insured) in order to cover rescue costs. He routinely flew when he was needed regardless of whether payment for his efforts was guaranteed, a policy that often left him empty-handed. Though bonding was a reasonable suggestion, the idea appeared to alarm some of the climbers. Gary Hansen immediately attacked the idea, saying it could restrict those who couldn't afford insurance for climbing, and might lead to clandestine climbs. Washburn joined Sheldon in pressing the question, suggesting that climbing would continue to grow in popularity, resulting in more possible losses to rescue organizations.

After the meeting, my father further explored the bonding idea and decided that Hansen was right.

"I explored all I could with everybody I could think of, including Lloyd's of London, the cost was too high. The people making the climbs generally were just doing it, they were just guys hanging around," he said. "They were just people who wanted to climb the damned mountain. They had no money, and they usually gave up their jobs to come up and climb."

Today Joe Wilcox splits his time between Seattle, Washington, and Kailua-Kona, Hawaii, where he teaches astronomy and oceanography at the University of Hawaii.

He is a spare man both in physical appearance and personality. Over the phone his voice is jovial—high yet soft, as if he is talking through a filter of cotton balls. In person he appears somber, with deep-set eyes and a face that, even at rest, seems intense and distracted by unspoken concerns. He has given the years no quarter. He is tall and fit, with the muscular legs of a runner; he is an avid competitor in Masters track and field competitions.

Pictures of Wilcox in his youth show a strapping man who played college football and scaled mountains. Today, after decades of strenuous activity, he has honed his body to a straight, lean, and sinewy version of his youthful self.

In person, his conversation is marked with long pauses and gazes toward the horizon. His impassive face and penetrating eyes are unsettling, but the combination is broken suddenly and frequently by a warm smile.

He still treks in high places, acclimating himself by hiking above 10,000 feet on the slopes of Mauna Kea volcano near his winter home in Kailua-Kona. His most recent climb was Mount Kilimanjaro. And when he isn't climbing, he is sailing *Shepherd Moon*, his Island Packet 350 harbored in Kona. He has already made the 5,000-mile round-trip sailing to Tahiti and back. Australia is next and he hopes to complete a circumnavigation of the planet. He is seventy years old.

When I visited him in Kailua-Kona, he drove a small convertible Geo Metro. The inside was cluttered but clean. His apartment was similar. The floor was covered with piles of books on astronomy, oceanography, and travel. Maps, vinyl records, and DVDs were stacked on his couch. Like his car, it looked more like the domain of a college student rather than a professor.

His life seems to be an exercise in practicality and restraint. He owns two identical baseball hats, one much dirtier than the other.

"I wear that one when I work on the boat," he explained. One afternoon we drank beer from big schooners at a bar near the harbor where he keeps his sailboat. Later at his cluttered apartment he poured me another beer in an identical schooner. "I liked their glasses so I got some for myself," he explained. "They're big and they stay cold."

I suggested he join me but he said, "No, I'll have one next week." He was not joking.

When I asked why he treated himself so sparingly, he replied, "People ask me if I ever let myself go. I like beer, I eat nasty hamburgers, I just do it once a month; I enjoy these things just like anyone else; I just don't do it constantly. When I tell people that, they think something is wrong with me. They don't understand."

I could only wonder if this ordered existence had been influenced by his experience on Denali or if the rigors of mountaineering had appealed to his ascetic nature. For a dozen years after the tragedy on Denali, Wilcox grappled with survivor's guilt. He divorced his first wife, Cheryl, and though he returned to Alaska to teach school in the village of Sand Point in the Shumagin Islands and later in McGrath, he never returned to Denali.

He pored over weather records and climbing journals to compare weather statistics with conditions experienced by climbers during windstorms and finally came to the realization that he could not have saved his friends, even if he had been with them when the storm hit. He wrote his own book about the climb titled *White Winds,* an effort he described to me as therapeutic. "At first I felt guilty, I thought I should have died myself. I'm convinced now that it doesn't matter, it wouldn't have made a difference."

During a climbing conference in the 1980s, Joe Wilcox and Brad Washburn met for the first and only time. Wilcox says they never talked about the infamous letter or the specifics of the climb but had a pleasant exchange. According to Washburn's biographer, Mike Sfraga, that was the closest semblance to an apology Washburn could muster.

"I never got the impression from Brad that he ever said, 'Hey, I'm sorry I wrote you that crappy letter,'" Sfraga told me. "He said that he had talked to Wilcox at some conference. That was about as good as it got, as close to an apology as I think you could get from Brad."

Howard Snyder is the director of the Remington Carriage Museum in Cardston, Alberta, Canada, and remains intensely interested in the expedition. He wrote a book about the climb called *The Hall of the Mountain King,* published in the early 1970s. In it, he was critical of Wilcox's leadership and the abilities of some of the Wilcox party members, but his attitude seems to have mellowed in the ensuing years.

"Joe is a real convenient target, but that's the nature of being the leader of an expedition. He has been, I think, attacked probably unfairly, probably more than anyone else by himself."

Of all the people interviewed, Snyder's memories were the most detailed and the most consistent with documentation from the incident. He and Paul Schlichter also seem to be the least affected of the survivors. "Paul and I have talked about it many times and we're glad we climbed it when we did because we were on a real adventure and we were on our own. Now it's overrun with people and regulations and rangers."

Schlichter went on to serve in Vietnam as a rescue and reconnaissance pilot and lost comrades there and in Laos. That experience, he said, had more of an impact on his life than the Wilcox Expedition, which he looks at as one small aspect of his early life.

"It's funny, we had some friends here that I knew from college, who knew I had been on the climb, and they introduced me to their friends like, 'Here's Paul, he climbed McKinley back in 1967 in a tragic situation.' All I could think was, Well, that was a long, long time ago and I'm not sure why they brought it up in a first introduction."

Of the three Colorado climbers, Jerry Lewis had the most difficulty during the climb, and Snyder said Lewis has tried to distance himself from the experience. "He suffered physically and emotionally way more than we did on this trip and really finds revisiting it to be unpleasant."

Lewis didn't respond to my requests to talk about the climb. Neither did Anshel Schiff, whom Joe Wilcox described as being in poor health and uninterested in talking about the past.

My father remained close to many of those who had worked on the Wilcox rescue. Vin and Grace Hoeman were frequent visitors at our home in the park and the one in South Anchorage for a couple of years following the tragedy. Though my father was ten years his senior, he and Hoeman both were avid letter writers and meticulous collectors. My father's interest was in polar history; Hoeman's was Alaska mountaineering. He maintained a card catalog noting the climbing accomplishments of nearly every serious mountaineer actively climbing at that time, and he was working on a comprehensive climbing guide to Alaska's mountains. Hoeman was thirty-three years old when he died in 1969, swept away by an avalanche on Mount Dhaulagiri in the Himalayas, along with five of America's finest mountaineers and two Sherpas. Vin's wife, Grace Jansen Hoeman, was denied the summit of Denali twice in 1967, both times due in part to altitude sickness, but in 1970, at age forty-nine, she led an all-female expedition to the top. She was traversing Eklutna Glacier north of Anchorage the following year when she met the same fate as her husband and was buried by an avalanche along with her climbing partner Hans Van Der Laan.

Ray Genet, who reached the summit twice in 1967, remained a

close family friend for many years. He presented me with my Eagle Scout Award in 1978, and we often visited him in his tiny cabin near Talkeetna—my father usually went in first to make sure that the attractive young women who often accompanied Genet were appropriately dressed for a family visit. Genet pioneered guided climbing on Denali, founding Genet Expeditions, and made more successful ascents of the mountain than any other climber before he died at age forty-eight on the slopes of Mount Everest, where his body remains.

The last time I saw Don Sheldon, he was wearing a wool watch cap and a down vest, ambling through the terminal at Anchorage International Airport. He and my father clasped hands like long-lost friends, and Sheldon gave me a wry smile and a vigorous handshake too. Then the two men stood there and talked for what seemed like an hour. Though Sheldon had cheated death scores of times while performing rescues on Denali and in the surrounding country, he died in bed, felled by cancer in 1975 at age fifty-four.

My father's friendships with these adventurers were always puzzling to me. He was not like them; he did not climb, nor for that matter was he much of an outdoorsman. After leaving the Park Service, my father wore suits and worked in an office, yet he remained close to some of the leading climbers of the '60s and '70s, and they treated him as if he were one of their own. I never understood why until after his death in 2005 at age eighty-one.

For as long as I can recall, a framed paper certificate hung on the wall of my father's office, an honorary lifetime membership in the Mountaineering Club of Alaska. Toward the end of his life, when his memory was poor, he told me he got it for keeping Denali open to climbing but the details eluded him. When he died and I was writing his obituary, I tried to learn more about the award, but his climbing friends were long dead and calls to several current club members revealed nothing. It wasn't until I was nearly finished with the research for this book that I learned the story.

My sister found the certificate among our father's belongings and read the faded signature of the MCA president, revealing the name Frank Nosek, now a well-known attorney still practicing law at age seventy-eight, and serving as the honorary consulate to the Czech Republic. When I went to his law firm in downtown Anchorage, he met me in the lobby and said, "My office is on the second floor; let's take the stairs, it keeps you young." By his fit appearance and sharp mind, I figured he knew what he was talking about and followed as he jogged up the steps.

"Your dad was a real friend to the climbing community," Nosek began as we settled into chairs in his slightly cluttered office. "I remember designing that certificate; it was one of a kind. We'd never given one before. We wanted to thank him."

The Wilcox tragedy was the worst climbing accident to occur on Denali or in North America when it occurred and the worst accident to take place in a national park. Understandably it hadn't gone unnoticed by higher-ups in the Park Service. In the fall of 1967 John Rutter, Alaska's San Francisco–based regional director, called my father and made an unprecedented demand: end climbing in Mount McKinley National Park.

Because a tragedy had occurred in July, and a near tragedy had occurred in the winter, Regional Director Rutter considered the mountain too dangerous for mountaineering, and his solution was to close it. The regional director didn't have the authority to ban climbing in the park himself, but the superintendent did.

My father refused.

In 1999 former superintendent George Hall told Park Service

historian Kristen Griffen about John Rutter's demand. "He wouldn't put it in writing. He wouldn't take any positive step. He wanted me to stick my neck out. Now, mountain climbing is a legitimate recreation program, it's just that there should be some more support and control to it."

Nosek was chairman of the Mountaineering Club of Alaska in 1967 and said the climbing community in Alaska and in the Pacific Northwest was well aware of the threat of closure yet unsure how to fight it.

"We wanted to show our opposition to that idea, but we didn't really have any place to show it, except your dad. And so we did. We felt like we had a connection, a reasonable connection, with a very, very unreasonable government agency. It was an agency we couldn't—we didn't have the ability to—fight. But we did have an open ear with their local representative, and he was sympathetic and reasonable."

The pressure to close the mountain eased as winter set in and the horror of the accident began to fade. Some time that fall, Rutter withdrew his demand. In December 1967 the Mountaineering Club of Alaska recognized my father with an honorary lifetime membership signed by Nosek. It hung on the wall of every office my father occupied after he left the Park Service, and in the last years of his life it adorned the wall of his den at our home in Anchorage and remained there until his death.

"The appreciation for your dad having that attitude was enormous in the climbing community here," Nosek said. "He worked with us. I don't know what he went through, but he was our front line against that movement to shut down the mountain, so we've always credited him with having defeated that very, very bad idea."

As my father had put it at the review meeting: "The people making the climbs generally were just doing it, they were just guys hanging around. They were just people who wanted to climb the damned mountain. They had no money, and they usually gave up their jobs to come up and climb."

He didn't want those people shut out of Denali.

CHAPTER 13

THIRTY YEARS AFTER

F our of the men simply vanished. The three bodies found on the mountain revealed few clues to their final hours. And over the decades since the storm engulfed them, no new evidence has turned up. But, as Brad Washburn predicted, climbing has grown in popularity and thousands of climbers can now say they have reached the summit of Denali. A few have returned with stories that might shed light on what it was like inside the storm that engulfed the mountain in late July 1967.

In late May 1997, longtime climbing guide Blaine Smith led a Denali expedition that bore remarkable similarities to the second Wilcox summit team: Smith's party also consisted of seven men; during their ascent two climbers chose to forego the summit and wait while five went to the top. Near the summit, those five were overtaken by an unexpected storm. And when the wind velocity approached 100 miles per hour and reaching the safety of their high camp became impossible, the party was caught above Denali Pass, unable to move and fighting to find a way to survive in the relentless wind.

Blaine Smith is in his early fifties, lantern-jawed, tall, and fit, with thin brown hair and the energy and mannerisms of a man half his age. His face has acquired some character since we first met more than forty years ago while attending Rabbit Creek Elementary School in Anchorage: his nose is scarred by frostbite picked up on Denali, and one brown eye is surrounded by a titanium socket thanks to a slap delivered by a grizzly bear near his home in the Anchorage suburb of Eagle River. His demeanor, however, remains remarkably unchanged: he is enthusiastic and cheerful, and when he talks about Denali, where he once made his living, Smith laces his descriptions with colorful imagery, humor,* and authority gained from decades of climbing and guiding there.

On May 29, 1997, Smith roused his clients at the 17,200-foot high camp on the West Buttress. Though the forecast called for good weather, Smith made his own observation before deciding whether to head out on the 3,000-foot climb to the summit.

The wind blew from the north, and the telltale signs of an approaching low—clouds, either creeping up the lower mountain or amassing around nearby peaks—were nonexistent.

"The lows usually come from the south," he said. "A lot of times that high ends up outcompeting the low and you're golden, not a big deal."

The north wind appeared to be doing just that.

With all signs looking promising, he and assistant guide Willy

---

* Blaine Smith's sense of humor is revealed by his behavior in a cross-country ski race in which we both competed in 2011. Moments before the starting gun, he pushed me over. He has a more philosophical side. After we talked about the storm he survived, he said, "There is no reward without risk. I can't imagine living life without it."

Peabody set out for Denali Pass around 9:15 A.M. leading five clients. The team carried two ropes, two steel shovels, a scoop shovel, a few snow saws, a stove, a pot, fuel, and extra food and water. Smith also carried an oversized bivouac sack, and each man had a sleeping bag and down pants and a parka. Smith's pack weighed close to 40 pounds; his clients carried 25-pound packs.

By the time they reached Denali Pass, the thin overcast sky had burned off, and the sun was out. Still, Smith was cautious.

"We were kind of creeping into this thing thinking that if we did get bad weather, that we turn around and bolt," he said.

They continued on to Archdeacon's Tower, a rocky 19,550-foot spur rising above Denali Pass, under sunny skies. After a short break, they reached the small plateau below the summit ridge at 19,200 feet known as the Football Field. The entire route was scoured by wind—hard packed and icy, with little loose snow. Where the wind had dislodged wands along the well-traveled route, they replaced them, though the icy crust made planting them difficult. The climbing here isn't technical, but the thin air, heavy packs, cold, and constant uphill pace is challenging even on a good day.

At the upper end of the Football Field, one of the climbers ran out of steam.

Peabody built a windbreak, fired up a stove to heat water and food, and the two men hunkered down at the foot of a last rise to the summit ridge known as Pig Hill to wait for the summit team to return.

The others continued with two rope teams, Smith in the lead, up the hill and onto the summit ridge.

"That's usually how it goes. If it's easy terrain, you usually are in front. If someone has trouble, you can belay him up," Smith said. "You've got a lot more mobility on the end than if you're tied in the middle."

When they reached the summit around 6:00 P.M. the skies were clear and the sun shined, but the wind had picked up to about 20 miles per hour. A bit brisk, Smith thought, but not enough to be too concerned.

"That's not that unusual on top," he said, "and it was still blowing from the north, which was good for us."

As his clients posed for photos and celebrated their success, Smith watched the sky begin to change and felt his heart drop.

"In the process of five or ten minutes of being on the summit, it went from clear to opaque to overcast. Then the wind built from twenty to twenty-five from the north. Then the wind all of a sudden shifted and came from the south. As soon as it shifted and the sky turned opaque, I was alarmed."

The clouds he had been watching for all day materialized as if by magic, and the southwest wind pushed a column of warm, damp air up against the icy mountain, creating a cloud cap with Smith and his team caught inside.

"It was the worst time for it to happen," he said. "It could have happened at any other time, but right then we were the farthest we could have possibly have been away from safety."

His first thought was to get the climbers off of the summit ridge as quickly as possible without endangering them.

"I didn't want us to go in two teams anymore because I didn't want to lose anybody."

He put the entire team on one rope and he clipped in last.

"So everybody was out ahead of me, and I was driving them like horses," he said. "I was yelling, 'It's time to go, let's go!' I was doing everything but putting my boot in their ass. They could tell I was serious."

Partway down the ridge, the rope slowed and finally stopped. The men were spread out at 50-foot intervals ahead of him, and from his vantage point at the back of the line, he couldn't tell what was happening.

"I'm like, Holy shit, let's get going! What's the fucking malfunction?"

At the other end of the rope, the lead climber had stopped at one of the most exposed parts of the ridge and began yelling for help. With mist hampering Smith's view, he had little choice but to unclip his harness from the rope, hook his arm around it, and begin running down the ridge.

"I've got my crampons on, my pack, the whole show," he said.

As he approached each man, he let go of the rope briefly, then hooked his arm around it again and continued running. It seemed to be a good idea until he tripped and went over the north side of the ridge. Suddenly he was sliding down on his knees hoping the rope would come tight. One of the clients saw him go down and jumped off the other side to counteract his fall.

The rope came tight and Smith pulled himself up to the trail.

"Dave was on the other side of the hill in the snow," Smith said. "It was a gutsy move, but I didn't have time to thank him. I yelled at him to get up and get going."

When Smith reached the lead climber he saw that the man's goggles had fogged up and he was unable to see. "So I calmed down and said, 'Let's take them off, let's put them someplace else.'"

Then he realized why the climber was panicking: ice had built up and the goggles had frozen to his face.

"So I took my fist and hit him in the goggles and the lens popped out," Smith said. "I grabbed the lens and said, 'How's that?' He said, 'OK.' I said, 'Let's go!' I could feel the window closing and I felt like, Oh man, we got to get going, we got to get going."

Once off of the precarious summit ridge and down Pig Hill, Smith took the lead position on the rope to set the pace.

"I just drug them down the hill. I was just ruthless."

They collected themselves on the Football Field, but the wind picked up and a full-on whiteout descended. After several desperate minutes spent searching for Peabody and his charge, the party reunited and continued on.

Near Archdeacon's Tower, two British climbers overtook them, also heading for the 17,200-foot camp on the West Buttress.

"We offered for them to join forces, that they could go down with us," Smith said.

They refused, saying they could move faster on their own, and disappeared into the fog and wind. As Smith and Peabody led their clients toward Denali Pass the wands grew sparse and they had to slow down. Here the trail leading to the West Buttress can be easily confused with one that leads to a part of the mountain known as the Orient Express, a slope of 40 to 45 degrees that drops 2,000 feet from the top of the West Rib to a crevasse field.

"It's super easy to get disoriented when you're in the blender like that," Smith said. "So, in the middle of this windstorm I dug in the top of my pack, pulled out my map—managed to hang on to my map—dug out my compass, and reoriented myself."

Soon they were picking up wands again, but as they approached Denali Pass the wind became overpowering. At about 19,200 feet Smith stopped his climbers and continued alone to a ridge that overlooked the pass. When he crested it, the wind knocked him down. "It usually takes a wind of eighty or so to push me over," he said. "It's a guess on my part; I only know that I couldn't stand up."

It was then that the two guides decided to hole up and wait out the storm.

"So I said, 'OK, gentlemen, it's time to dig in.' Then the adventure started, the fun and games were over, and now it was going to get serious."

They broke out the steel shovels and discovered that the wind had denuded the slope of snow.

"It was as hard as this table," Smith said, rapping his knuckles on the wood under his cup. "There is no place to dig in. We thought we'd find a drift someplace."

But no matter where they probed, they found only ice and rock. Meanwhile the storm was battering his clients.

When one man turned his back to the gusts, the wind filled his mittens and carried them away. Minutes later, both of his hands were frozen. Another's goggles frosted up, so he removed them and made the mistake of looking into the wind. In a matter of minutes his corneas froze, blinding him.

"We lost two sleeping bags right out of the gate," Smith continued. "They were trying to get their sleeping bags out and all of a sudden the thing inflates like a balloon. One guy was just hanging on to it and he was getting drug off, he was going to go away. I had to yell, 'Let go of the sleeping bag!' and that's it. It's gone."

The guides continued to brainstorm ways to create a shelter; even a windbreak would have helped. But the storm made it nearly impossible to even manipulate a shovel.

"Gravity had totally shifted. The shovel was all over the place. Every time it went crossways to the wind it flipped up in the air and hit somebody in the head."

Finally, Smith got three men into the large bivouac sack. When he looked up, one of the others was walking away.

"I didn't know what the hell he was doing. I've got to get him back because if he gets a few more feet away, I was not going to be able to find him."

Desperate to block the wind, he considered emptying the packs and filling them with snow to make a buttress. It would have been a feeble shelter, but better than nothing. Then Peabody found a thick layer of snow that had collected in a small depression. It was hard and deep enough to make blocks, so they pulled out their snow saws and started building an igloo. An hour and a half later, three men were huddled inside the igloo and two were tucked into the bivouac sack.

The diameter of the igloo was about three feet and the men were packed in, elbow to elbow. Spindrift blew through the door, creating a minor snowstorm inside. One man checked the temperature in the igloo; it was 30 degrees below zero.

Outside, Peabody and Smith ran out of snow-block material.

Their clients were safe, but they were not. The wind was moving so fast that it was becoming difficult to breathe.

"You'd have to get a kind of bubble just to breathe," Smith said. "If you face into the wind, it would pile-drive you, like drinking from a fire hose. If you face downwind then you'd get all of these vortices; you couldn't even pull air into your lungs. So you try to position your face so you can just take a breath."

The seriousness of the situation was lost on no one. By now, everyone realized the precariousness of their position, and one of the men in the igloo, overcome by claustrophobia, stood up, bursting through the snow blocks like a girl popping out of a cake.

"So now there's a hole in the igloo and I'm patching it up again," Smith says.

Over the next several hours, the two men struggled to build shelter for themselves, but each time they got close the wind destroyed it or one of them knocked it over.

"We were getting punchier and punchier and punchier. It finally got to the point where we dug a ranger trench. It was only deep enough for one of us. So Willy got into it and I put a top over it."

He didn't stay inside long, saying being buried in the long, shallow pit was too much like lying in a grave. Finally, after hours out in the wind they gave up on the structure and sat with their arms around each other. Their noses were frozen porcelain white, they were exhausted, and they came to think that they weren't going to make it.

"I was trying to think how could we salvage the best thing out of this," Smith said. "We had one client named Andy who was doing really well. He was our strongest client, and I thought that Willy and he could probably make it down."

Though he was fully capable of descending too, Smith would stay behind.

"I had always wondered, if things got really, really bad, if I would just save myself," he said. "Could I just say, 'Well, this didn't work out,' and stay alive and everyone else would just croak. So that was a big thing for me. I decided I wouldn't leave my clients, I decided no matter what it took—even if it cost me my life—I would stay."

He sat there, huddled against the chaos around him, and thought about his wife, and the burden she would have to shoulder without him.

"I remember thinking, Well, who's going to finish the house? Boy, I'm really going to leave Deb in the lurch here if I don't pull this one out of my ass—that's what I was thinking."

The guides hugged and said good-bye for what they believed would be the last time, then walked over to roust Andy from the bivvy sack.

"Well, instead of saying, 'Andy, get up, you're going down,' I said, 'Andy, how you doing?' He said, 'We're doing pretty good, we're staying pretty warm, I think we're going to make it.'"

Then they went to the igloo and got a similar response from the men shivering inside.

"We weren't any better off than we were a few minutes earlier, but still, just hearing them say they're going to make it turned the table for me."

So the two guides went back to the task of trying to build a shelter for themselves. In retrospect, Smith believes it was the constant activity that had kept them alive through the storm. Then, minutes after returning to the task of building a shelter, they felt the wind begin to diminish. By 11:00 A.M., it was over.

"If it had lasted a few more hours," he said, "we would have died."

Smith, Peabody, and their party had spent twelve hours in the heart of the storm and had barely survived. One man was blind, all suffered frostbite on their faces, and most had frozen feet or hands, or both. Getting back to camp and off of the mountain without further injury was an odyssey in and of itself, but they all survived. A few fingers and toes were lost to the mountain, and the blind man regained his sight when his corneas thawed. They knew how close they had come to not coming down at all.

At the time of the storm, the National Park Service had a contingent of climbing rangers on the mountain as well as a Lama high-altitude helicopter parked in Talkeetna, ready to fly. Rangers knew where the climbers had been when the storm hit, and they knew that Smith and his party were overdue. Yet no aircraft flew and no rescuers were dispatched.

Daryl Miller, Denali National Park's South District ranger, was at the Talkeetna ranger station and in charge of the mountain at the time. Smith and Peabody were popular guides and friends with many of the climbing rangers, including Miller. Deb, Smith's wife, was with Miller at the ranger station while he fielded calls from rangers on the mountain and monitored the storm. As difficult as it was to do, especially with Deb right there, Miller forbade rescuers from searching until the storm broke. The wind and whiteout made flying out of the question.

"Too many rescuers are killed in the world today," he said. "It's a hero thing. Sometimes people, especially volunteers, practice and practice and they don't want to see anybody suffer, they want to help. It was great that I had a ranger willing to go. I wasn't willing to get anyone killed; I didn't want to make a bad situation a tragedy by killing rescuers. It was hard, but that's what I had to do to protect my field operations, I had to say, We're not going, I don't want anybody else killed or hurt."

Smith carried a radio through the entire event, yet he didn't call for help. In retrospect, he said a call might have alleviated some concern, then again he said it would have been hard to sugarcoat the situation, and it might have made things worse.

"I never even considered calling on the radio, to be quite honest with you. We might as well have been on the moon," Smith said. "What was I going to call somebody for? What were they going to do for me? I'm in the middle of this huge whiteout with the wind blowing eighty miles an hour. What was I going to say? 'Hi, things really suck here. Wish I wasn't here. OK, thanks, bye.' I didn't see any use for it at all."

The emergency response system on the mountain is a lifesaver in many climbing accidents, but in a windstorm like the one Smith's party endured, it couldn't help.

"There was no way help could come to me. There was no help that I would want. I would never ask anybody to come out there in the types of conditions we were in. I mean it's asinine; I was in the spot, I better figure it out, I got to make it on my own. Then, once I can get help, then I'll talk on the radio, and that's what I did.

Once he got his team back to the high camp at 17,200 feet, he broke out the radio. "I called down to fourteen [the camp at 14,000 feet] and said, 'My clients are beat up, we need some help, they're blasted, frostbit bad, they need to go to the hospital.' Then, the Park Service was good; they worked it out. We got the helicopter to come in twice, they took the clients away, and it was great."

Smith guided for six more years but only one more season on Denali. Peabody never guided on the mountain again. The two British climbers they encountered near Archdeacon's Tower followed the wrong trail. Instead of reaching the West Buttress they walked off the West Rib and plunged down the Orient Express. One died and the other lost both hands to frostbite.

Though the 1997 party bore some similarities to the second Wilcox summit team, it had two elements in its favor that the Wilcox team did not: a leader with ten years of experience on Denali, and a short storm.

Back in the NOAA forecast center, meteorologist Jim Nelson ran a model for me of the 1997 storm and compared it to July 1967. "The winds were only half what they were in the '67 storm, and it lasted twelve hours. The '67 storm lasted seven days. If they barely survived this"—he pointed to the 1997 weather map and paused, then he put the '67 storm on the screen—"can you imagine what *this* was like?"

MEMORY IN A LIFETIME

I never learned the identity of the poncho-wearing climber who chased my father and me along the river all those years ago. He was not one of the Wilcox survivors and neither was he a member of the Mountaineering Club of Alaska Expedition. Most of them hiked out to Wonder Lake, with the exception of the four Wilcox survivors and Grace Hoeman, who were picked up by helicopter after the rain-swollen McKinley River blocked their escape from the mountain.

But still, the climber in the poncho haunts me. No matter who he was, he vividly transports me back to those gray, rainy days when my dad wasn't his usual cheerful self and there seemed a tension in the air that even as a five-year-old I could sense.

I probably associate the Wilcox tragedy with that mysterious encounter because whenever I brought up the man who chased us along the riverbank, Dad would chuckle about how difficult it was to jog with me dangling from one of his arms—and then launch into his memories of the Wilcox tragedy and his difficult discussions with the parents of the lost climbers. I never thought to ask who that young man actually was and what connected him to that ill-fated climb. Ranger Wayne Merry had no recollection of the encounter; neither did Bob Hafferman, the Park Service engineer who lived next door to us; nor Wally Cole, the former hotel manager and long-time owner of Camp Denali near Wonder Lake. Was it a figment of my imagination? No. That much I know. My dad was there, and so was I. No matter who that man was, to me, he represents the ghosts of those lost souls, those men whose lives had barely begun.

The storms that hammered Denali in late July and early August 1967 deluged the park and much of interior Alaska with rain. On the twenty-fourth of July, boulders and washouts closed the Park Road, stranding ten vehicles and thirty tourists at Eielson Visitor Center. Other park visitors were trapped on the road between washouts and had to hike to safety; I suppose the stranger could have been one of them, though it wouldn't explain the conversation we had on the long drive home.

On July 25, my sister and I put on our boots and raincoats, climbed into my dad's green Park Service sedan, and drove down the long, arcing hill to the park entrance where the road crossed Riley Creek. The usually sedate stream was a raging brown torrent that day and had already jumped its banks and undermined the small bridge. As we watched from a safe distance, the bridge spanning Riley Creek slumped into the roiling water, temporarily cutting off road access to the park.

It was a demonstration of Nature's power and the kind of lesson our dad often liked to expose us to: he knew a firsthand experience would be much more powerful than reading it in a book or watching it on television. I've never seen another bridge collapse, and though it happened forty-five years ago, the memory is still large in my mind.

The rains continued into August, and by the middle of the month, the Chena River rose to inundate the city of Fairbanks, displacing hundreds of people in an event still known as the "Great Flood."

Who was the young man who walked out of the wilderness on that cool, rainy evening, and what was his relationship to the tragic climb? I doubt I'll ever know. If I've learned anything through the process of writing this book, it is that memory is fleeting and flawed at best. Some of the subjects I interviewed are sure that they remember things clearly, yet their accounts don't match the documentation and, in many cases, their own journals written at the time of the incident. Others think their memories are flawed, yet they match up almost perfectly with the documentation I was able to find. A few think they are fuzzy on the details, and follow-up research shows they're right. Rarest is the one who believes his memory is accurate and follow up confirms that he is right.

Where I fall on this spectrum I am not sure.

ACKNOWLEDGMENTS

No book is written alone, and this one is no exception. I had no idea how much work it would entail when I embarked on the venture—if I had, I may never have started. My wife, the author Melissa DeVaughn, knew what was in store and she never wavered in her belief in me—even when I did. For that I'll be forever grateful.

My sister, Gerianne Thorsness, helped me with recollections of our childhood in Mount McKinley National Park and the events that took place during that tragic summer. She also broke the ice for me with several sources and helped in innumerable ways, not the least of which was her certainty in the importance of telling our father's story and that of the other rescuers. Her husband, John Thorsness, traversed Denali, ascending the West Buttress to the summit and descending via the Muldrow. When I got lost in the pile of research, he helped me find my way more than once.

My mom, Eileen; sister Marietta; and brother, Kevin also supported me both emotionally and financially when things got tight. I doubt I'll ever be able to repay them, and I'm not talking about the money.

Daryl Miller, Denali's former South District ranger, is quoted only sporadically in this book, but he was a guiding influence throughout the research and writing process and was a trusted source when attempting to see the crisis through the eyes of a rescuer.

Joe Wilcox revisited with me what is obviously a painful chapter in his life and has put up with innumerable follow-up questions. Howard Snyder gave me hours of his time, helping me parse through the hundreds of pages of documents and generously allowed the use of his photos taken during the expedition,

Frank Nosek and Gary Hansen, who led the Mountaineering Club of Alaska and the Alaska Rescue Group in 1967, provided unique insight into the climbing culture that existed in Alaska in the 1960s. Their matter-of-fact descriptions of their Herculean rescue efforts, and those of their Alaska Rescue Group compatriots—all done on a volunteer basis—were humbling. Gayle Nienhueser and Bill Babcock, members of the MCA Expedition whose members put themselves at risk in hopes of finding survivors, were generous both with their time and their journals and photos, sharing memories that were clearly painful to relive.

The memories of the incident also weigh heavily on Wayne Merry, who was the Wonder Lake District ranger in 1967. In spite of that, he invited me into his home and spoke frankly about his experiences. I hope this book casts some light on the efforts that took place beyond his isolated outpost at Wonder Lake and helps him shed some of that weight.

Paul Schlichter, Dave Johnston, Bob Hafferman, Butch Farabee, Bob Gerhard, and Louis Reichardt each assisted with details that helped me flesh out aspects of the expedition, the search, the park, the regulatory atmosphere, the weather, and the climbing zeitgeist of the era.

Chuck Sassara drew on more than fifty years of flying in Alaska to portray the perils of mountain flying and what makes pilots do it anyway.

Don Sheldon's son, Robert, helped me determine which airplanes were used during his father's flights and offered insights into what motivated Don to put himself at risk time and time again to help others.

My old friends Blaine Smith and Charlie Sassara kept me in line when I was trying to describe the intricacies of mountaineering, something they both did professionally and I pursue only recreationally.

Brian Okonek, the renowned mountain guide and all-around student of Denali, gave me hours and hours of his time, sharing his comprehensive knowledge of the mountain's history and geography.

Frank Norris's excellent two-volume administrative history of Denali National Park was a resource I visited repeatedly early in the writing process. The only resource I tapped more while trying to decipher the intricacies of rescue history and jurisdiction was probably Frank himself.

Mike Sfraga, PhD, brought Brad Washburn to life for me in a way that only a confidante to the great man could.

Dave McMahan and I met during the Exxon Valdez oil spill and we've seen each other only occasionally since. It was a pleasure to reconnect and again tap the forensic knowledge he's gained during a truly unique career as Alaska's state archaeologist.

Meteorologists John Papineau, Jim Nelson, and the late Ted Fathauer collectively painted a picture of the tremendous storm that engulfed the mountain and the Wilcox team. I could not have accurately portrayed it without their assistance.

Kirk Dietz was the archivist at Denali National Park and Preserve when I started the project. He delayed his vacation and took the time to teach me how to properly collect and document my findings; if I hadn't started this with Kirk, this thing would be a mess.

While writing *Denali's Howl,* I reconnected with Lloyd Johnson, a friend from college who is battling Lou Gehrig's disease. I sent him an early draft of the manuscript and asked for his opinion. I wasn't sure what to expect when he asked me to call him on a Sunday afternoon a few weeks later. When we connected he got right to the point, suggesting I work on character development to differentiate the story's various players since there are so many. I took his advice and the book is better for it.

Dave Cooley, John Russell's childhood friend and early climbing partner, shared his memories of the man whom I found to be the most compelling of all the characters in this story. My dad once told me that if anyone could have survived, it would have been Russell. I don't know what prompted the statement, but I half hoped I'd discover Russell alive and well somewhere during the research process. Alas, it didn't happen.

Wally Cole, who with his wife, Jerryne, have been pillars in the Denali community for nearly fifty years, allowed me to hole up in their home on Deneki Lakes near Denali National Park in order to kick-start the writing process. The week I spent there got the book moving. Wally also proved to be a font of knowledge regarding the workings of the park during the 1960s. From the phone system, to the old hotel, to mail service, to park staffing, his answers were impressive in their swiftness and detail. He also has a vast collection of mountaineering books, and ready access to them was an unexpected boon during my stay.

I owe Vin Hoeman a debt of gratitude, though he died not long after the Wilcox victims, while I was still in single digits. In the fall of 1967, he began work on his own book about the Wilcox Expedition tragedy, to be called *Denali—Triumph and Tragedy.* Vin wrote to the families and friends of the lost climbers and had collected a trove of background information about them when he was killed while climbing in the Himalayas. His research languished for more than forty years until it was archived and made available to researchers at the University of Alaska–Anchorage's Consortium Library. The material he gathered, and his own insights revealed in his correspondence with the parents of the victims, were invaluable to me. I hope my book does what he had hoped to do when he set out to write his own.

Nick Jans, the noted Alaskan author and my good friend, was one of my earliest supporters, and if he hadn't introduced me to my fantastic literary agent, Elizabeth Kaplan, this book wouldn't have happened. Under Elizabeth's tough love, the proposal came together and caught the eye of Stephen Morrow at Dutton.

Stephen and his assistant, Stephanie Hitchcock, have patiently and skillfully massaged my crude early drafts into a real narrative. I'm indebted to them and will try to pay them back with fresh salmon and dogsled rides if they ever make it to Alaska.

—Andy Hall

CHUGIAK, ALASKA

223

NOTES

The Wilcox Expedition

xii **Auburn, Washington:** E-mail exchange with David Cooley, childhood friend and climbing partner of John Russell, December 2013.

CHAPTER 1: Those Who Came Before

9 **the Big One, the High One, the Great One:** Donald J. Orth, ed., *Dictionary of Alaska Place Names* (Washington, DC: US Government Printing Office, 1971), 610.

10 **superstitious horror of even approaching glacial ice:** A. H. Brooks, "An Exploration to Mt. McKinley, America's Highest Mountain," *Journal of Geography* 2, no. 9 (1903): 441–69.

10 **Ruth Gap marks its southern edge:** Author interview with Denali guide Brian Okonek, Talkeetna, AK, October 2013.

10 **12,000 feet from base to summit:** Bryce S. Walker, ed., *Reader's Digest Illustrated World Atlas* (Pleasantville, NY: The Readers Digest Association, 1997), 122.

11 **lowlands of interior Alaska:** Orth, *Dictionary of Alaska Place Names,* 61.

11 **35-million-year-old granite intrusion:** Bradford Washburn, *Guide to the Muldrow Glacier,* unpublished, Daryl Miller Collection, 2.

11 **Bolshaya Gora, or Big Mountain:** Orth, *Dictionary of Alaska Place Names,* 345.

11 **"bounded by distant stupendous snow mountains":** Ibid., 610.

11 **known among prospectors as Densmore's Peak:** Ibid.

12 **was for exploration and mountaineering:** Frank Norris, *Crown Jewel of the North: An Administrative History of Denali National Park and Preserve,* vol. 2 (Anchorage: Alaska Regional Office National Park Service, 2006), 253.

12–13 **"At my request he tells them":** James Wickersham, *Old Yukon: Tales—Trails—and Trials* (Washington, DC: Washington Law Book Co., 1938), 223.

14 **"I was then convinced":** Diary of James Wickersham, June 21, 1903, entry, Alaska State Library, Juneau, AK, Historical Collections, MS 107, Diary 6, 13.

14 **Snow falls down to 6,000 feet:** National Park Service, "Denali: Photography," nps.gov/dena/planyourvisit/photography.htm [accessed December 6, 2013].

14 **permanently snow-covered vertical reliefs:** Washburn, *Muldrow Glacier,* 2; Okonek interview, October 2013.

15 **the fourth relying on a tent pole:** Okonek interview, October 2013.

16 **"As I brushed the frost":** Belmore Browne, *The Conquest of Mount McKinley* (New York: GP Putnam and Sons, 1913), 344.

17 **just 200 feet lower than the summit:** Okonek interview, October 2013.

18 **"Cold & Clear. 'Hurrah'":** Harry Karstens, *The First Ascent of Mount McKinley, 1913. A Verbatim Copy of the Diary of Harry P. Karstens, Preface and Footnotes by Bradford Washburn* (New York: American Alpine Journal, 1969), 347.

18 **"it was plain and prominent":** Hudson Stuck, *The Ascent of Denali (Mount McKinley)* (New York: Charles Scribner's Sons, 1918), 173.

21 **Shakshanee Ish had lived in Sitka:** Arrest record for Shakshanee Ish from the Sitka jail, undated, George Hall collection.

22 **already listed our house with a Realtor:** George Hall, interview by Kristen Griffen, tape recording, June 3, 1999, Alaska Regional Curatorial Center, Anchorage, DENA40001, Series II Box 31, Folder 17.

CHAPTER 2: What Makes an Expedition?

24 **"I was rather non-gregarious":** Joe Wilcox, *White Winds* (Los Alamitos, CA: Hwong Publishing Company, 1981), 14.

24 **in a snowcat measuring ice thickness:** Undated letter from Jerry Clark to Joe Wilcox, Denali National Park and Preserve Museum Collection, DENA13611, 1967 Wilcox Expedition, Folder 110.

24 **he was a smart and careful climber:** Handwritten letter from Joe Wilcox to Vin Hoeman, October 25, 1967, Grace and John Vincent

Hoeman papers, Archives and Special Collections, Consortium Library, University of Alaska–Anchorage.

25 **"Every person will be expected":** Pretrip update letter from Joe Wilcox to potential expedition members November 16, 1966, Denali National Park and Preserve Museum Collection, DENA13611, 1967 Wilcox Expedition, Folder 107.

25 **"primarily because I conceived of it":** Wilcox, *White Winds,* 14.

25 **"I was a bit uncomfortable":** Ibid., 15.

26 **longtime editor of *National Geographic*:** Norris, *Crown Jewel of the North,* 258.

26 **photo expeditions to the mountain in 1937 and 1938:** Ibid., 259.

27 **looking for a new route to the summit:** Author interview with Mike Sfraga, PhD, Anchorage, December 2012.

29 **"Dear Dr. Washburn":** Letter from Joe Wilcox to Bradford Washburn, May 12, 1967, Denali National Park and Preserve Museum Collection, DENA13611, 1967 Wilcox Expedition, Folder 111.

29–30 **"Dear Mr. Wilcox":** Letter from Bradford Washburn to Joe Wilcox, May 17, 1967, Denali National Park and Preserve Museum Collection, DENA13611, 1967 Wilcox Expedition, Folder 111.

31 **"Here I've got this guy":** Hall, Griffen interview, June 3, 1999.

31 **"In chatting with Mr. Wilcox":** Letter from Bradford Washburn to George Hall, June 12, 1967, Denali National Park and Preserve Museum Collection, DENA13611, 1967 Wilcox Expedition, Folder 111.

32 **"crevasse rescue, belays":** Letter from Chief Ranger Art Hayes to Joe Wilcox, May 10, 1967, Denali National Park and Preserve Museum Collection, DENA13611, 1967 Wilcox Expedition, Folder 111.

33 **"It is my intention":** Letter from Howard Snyder to Jerry Clark, May 11, 1967, Denali National Park and Preserve Museum Collection, DENA26657, Box 18.

33 **"We had to either combine":** Howard Snyder, *The Hall of the Mountain King* (New York: Scribner, 1973), 10.

33 **left Boulder for Mount Rainier:** Ibid., 13.

CHAPTER 3: A Dozen Kids

35 **stores gathering last-minute supplies:** Wilcox, *White Winds,* 44.

36 **Humorous yet functional garb:** Ibid., 47.

36 **"I just don't feel good about it":** Ibid., 49.

37 **"like a Hong Kong tailor":** Snyder, *The Hall of the Mountain King,* 13.

37 **"You've got two guys ":** Author telephone interview with Paul Schlichter, February 2013.

37 **Some of Steve's reasons:** Wilcox, *White Winds,* 52.

37 **"apparent lack of basic mountaineering knowledge":** Snyder, *The Hall of the Mountain King,* 17.

37 **"Wilcox was under no obligation":** Author interview with Wayne Merry, Atlin, British Columbia, March 2012.

38 **and finally waved them through:** Author telephone interview with Howard Snyder, May 1, 2013.

39 **climbed to get high:** Author telephone interview with Joe Wilcox, September 2013.

39 **"The Hankmobile and the Green Bomb":** Wilcox, *White Winds,* 55.

41 **stopped for the night at Wolf Creek:** Snyder, *The Hall of the Mountain King,* 19.

42 **was a McLaughlin creation:** Wilcox to Hoeman, October 25, 1967.

42 **"This last fall":** Undated Letter from Mark McLaughlin to Joe Wilcox, Denali National Park and Preserve Museum Collection, DENA13611, 1967 Wilcox Expedition, Folder 110.

42 **took a more conservative approach:** Wilcox to Hoeman, October 25, 1967.

42 **"If all goes well, I should have the THING":** Letter from Dennis Luchterhand to Joe Wilcox, Denali National Park and Preserve Museum Collection, DENA13611, 1967 Wilcox Expedition, Folder 110.

43 **"Sometime in the next few years":** Ibid.

43 **"some of the greatest moments of my life":** Letter from Hank Janes to Joe Wilcox, Denali National Park and Preserve Museum Collection, DENA13611, 1967 Wilcox Expedition, Folder 110.

43 **"I feel that I can be of more help":** Ibid.

44 **"My parents don't think it such a swinging idea":** Letter from Steve Taylor to Joe Wilcox, Denali National Park and Preserve Museum Collection, DENA13611, 1967 Wilcox Expedition, Folder 110.

44 **"Brad is a no gooder":** Wilcox, *White Winds,* 56.

44 **"I first learned to water ski":** Letter from Walt Taylor to Joe Wilcox, Denali National Park and Preserve Museum Collection, DENA13611, 1967 Wilcox Expedition, Folder 110.

45 **"scrambling as opposed to climbing":** Letter from Anshel Schiff to Joe Wilcox, Denali National Park and Preserve Museum Collection, DENA13611, 1967 Wilcox Expedition, Folder 110.

45 **not to reach the summit:** Author interview with Joe Wilcox, Kailua-Kona, HI, March 2012.

45 **"He was a fighter from conception":** Handwritten letter from Jane O. Russell to Vin Hoeman, October 15, 1967, Grace and John Vincent Hoeman papers, Archives and Special Collections, Consortium Library, University of Alaska–Anchorage.

45 **began calling himself John Russell:** Author telephone interview with David Cooley, May 2013.

46 **"at which time he was a complete beatnik":** Russell to Hoeman, October 15, 1967.

46 **"I have in the past carried load[s]":** Letter from John Russell to Joe Wilcox, Denali National Park and Preserve Museum Collection, DENA13611, 1967 Wilcox Expedition, Folder 110.

46 **had meandered off of the road in his sleep:** Wilcox, *White Winds,* 56.

47 **"Gee, maybe I'd be happier":** Schlichter telephone interview, February 2013.

48 **"Look there":** Snyder, *The Hall of the Mountain King,* 20.

48 **"The ranger at the Information Center":** Ibid., 21.

CHAPTER 4: Trouble at the Base

52 **including communications with climbers:** Author telephone interview with William Babcock, April 2013.

52 **The radios weren't compatible:** Denali National Park and Preserve Museum Collection, DENA13611, 1967 Wilcox Expedition, Folder 107.

52 **Hayes arranged to borrow a CB radio:** Letter from Arthur Hayes to Jerry Clark, May 18, 1967, Denali National Park and Preserve Museum Collection, DENA13611, 1967 Wilcox Expedition, Folder 111.

53 **With the rough communications schedule mapped out:** Wilcox, *White Winds,* 59.

53 **"After reading Brad Washburn's unusually hot letter"** . . . **"Basically, Wilcox ran afoul":** Memorandum from Wayne Merry to George Hall, May 22, 1967, Denali National Park and Preserve Museum Collection, DENA13611, 1967 Wilcox Expedition, Folder 111.

53 **"On paper, you are the best organized party":** Wilcox, *White Winds,* 60.

54 **"We seem to be a loose collection":** Ibid., 61.

54 **"No one even opens cans with gusto":** Snyder, *The Hall of the Mountain,* 23.

54 **beyond the means of the young men:** Wilcox interview, March 2012.

56 **"Dad told us they weren't happy":** Author interview with Baxter Mercer, Healy, AK, November 2012.

57 **"in a continual state of depression"** . . . **"literally worrying him sick":** Snyder, *The Hall of the Mountain King,* 25.

57 **"I think psychologically he just wasn't ready":** Schlichter telephone interview, February 2013.

57 **"At a couple of places going up there":** Mercer interview, November 2012.

58 **dawdled incompetently:** Snyder, *The Hall of the Mountain King,* 28.

58 **he had been goaded, ridiculed, insulted:** Wilcox, *White Winds,* 70.

58 **"It seems you're still the Colorado Group":** Ibid., 32.

58 **"We both appreciated the position":** Ibid., 33.

59 **"C'mon, sun!":** Ibid., 35.

61 **"I want four days of food":** Wilcox, *White Winds,* 74.

61 **Wilcox refused:** Snyder, *The Hall of the Mountain King,* 37.

61 **"Tell you what, Joe":** Ibid., 38.

62 **"I know the rules are conservative"** . . . **"if I have your full support":** Wilcox, *White Winds,* 78.

62 **"I didn't have any":** Ibid., 79.

63 **"Consequently, the Colorado group's shovel":** Snyder, *The Hall of the Mountain King,* 36.

63 **snow saws and steel spades became mandatory equipment:** Beat Niederer, "Management Evaluation Report of the Accident Investigation on a mountaineering accident involving the Mountain Trip Concession Guide David Staehli and Death of Client," March 22, 2012.

64 **"I didn't see us as very separate":** Schlichter telephone interview, February 2013.

64 **"We were three guys from Colorado":** Author telephone interview with Howard Snyder, October 2012.

64 **"Well, you take twelve people":** Schlichter telephone interview, February 2013.

64 **"We had a couple of meetings":** Wilcox interview, March 2012.

64 **"I had the last word":** Ibid.

65 **"It's not like a military organization"** . . . **"the people who are up there":** Schlichter interview, February 2013.

CHAPTER 5: From a Crevasse to Brotherhood

68 **hard to spot, even by experienced mountaineers:** Author interview with Denali climbing guide Blaine Smith, Eagle River, AK, December 2012.

68 **"I have often seen huge chunks":** Washburn, *Muldrow Glacier,* 19.

69 **"Come back here, Anshel":** Snyder, *The Hall of the Mountain King,* 39.

70 **Bunny Boot:** Extreme Cold Vapor Barrier Boots developed at the Navy Clothing and Textile Research Center in Natick, Massachusetts, for use during the Korean War. Nicknamed Bunny Boots, the bulbous white boots retain warmth by sandwiching up to one inch of wool and felt insulation between two layers of rubber. The addition of a valve sometime after the Korean War made them useable at altitude and popular with climbers.

71 **"I wish there was enough light":** Snyder, *The Hall of the Mountain King,* 41.

71 **"Our Fearless Leader":** Snyder, *The Hall of the Mountain King,* 42.

72 **"The concealing snowfall":** Wilcox, *White Winds,* 84.

72 **"became chronic whenever he got within two blocks":** Ibid., 85.

74 **"I didn't mind carrying it":** Snyder, *The Hall of the Mountain King,* 52.

74 **Wilcox said Schiff appeared:** Wilcox interview, March 2012.

75 **Luchterhand's camera wasn't working:** Wilcox interview, March 2012.

75 **The group photo:** Black-and-white print, Denali National Park and Preserve Museum Collection, DENA13611, 1967 Wilcox Expedition, Folder 110.

76 **The advance team of Wilcox, Russell, Snyder:** Snyder, *The Hall of the Mountain King,* 192.

78 **lethal tendency to shatter in extreme cold:** Author interview with Charlie Sassara, president of the American Alpine Club, Anchorage, September 2013.

78 **with a red, braided outer sheath:** Author telephone interview with Howard Snyder, September 2013.

78 **50-degree-steep stretch of white ice:** Washburn, *Muldrow Glacier,* 26.

78 **"Anshel, there's a rumor":** Snyder, *The Hall of the Mountain King,* 79.

79 **to Wilcox one-on-one:** Wilcox interview, March 2012.

79 **"Richie was worthless" . . . "He wanted to beat it":** Cooley telephone interview, May 2013.

79 **"In my mind [Walt] was the most mature":** Author telephone interview with Paul Schlichter, March 2013.

80 **meals averaged 4,505 calories per day:** Expedition newsletter M8, March 7, 1967, Denali National Park and Preserve Museum Collection, DENA13611, Folder 108.

80 **"witty humorist, tactful conciliator":** Wilcox, *White Winds,* 93.

80 **"wanted to be viewed as independent":** Wilcox interview, March 2012.

80 **Calls of "Muthah":** Ibid.

80–81 **"As the trip progressed":** Wilcox to Hoeman, October 25, 1967.

81 **"John gave it all he had":** Wilcox, *White Winds,* 208.

CHAPTER 6: A Run for It

84 **Obvious symptoms of acute mountain sickness:** Copy of Joe Wilcox's journal, Grace and John Vincent Hoeman papers, Archives and Special Collections, Consortium Library, University of Alaska–Anchorage.

84 **and swollen hands and feet:** Jonathan Waterman, *Surviving Denali* (Golden, CO: The AAC Press, Second edition, revised 1991), 26.

84 **dramatic brain swelling:** Author e-mail interview with Dr. Peter Hackett, September 2013.

84 **exhaustion, drowsiness, and weakness:** Ibid.

84–85 **five days to top Karstens Ridge:** Snyder, *The Hall of the Mountain King*, 85.

85 **causing noticeable weight loss:** Wilcox interview, March 2012.

85 **exhibited extreme exhaustion:** Snyder, *The Hall of the Mountain King*, 84.

85 **before the symptoms become life threatening:** Waterman, *Surviving Denali*, 25.

85 **"The next two days will be perfect":** Wilcox, *White Winds*, 114.

86 **"My feeling is that we should make a run for it":** Ibid., 115.

87 **"a bit apprehensive":** Snyder, *The Hall of the Mountain King*, 94.

87 **two shovel scoops minus their handles:** Snyder telephone interview, September 2013.

87 **Blazo fuel, and the five-watt CB radio:** Wilcox, *White Winds*, 116.

87 **"There are a number of treacherous crevasses":** Washburn, *Muldrow Glacier.*

88 **"The men in the tent":** Snyder, *The Hall of the Mountain King*, 94.

88 **"At 8:00 A.M.":** Wilcox, *White Winds*, 116.

88 **"I think I've still got my 111B":** Author interview with Frank Nosek, Anchorage, April 2013.

89 **"but by the time he got there the wall was gone":** Snyder, *The Hall of the Mountain King*, 95.

89 **"There's one thing that didn't burn":** Ibid.

90 **"God dammit, slow down!":** Wilcox, *White Winds*, 119.

90 **"Seeking shelter here":** Ibid.

91 **in order to digest rich foods:** Klaas Westerterp, "Energy and Water Balance at High Altitude," *News Physiology Sciences* 15 (June 2001): 134–37.

91–92 **"I'm afraid we don't have any new weather" . . . "Well, it was snowing":** Cassette tapes of radio transmissions from the collection of Michael Sfraga, PhD, transcribed by author.

93 **"It was primitive then":** Author interview with Ted Fathauer, Fairbanks, AK, October 2012.

93 **"They could look at the mountain":** Nosek interview, April 2013.

CHAPTER 7: Four Months Before and 15,000 Feet Below

96 **Neither Johnston nor Davidson can recall:** Author telephone interview with Dave Johnston, October 2013.

97 **notified the Alaska Rescue Group (ARG):** The Alaska Rescue Group was formed in the wake of the 1960 Day Bading rescue by a group of mountain climbers, skiers, riverboat enthusiasts, and skin divers. An offshoot of the Mountaineering Club of Alaska, the ARG was based in Anchorage. Now called the Alaska Mountain Rescue Group, the volunteer rescue organization continues to provide rescue support for the Alaska State Troopers.

97 **"Nothing moved":** Author telephone interview with Gary Hansen, November 2012.

98 **"He had a great guilt":** Author interview with Robert Sheldon, Talkeetna, AK, December 2013.

98 **"Yeah, I was hucklebuck'n":** Art Davidson, *Minus 148 Degrees: The First Winter Ascent of Mt. McKinley* (Seattle: The Mountaineers, 1999), 215.

98 **"His parting comment was":** Hansen telephone interview, November 2012.

98 **spotted three men descending near 18,000 feet:** "Decisions Effecting the Conduct of Search and Rescue Activity on Mount McKinley Rescue, 5–9 March 1967," ARG project no. 6703, Alaska Mountain Rescue Group files.

99 **before heading back to report their position:** Davidson, *Minus 148*, 198.

99 **the Mountaineering Club of Alaska:** The Alaska Rescue Group was part of the Mountaineering Club of Alaska. All ARG members also were members of the MCA, although not all members of the MCA were part of the ARG. Babcock telephone, interview, April 2013.

99 **"That one set us back on our heels":** Nosek interview, April 2013.

99 **"The club had fairly high requirements":** Wayne Merry, interview by National Park Service historian Frank Norris, May 7, 2007.

100 **"When it came to the summertime":** Nosek interview, April 2013.

100–101 **"We thought that for the Wilcox party":** Ibid.

101 **"where the climbers ascended one-hundred-foot ice walls":** Mountaineering Club of Alaska letter to NPS seeking permission to climb Mount McKinley, Alaska Mountain Rescue Group archives.

101 **"Each member of the group":** Ibid.

101 **they went out without their sleeping bags:** Ibid.

102 **"You have to practice" . . . "Our first seven days":** Babcock telephone interview, March 2013.

102 **Don Haglund and Barney Seiler were spooked:** Ibid.

102 **"Don moody and fearful" . . . "Barney took off":** Bill Babcock's original journal kept during the 1967 MCA expedition, Bill Babcock Collection.

103 **He told me he was in poor physical condition . . . "I didn't pay much attention to it":** Author interview with Don Haglund, Anchorage, August 2012.

103 **"The map and book":** Babcock journal.

103–104 **"Everything was soaked":** Author interview with Gayle Nienhueser, Anchorage, August 2012.

104 **"Hot weather made relays" . . . "Mistake to leave big shovel":** Babcock journal.

104–5 **"It was Gayle and Leo" . . . "Don and Barney just came to me":** Author telephone interview with William Babcock, March 2013.

105 **"several pair of broke":** Denali National Park and Preserve Museum Collection, DENA13611, 1967 Wilcox Expedition, Folder 113. Synopsis of climb signed by Bill Babcock.

105 **leaving the food and fuel behind was foolish:** Babcock journal.

106 **"I think the smartest thing":** Babcock interview, March 2013.

CHAPTER 8: Howling

108 **"Here we are, Jerry Lewis" . . . "Well, they knew":** Snyder telephone interview, October 2012.

109 **"I thought it strange":** Wilcox interview, March 2012.

109 **"I think that was where Joe":** Schlichter telephone interview, February 2013.

109–10 **"In Joe's defense":** Snyder telephone interview, October 2012.

110 **"What a blunder, I thought":** Wilcox, *White Winds,* 122.

111 **"We did not inspect" . . . "We chose to follow these wands":** Narrative report by Joe Wilcox, Alaska Mountain Rescue Group files.

111 **"It was not well wanded":** Author telephone interview with Howard Snyder, January 2014.

111 **"I remember we got":** Schlichter telephone interview, February 2013.

111 **"On this day the summit ridge":** Snyder, *The Hall of the Mountain King,* 104.

112–13 **"How far now to the summit?" . . . "All kinds of them":** Cassette tapes of radio transmissions from the collection of Michael Sfraga, PhD, transcribed by author.

113 **"When the party Russell was with":** Letter from Howard Snyder to Vin Hoeman, September 11, 1967, Grace and John Vincent Hoeman papers, Archives and Special Collections, Consortium Library, University of Alaska–Anchorage.

114 **"While the first party of eight":** Ibid.

115 **"I think we'll just wait":** Wilcox, *White Winds,* 131.

115 **Jerry Lewis's condition continued to worsen:** Snyder, *The Hall of the Mountain King,* 113.

116 **whenever he'd try to eat, he'd throw up:** Ibid., 114.

116 **"I knew John was sick":** Snyder interview, October 2012.

116 **"Anshel had a realistic view":** Wilcox interview, March 2012.

116 **"Lewis asked specifically":** Snyder to Hoeman, September 11, 1967.

117 **"He was so damn sick":** Snyder telephone interview, October 2012.

117 **"I was tired after staying up":** Wilcox interview, March 2012.

117 **"I'll stay here" . . . "That really won't be necessary":** Wilcox, *White Winds,* 131.

117 **"I felt that I should stay":** Wilcox to Hoeman, October 25, 1967.

117 **fuel that had been left outside and lost:** Wilcox McKinley Expedition partial log by Howard Snyder, Grace and John Vincent Hoeman papers, Archives and Special Collections, Consortium Library, University of Alaska–Anchorage.

117 **"Don't take any chances" . . . "Don't worry":** Wilcox, *White Winds,* 132.

118 **the expedition's only complete shovel:** Snyder telephone interview, October 2012.

118 **"We could see the camp":** Schlichter telephone interview, February 2013.

118 **and 150 wands for trail marking:** Wilcox to Hoeman, October 25, 1967.

118 **the only food they carried was lunch . . . "It is possible":** Snyder telephone interview, October 2012.

119–25 **"ETA is approximately forty-five minutes" . . . "Thanks very much. KHD6990 Unit One clear":** Cassette tapes of radio transmissions from the collection of Michael Sfraga, PhD, transcribed by author.

126 **"I could imagine him":** Wilcox interview, March 2012.

126 **one that was narrow but apparently bottomless:** Snyder, *The Hall of the Mountain King,* 104.

CHAPTER 9: Split Apart

127 **"Radio contact with Eielson":** Copy of Joe Wilcox's journal, Grace and John Vincent Hoeman papers, Archives and Special Collections, Consortium Library, University of Alaska–Anchorage.

128 **"As feared, the weather turned foul":** Louis Reichardt journal from the July 1967 Western States Expedition, courtesy Louis Reichardt.

128 **"Mountain clear from 6:30":** Wonder Lake logbook, Denali National Park and Preserve Museum Collection, DENA26382.

128 **a saucerlike lenticular cloud:** Author telephone interview with Howard Snyder, May 2013.

129 **"Light snow and fog all day":** Boyd N. Everett Jr., "The A-67 M. McKinley Expedition 1967," Alaska Mountain Rescue Group archive.

129 **since they carried no intact shovels:** Snyder telephone interview, October 2012.

130 **"Listen . . . I hear voices":** Wilcox, *White Winds,* 140.

130 **"Wed. July 19. Strong winds":** Wilcox journal.

131 **"The wind picked up":** Reichardt journal.

131 **"Lloyd's prognosis was favorable":** Lloyd Price was a member of the expedition. He went on to work as a ranger in Yosemite. E-mail exchange with Louis Reichardt, December 28, 2013.

131 **"Denali visible briefly":** Wonder Lake logbook, Denali National Park and Preserve Museum Collection, DENA26382.

131 **"The failure to establish radio contact":** Narrative report by Joe Wilcox, Alaska Mountain Rescue Group files.

131 **"We knew they got to the top":** Schlichter telephone interview, February 2013.

132 **"How long should we wait" . . . "Two days":** Wilcox, *White Winds,* 144.

132 **foot-deep powder:** Wilcox McKinley Expedition partial expedition log, 14 July through 26 July, written by Howard Snyder in Anchorage, evening of July 29, 1967, Grace and John Vincent Hoeman papers, Archives and Special Collections, Consortium Library, University of Alaska–Anchorage.

132 **"With our trail obliterated":** Wilcox, *White Winds,* 144.

132 **"We stood still":** Snyder, *The Hall of the Mountain King,* 128.

132 **"I thought he shouldn't have left it":** Snyder telephone interview, January 2014.

133 **"He said I was not to leave her":** Hall, Griffen interview, June 3, 1999.

133 **"The ranger said to me":** Ibid.

134 **"At about noon Wilcox exp.":** Wonder Lake logbook.

134 **By 4:30 P.M., Hansen had received his briefing:** Alaska Rescue Group diary written by Gary Hansen, Howard Snyder collection.

134 **"The same spirit of preparation":** E-mail exchange between author and Gary Hansen, January 2013.

135 **"the ARG had been alerted" . . . "a 'go-ahead'":** Log of Wilcox Expedition rescue by Wayne Merry, Denali National Park and Preserve Museum Collection, DENA13611, 1967 Wilcox Expedition, Folder 108.

135–36 **"If a flight is required" . . . "Report from the mountain":** Hansen ARG diary.

136 **stripped-down bare aluminum Cessna 180:** Don Sheldon was so conscious about the weight of his aircraft when flying in the mountains that he didn't paint many of them, saving as much as 80 pounds.

136 **Sheldon, who reported poor weather:** Hansen ARG diary.

137 **50 miles per hour with gusts to 65:** Merry, Wilcox Expedition rescue log.

137 **"The storm, which had been battering":** Wilcox McKinley Expedition partial expedition log.

137 **"The day was cold and clear":** Reichardt journal.

137 **"Unfortunately, the weather did not break":** Ibid.

138 **"Storm appears to be roaring" . . . "We build huge snow walls":** Babcock journal.

138 **"When visibility improved":** Draft of report by Bill Babcock, undated, Denali National Park and Preserve Museum Collection, DENA13611, Folder 113.

138–39 **"I knew there was a problem" . . . "I didn't know what it was":** Babcock telephone interview, March 2013.

139 **"You know . . . I think to not try the summit":** Wilcox, *White Winds,* 148.

140 **"We Gotta Get Out of This Place":** Snyder telephone interview, May 2013.

140 **"I remember thinking, It's only a matter of time":** Schlichter telephone interview, February 2013.

140 **having difficulty moving his hands:** Snyder telephone interview, May 2013.

140 **three sick men who couldn't care for themselves:** Snyder, *The Hall of the Mountain King,* 150.

141 **"Not more than one of us would feel like going up":** Wilcox, *White Winds,* 154.

141 **"We have three people":** Ibid., 151.

141 **"They understand that they were the closest":** Wonder Lake logbook.

141–42 **"It was such a surprise"** . . . **"A few hundred yards":** Reichardt journal.

143 **"Climbing alone unroped":** Wilcox, *White Winds,* 157.

143 **"When Lewis would fall":** Snyder, *The Hall of the Mountain King,* 155.

143 **"You'll just have to leave me":** Ibid., 159.

144 **"We see a party of 5":** Grace Jansen Hoeman's journal, Grace and John Vincent Hoeman papers, Archives and Special Collections, Consortium Library, University of Alaska–Anchorage.

144 **"They literally drank":** Babcock telephone interview, March 2013.

CHAPTER 10: An Ice Ax in the Snow

145 **he urged Joe Wilcox to call an all-out rescue:** Babcock journal.

145 **"To me, it was blatantly obvious":** Babcock telephone interview, March 2013.

145 **"Bill will go up in forced ascent":** Hoeman journal.

145 **"Wilcox reached MCA":** Wonder Lake logbook, Denali National Park and Preserve Museum Collection, DENA26382.

146 **"Somehow, there was the idea":** Wilcox interview, March 2012.

146 **"I got the sense that":** Author interview with Frank Nosek, Anchorage, May 2013.

146 **was worried about the cost:** Nienhueser interview, August 2012.

146 **"There's a full-scale rescue":** Snyder, *The Hall of the Mountain King,* 162.

147 **"Merry again recommended":** Wonder Lake logbook, Denali National Park and Preserve Museum Collection, DENA26382.

147 **"I remember we mobilized":** Nosek interview, May 2013.

147 **"You have to be moving faster"** . . . **"You simply can't get it down":** Author interview with Chuck Sassara, Anchorage, October 2013.

148 **"He just wanted to take off":** Babcock telephone interview, March 2013.

148 **"Winds began to pick up":** Babcock journal.

148 **"MCA report good flying weather":** Wonder Lake logbook.

148 **dropping a radio and food 500 feet below:** Itemized account of hours
flown for reconnaissance and search, Wilcox Expedition, bill submitted
to the ARG for reimbursement on September 2, 1967 by Don Sheldon's
Talkeetna Air Service, Grace and John Vincent Hoeman papers,
Archives and Special Collections, Consortium Library, University of
Alaska–Anchorage.

149 **"We awoke at 3:30 A.M.":** Reichardt journal.

149 **"Would you like to see the storm?":** Author interview with John
Papineau, Meteorologist, NOAA, National Weather Service,
Anchorage, October 2011.

151 **"They were where the wind"** . . . **"the worst when people were on it":**
Fathauer interview, October 2012.

152 **"Spent several hours digging":** Babcock journal.

152 **"We were still planning to relay"** . . . **"I had been very happy":**
Babcock telephone interview, March 2013.

152 **"The going was extremely difficult":** Draft of report by Bill Babcock,
undated, Denali National Park and Preserve Museum Collection,
DENA13611, Folder 113.

153 **"Never should have done it":** Babcock journal.

153 **"We had this crazy way"** . . . **"Today, you can have a conversation":**
Babcock telephone interview, March 2013.

154 **Sheldon spent two hours searching:** Talkeetna Air Service invoice,
September 2, 1967.

154 **"Bill exhausted":** Babcock journal.

154 **the A-67 Expedition spotted Sheldon's shiny Cessna:** Everett, "The
A-67 Mt. McKinley Expedition."

155 **"The snow was hard enough"** . . . **"Around that . . . there was a
sleeping bag":** John Ireton, interview by the National Park Service,
tape recording, July 1967, Denali National Park and Preserve Museum
Collection, NPS 7187, transcribed by author.

155 **"We hollered":** Babcock telephone interview, March 2013.

155 **"a ghastly sight":** Babcock journal.

155 **"He was blown over":** Ireton NPS interview.

156 **"I was twenty-six":** Nienhueser interview, August 2012.

156 **the cold begins to penetrate the skin:** J. L. Harrison and K. D. Davis,
"Cold-Evoked Pain Varies with Skin Type and Cooling Rate: A
Psychophysical Study in Humans," *Pain* 83, no. 2 (November 1999):
123–35; A. Kreh, F. Anton, H. Gilly, and H. O. Handwerker, "Vascular
Reactions Correlated with Pain Due to Cold," *Experimental Neurology*
85, no. 3 (September 1984): 533–46.

157 **renders brain enzymes less efficient:** Peter Stark, *Last Breath: Cautionary Tales from the Limits of Human Endurance* (New York: Ballantine Books, 2001), 11–25.

157 **blood surges into the nearly frozen flesh:** "The Word: Paradoxical Undressing," *New Scientist* 194, no. 2,600 (April 21, 2007): 50.

158 **"It was a nightmarish thing":** Babcock telephone interview, March 2013.

158 **"We give negative":** Babcock journal.

158 **"Not likely" . . . "Can this be accomplished commercially":** Hansen ARG diary.

159 **"It's not the kind of rig":** Author interview with Dave Johnston, Talkeetna, AK, November 2012.

159 **"Well, the plane flew over":** Babcock telephone interview, March 2013.

160 **"By three fifteen we also reach the summit":** Babcock journal.

160 **this time in his Super Cub:** Talkeetna Air Service invoice, September 2, 1967.

160 **The plane circled the slope . . . they wait and discuss it with Babcock:** Description of flight pattern and note from interview with Chet Hackney, reel-to-reel tape, George Hall Collection, transcribed by author.

160 **"I really tried very hard":** Babcock telephone interview, March 2013.

161 **orange wind pants, and green overboots:** Ireton NPS interview.

161 **"The body was in a sitting position":** Hackney e-mail interview, September 2013.

161–63 **"He again was in a position" . . . "We looked into the cans":** Ireton NPS interview.

163 **"Mysterious clouds spill over":** Babcock journal.

163 **"If we had dillydallied a half an hour":** Babcock telephone interview, March 2013.

163–64 **"I didn't have enough knowledge":** Wilcox interview, March 2012.

165 **"Let's go. They've found two more bodies" . . . it took a half an hour to dig their way out:** Wilcox, *White Winds,* 158.

165 **leaving the body where it sat:** Babcock telephone interview, March 2013; Ireton NPS interview.

166 **"Would you fellows consider":** Babcock journal.

166 **"I think I yelled at Gayle":** Babcock telephone interview, March 2013.

166–67 **"We had no feeling toward him":** Babcock journal.

167–68 **"24 July: The Colorado Party" . . . "Grace says not true . . . VH":** Wilcox McKinley Expedition partial expedition log, 14 July through 26 July, written by Howard Snyder in Anchorage, evening of July 29, 1967, handwritten note added by Vin Hoeman, Grace and John Vincent Hoeman papers, Archives and Special Collections, Consortium Library, University of Alaska–Anchorage.

168–69 **"We weren't there"** . . . **"with no divided channels":** Snyder telephone interview, January 2014.

170 **"My question was, are they alive":** George Hall, interviewed by Karen Brewster, April 16, 1999, Anchorage, H98-39-12, Part 1 Project Juke Box, University of Alaska Fairbanks oral history program, http://jukebox.uaf .edu/Sitka/program/htm/GeHa.htm [accessed January 5, 2014].

CHAPTER 11: Whose Son?

171 **"Luchterhand's nineteen-year-old sister, Erika":** Letter from Pat Luchterhand to Vin Hoeman, October 6, 1967, Grace and John Vincent Hoeman papers, Archives and Special Collections, Consortium Library, University of Alaska–Anchorage.

171 **"Further information came":** Letter from Elmer Luchterhand to Vin Hoeman, June 17, 1968, Grace and John Vincent Hoeman, papers, Archives and Special Collections, Consortium Library, University of Alaska–Anchorage.

172 **"and that he had contacted Senator Edward Kennedy"** . . . **"Capt. Gordon has talked":** Hansen ARG diary.

172 **"the generally slight prospects":** E. Luchterhand to Hoeman, June 17, 1968.

172 **Steve Taylor's parents:** Author interview with Wally Cole, park hotel manager in 1967, Deneki Lakes, AK, March 2013.

173 **"could be of any assistance"** . . . **return to the upper mountain to continue searching:** Hansen ARG diary.

173 **"Send the Air Force"** . . . **"Whose son should I send?":** Author interview with George Hall, Anchorage, August 1999.

174 **Against the wishes of the regional director:** Hall, Griffen interview, June 3, 1999.

174–76 **"to find and bury"** . . . **"Little was added":** Notes on the Humanitarian Climb, written by Vin Hoeman, Denali National Park and Preserve Museum Collection, DENA13611, 1967 Wilcox Expedition, Folder 109.

176–77 **"Dear Vin and Grace":** Letter from Perry Taylor to Vin Hoeman, June 20, 1968, Grace and John Vincent Hoeman papers, Archives and Special Collections, Consortium Library, University of Alaska–Anchorage.

177 **"I know that considerable effort"**: Letter from S .P. McLaughlin to George Hall, September 6, 1967, Denali National Park and Preserve Museum Collection, DENA13611, 1967 Wilcox Expedition, Folder 108.

178 **"naïve but unlimited determination"**: E. Luchterhand to Hoeman, June 17, 1968.

178–79 **"Radio communication is a great thing"**: Letter from Vin Hoeman to Elmer Luchterhand, June 20, 1968, Grace and John Vincent Hoeman papers, Archives and Special Collections, Consortium Library, University of Alaska–Anchorage.

180 **moved too quickly for observers to effectively search:** Johnston interview, November 2012.

181 **"On the 17th and 18th"**: Wilcox to Vin Hoeman, October 25, 1967.

181–82 **"The six climbers made the push"**: Babcock journal.

182–83 **"It would appear to me"**: Letter from Brad Washburn to Perry Taylor, September 22, 1967, Denali National Park and Preserve Museum Collection, DENA13611, 1967 Wilcox Expedition, Folder 108.

183–84 **"you have to dig a snow cave"**: Hoeman to E. Luchterhand, June 20, 1968.

184 **frozen and matted hair:** Author interview with Gayle Nienhueser, Anchorage, May 2013.

185 **hold his tent upright in the "blowhole":** Babcock journal.

185 **"As soon as there is any kind of infarction"**: Smith interview, December 2012.

186 **Snyder put forth a similar scenario:** Author telephone interview with Howard Snyder, April 2013.

186 **If so, he said, decomposition would:** Author interview with Dave McMahan, Alaska state archaeologist, retired, Anchorage, May 2013.

187 **"The big difference"**: Okonek interview, October 2013.

CHAPTER 12: What Changed

189 **the National Park Service convened a "critique" meeting:** Letter from George Hall to parents of the Wilcox victims, September 21, 1967, Denali National Park and Preserve Museum Collection, DENA13611, Folder 109.

190–91 **group strength is not measurable . . . "not always as described":** Handwritten notes from critique meeting, undated, Denali National Park and Preserve Museum Collection, DENA13611, Folder 109.

191 **"Whether we could do anything"**: Merry interview, March 2012.

191–92 **"This I don't know":** Ibid.

192 **"Radio system funding and Climbing personnel":** Notes from critique meeting, undated, Denali National Park and Preserve Museum Collection, DENA13611, Folder 109.

192–93 **"The critique meeting":** Hall to parents of the Wilcox victims, September 21, 1967.

193 **He routinely flew when he was needed:** Nosek interview, May 2013.

193 **"I explored all I could":** Hall, Griffen interview, June 3, 1999.

195 **"I wear that one" . . . "At first I felt guilty":** Wilcox interview, March 2012.

196 **"I never got the impression":** Sfraga interview, December 2012.

196 **"Joe is a real convenient target" . . . "Paul and I have talked about it":** Snyder telephone interview, May 2013.

196–97 **"It's funny, we had some friends":** Schlichter telephone interview, February 2013.

197 **"He suffered physically":** Snyder telephone interview, April 2013.

197 **He maintained a card catalog:** Author interview with Jed Williamson, editor of *Accidents in North American Mountaineering*, published by the American Alpine Club. Hoeman's card catalog is part of the Grace and John Vincent Hoeman papers in the Archives and Special Collections at the University of Alaska–Anchorage Consortium Library.

197 **five of America's finest mountaineers and two Sherpas:** Author telephone interview with Bob Gerhard, April 2013.

197 **she met the same fate as her husband:** Author telephone interview with Gary Hansen, February 2012.

198 **Mount Everest, where his body remains:** Ray Genet death certificate, George Hall collection.

199 **"My office is on the second floor" . . . "We wanted to thank him":** Nosek interview, April 2013.

199–200 **end climbing in Mount McKinley National Park . . . "He wouldn't put it in writing":** George Hall, Griffen interview, June 3, 1999.

200 **"We wanted to show our opposition" . . . "The appreciation for your dad":** Nosek interview, April 2013.

CHAPTER 13: Thirty Years After

204–12 **"The lows usually come" . . . "If it had lasted a few more hours":** Smith interview, December 2012.

213 **"Too many rescuers are killed":** Author interview with Daryl Miller, Anchorage, November 2012.

213–14 **"I never even considered calling"** . . . **"I called down to fourteen":** Smith interview, December 2012.

214 **"The winds were only half":** Author interview with James Nelson, science and operations officer, NOAA, National Weather Service, Anchorage, March 2013.

EPILOGUE: *Memory in a Lifetime*

216 **Merry had no recollection of the encounter:** Merry interview, March 2012.

216 **neither did Bob Hafferman:** Author telephone interview with Bob Hafferman, Kalispell, Montana, November 2012.

216 **nor Wally Cole:** Cole interview, March 2013.

216 **thirty tourists at Eielson Visitor Center:** Wonder Lake logbook, July 24, 1967, entry, Denali National Park and Preserve Museum Collection, DENA26382.

216 **temporarily cutting off road access to the park:** Wonder Lake logbook, July 25, 1967, entry, Denali National Park and Preserve Museum Collection, DENA26382.

INDEX

A **150**-YEAR PUBLISHING TRADITION

•━━━━━━━━━━•

In 1864, E. P. Dutton & Co. bought the famous Old Corner Bookstore and its publishing division from Ticknor and Fields and began their storied publishing career. Mr. Edward Payson Dutton and his partner, Mr. Lemuel Ide, had started the company in Boston, Massachusetts, as a bookseller in 1852. Dutton expanded to New York City, and in 1869 opened both a bookstore and publishing house at 713 Broadway. In 2014, Dutton celebrates 150 years of publishing excellence. We have redesigned our longtime logotype to reflect the simple design of those earliest published books. For more information on the history of Dutton and its books and authors, please visit www.penguin.com/dutton.